Shailendra Pratap Jain, Ph.D., Shalini Sarin Jain, Ph.D.
Managing Brand Transgressions

Shailendra Pratap Jain, Ph.D.
Shalini Sarin Jain, Ph.D.

Managing Brand Transgressions

8 Principles to Transform Your Brand

DE GRUYTER

ISBN 978-1-5015-2108-9
e-ISBN (PDF) 978-1-5015-1733-4
e-ISBN (EPUB) 978-1-5015-1735-8

Library of Congress Control Number: 2024932303

Bibliographic information published by the Deutsche Nationalbibliothek
The Deutsche Nationalbibliothek lists this publication in the Deutsche Nationalbibliografie;
detailed bibliographic data are available on the internet at http://dnb.dnb.de.

© 2024 Walter de Gruyter Inc., Boston/Berlin
Cover image: Hybert Design
Typesetting: Integra Software Services Pvt.

www.degruyter.com

Dedication
To Daisaku Ikeda, our mentor
To Sudesh and Mahendra Pratap Jain & Sushila and Manohar Lal Sarin, our parents
To Naira Sarin Jain, our child and inspiration

Acknowledgments
Indian Institute of Management, Ahmedabad
Sridhar Ramakrishnan, Research Editor
Lalita Daikoku
Paul Baines
Sunil Gulati
Sachin Gupta
Hemant Mishra
Ramón F. Rosales, Esq.

Advance Praise for *Managing Brand Transgressions*

"Profs. Shailendra Jain and Shalini Jain's book is timely and very much needed to protect valuable brands from transgression. Their eight principles will indeed help a brand to grow without any hiccups."

— **N.R. Narayana Murthy**, Founder and Chairman Emeritus, Infosys

"*Managing Brand Transgressions: Eight Principles to Transform Your Brand* stands as a revolutionary exploration, transcending the conventional boundaries of brand evolution. It meticulously dissects the essence of trust across four crucial human dimensions: Physical, Emotional, Digital, and Financial. This narrative unfolds with unprecedented power, incorporating point-in-time case studies of iconic brands such as Cadbury, Boeing, Tylenol, Starbucks, Fox News, Patagonia, and more. By skillfully interweaving these real-world examples, the authors not only illuminate the intricacies of trust but provide a commanding blueprint for brand survival and triumph. This transformative manifesto reshapes the very paradigm of trust and brand success, making it an indispensable guide for navigating the complexities of the modern business landscape. A must read!"

— **Fatima Laher**, Global Senior Partner and Board Director of Deloitte Canada & Chile

"When their brands mess up, marketers need to reach into their shelves for a ready playbook, rather than try to wing it as they most often do. Until now, there was no such thing; but with *Managing Brand Transgressions*, Jain and Jain have filled that gaping hole in the marketer's arsenal. This is a must read and must have. It could one day save a precious life – your brand's!"

— **Sandeep Dayal**, author of *Branding Between the Ears*, and Managing Director, Cerenti Marketing Group

"Firms spend decades building brand equity only to see it disappear in the wake of a single transgression. In this important book, Shailendra and Shalini Jain offer informative case studies as well as actionable guidance on how brands can effectively recover."

— **Michael Norton**, Professor, Harvard Business School; author of *The Ritual Effect: From Habit to Ritual, Harness the Surprising Power of Everyday Actions*

Foreword

There are simply countless instances when a company or its brands materially fail to deliver on their core promise – provide safe and effective products or services. Many of the world's best companies have fallen short, eroding the emotional bond they have worked hard to nurture.

This phenomenon called brand transgressions is what this book is about. From a purely financial level, a poorly managed transgression can be disastrous for the brand. However, very often, the real damage to the business is intangible – loss of focus on the strategic priorities, and months or years spent in dealing with the crisis and recovering from it, and the inevitable loss of trust from its suppliers, customers, shareholders, and most importantly, its employees. For students of business, understanding why we still find examples of brand transgressions every other day, if and how they can be avoided, and managed better is as important as a Discounted Cash Flow (DCF) analysis. Having worked in a large global business for over three decades, I have witnessed firsthand several instances of such transgressions in my own company.

Besides exploring the anatomy of a brand transgression, this book serves a very important purpose no other book does. It elevates the topic to more than just an idea for public relations and crisis managers to worry about and makes it the very soul of good brand management. To accomplish this, the authors carve out a roadmap of what they call '8 Principles to Transform Your Brand'. Each principle is captured in a separate chapter and is based on a handful of notable case studies carefully culled from different parts of the world. What I find impressive also is the extent to which the authors have gone into the weeds through deep research underlying each of the 25+ case studies and brought them to life for practicing managers and CEOs.

Whatever your reasons for picking up this book, I believe you have made a good choice . . . because it's hard for a brand to escape facing a transgression. By following the 8 principles laid out in the book, I have no doubt that you will be better equipped to deal with the situation and prevent significant financial and reputation damage.

Rakesh Kapoor
Founder & CEO 12 Flags Group
Former Global CEO, Reckitt Plc

https://doi.org/10.1515/9781501517334-202

Foreword

This book could save you.

You read about some transgression getting a brand into serious trouble almost every day. Chances are that one day your brand will face such a crisis. As this valuable work illustrates, it's happened to Cadbury, Boeing, Johnson & Johnson, Volkswagen, Samsung and many other brands you might have believed were invulnerable.

As far as I know, this is the first book to focus on "brand transgressions" and their solution with a rounded brand marketing approach: eight principles to follow with an excellent range of case histories to bring each to life. The authors demonstrate how, without a good understanding of how to deal with a crisis, the investment over years in brand building can be lost in a matter of days.

It is impossible to predict how, or from where, a transgression will threaten the future of a brand. In Donald Rumsfeld's unfortunate phrase, "stuff happens", and you have to be ready to deal with it, whatever form it takes. In my years in advertising, working with more than a hundred brands, I saw it happen again and again. Some were own-goals – corporate malfeasance covered up; some were attacks from outside – product tampering (as the book describes) faced Johnson & Johnson's Tylenol; some involved the personality championing the brand getting into trouble . . . and many others.

Of course, the best way to deal with brand transgressions, as this book shows, is to have built a strong degree of trust in the brand in the first place, and a corporate culture of transparency and openness that takes ownership of the crisis when it strikes, and deals with it openly and at lightning speed. The eight principles in this book give the basis for company protocols that will lead to effective handling of such emergencies. Cadbury, Johnson & Johnson, and Starbucks among the case studies described in this book managed to come out stronger from a well-handled transgression that they were facing. Brand management should learn from these cases how to snatch such victories from the jaws of imminent defeat. In contrast, knee jerk attempts to defend profit by defensive denial, cover up, or blame shifting achieve the opposite of what they set out to do.

It will be a transgression if brand managers and CEOs have not studied this unique guide.

Sir Chris Powell
Former CEO, BMP DDB

Note: Boase, Massimi, and Pollitt merged with Doyle, Dane, and Bernbach advertising to become BMP DDB.

https://doi.org/10.1515/9781501517334-203

Contents

Introduction

The Eight Principles

Circa September 2003. India.

The world's second largest democracy, a teeming land of more than 1.1 billion people (population in 2003), was busy preparing for Diwali, India's festival of lights, slated for the end of October. Being a festive season, this time of the year happens to be prime for consumer goods marketers expecting an indulgent consumer and consequent sales spike. Cadbury, the British chocolate behemoth, was buzzing with anticipation as it had been experiencing a 15 percent hike in revenues during this period year on year (Vaid, 2006). Little did it expect the situation that was about to unravel, the likes of which it had never experienced in its glorious history, and that carried the threat of severe consequences down the line.

The Transgression, Cadbury's Response, and the Outcome

In October 2003, a handful of customers in Mumbai complained about live worms in Cadbury's flagship Dairy Milk chocolate bars. Later, live worms were found in a few bars in the nearby city of Pune as well. In response, the local Food and Drug Administration (FDA) seized the entire chocolate stock manufactured at the company's plant in Pune and threatened legal action.

Cadbury's first reaction to the perceived transgression was defensive, seeming to distance itself from assuming responsibility for the infestation during manufacturing and, instead, attributing blame on poor storage by the retailers (Vaid, 2006). FDA on the other hand called out the possibilities of inadequate packaging, a manufacturing defect, or unhygienic storage conditions (Avila, Parkin, & Galoostian, 2019). These publicly aired allegations and counter-allegations between Cadbury and the FDA received adverse media coverage for the brand, which touched close to 1,000 clips in print and 120 on TV news channels over the ensuing three-week period (Francis, 2010). Seemingly, many consumers decided to put their chocolate cravings on hold, angry at the apparent transgression committed by an iconic brand they had a deep emotional bond with. Following the event, for the first time in the company's Indian history since 1948, Cadbury's advertising went off the air for a month and a half. The conflict between Cadbury and the FDA, the heat of negative brand publicity, and the lack of advertising led to Cadbury's sales and profits plummeting by an estimated 30 to 45 percent (Shah, 2020). The brand's task was to restore consumer, retailer, public, and regulator trust in its manufacturing and packaging processes, and rebuild the credibility and equity of its brand, Dairy Milk bars as well as the umbrella brand Cadbury. It also had to respond to shareholders' concerns in an effort to bring its sales and profit back to where they were before the transgression.

https://doi.org/10.1515/9781501517334-001

It was evident that the company's initial response of denial and distancing itself from the situation by passing the buck was not working (Shah, 2020). Soon thereafter the company launched a multi-pronged initiative comprising of a public relations (PR) campaign, new packaging, and new advertising. The PR campaign titled Project Vishwas (meaning 'assurance') aimed at internal quality control, monitoring, educating, and building confidence with its close to 200,000 retailers who, too were under the microscope. Its revamped packaging featuring a more expensive poly-flow technique cost more than $5 million (at today's prices), a cost which apparently was not passed on to the consumer (Vaid, 2006). Three months later came an ad campaign featuring Bollywood icon Amitabh Bachchan, whose personal brand associations of being trustworthy and a benchmark in his profession were expected to help the brand Cadbury garner these associations.

Within six months of the launch of Project Vishwas, the brand's sales climbed back to where they were prior to the crisis and the brand's credibility was restored to a great extent (Vaid, 2006). Clearly, Cadbury's strong and positive brand equity and emotional connection with the consumer before the transgression cushioned it against more severe and longer-term damage. A weaker brand may not have been as successful in turning things around as quickly. Nevertheless, through its process and packaging innovation, work with the retailers and the local FDA, the public relations (PR) campaign, and many other steps it took that are not covered in this book, the brand transformed into a more consumer and retailer friendly brand. The transgression and the brand's response had led to this transformation.

Brand Transgressions Can Result in Crises

Cadbury is one of innumerable brands that have invested a great deal of resources in brand building, and yet find themselves in hot water at some time in their existence, and predictably so. Such brand building is an ongoing and continuous process central to a brand's market position, consumer loyalty, and its business objectives. One of the consequences of brand building is that consumers form relationships with brands that serve as implicit contracts that can drive longevity and profitability of the relationships. However, at certain times, these relationships hit a road bump, as when the brand is perceived to have committed a transgression, that is, *a harm-causing violation of some fundamental rules and norms of the relationship.* And depending on their nature and severity, these transgressions can lead to brand crises.

Our research reveals that brand transgressions are routine and global. Even the world's most well-known, well-respected, well-loved, and pre-eminent brands have faced or will face highly visible and defining crises. Uber's well-publicized transgressions (sexual assault and even murder of customers by Uber drivers) led to a loss of about 200,000 users in the wake of #DeleteUber and Google suing it for using stolen technology (Taylor & Goggin, 2019). United Airlines' (UA's) stock lost an estimated $1 billion in value in a few hours due to a paying customer's well-publicized bloodying and dragging off an overbooked flight so a standby staff could get a seat (BBC News, 2017). Boeing's 737 MAX back-to-back crashes in 2018 and 2019 (which we cover in detail in a later chapter) led to 346 deaths and the cost of the ensuing crisis is estimated at approximately $20 billion until date (Isidore, 2020). Samsung's much-touted Note 7 Smartphone launched in 2016 was reported by its South Korean consumers to catch fire. Some units even exploded, and replacement units launched in October had the same fiery problem as well! Consequently, the company's stock crashed in value by around $26 billion (Tsukayama, 2018). Volkswagen (VW), a hallowed German automobile brand, was found to have rigged diesel emissions tests in 2015, a discovery that led to a loss of brand trust. The price of the company's stock dropped from $38 to $23 within two weeks of this revelation even as it was suspended from the Dow Jones Sustainability Index (DJSI). VW faced criminal charges in several countries, and its own reports suggest that, in fines and settlements alone, "Dieselgate" has cost the company upwards of $32 billion to date (NDTV, 2021).

Human Brands Face Crises Too

Even "human" brands can be perceived as transgressive and can face crises. Eldrick Tont "Tiger" Woods, by far the most successful golf player of his generation and considered by many to be the greatest ever, was a child prodigy, and at the top of the sport from an early age. His winning streak throughout the first decade of this century gave him an air of unattained invincibility. His huge fan following enabled him to bag several lucrative brand endorsement deals that made him one of the richest sports persons in the world. However, in 2009, Tiger found himself in deep crises. Allegations of infidelity stemming from frequent and lurid sexual transgressions saw his personal brand damaged unrecognizably. His reputation as the world's leading and most loved golfer witnessed a relentless downward slide. Some of the brands he endorsed, including Nike and Gatorade, lost between $5 billion and $12 billion collectively due to their association with him (Morain, 2009). Not surprisingly, he lost virtually every brand endorsement deal he had before the transgressions came to light.

Linked with the Tiger Woods' story is what has come to be known as the #MeToo movement. Hundreds of well-known people in various professions all over the planet are under scrutiny regarding their sexual (mis)conduct. Many of them have lost their livelihoods, a few are in jail, and at least one (Jeffrey Epstein) has died under suspicious circumstances. Some are hoping for a miracle even as their cases undergo further deliberation and unravel. Each of them is facing a crisis—a personal, human brand crisis.

From Brand Transgression to Brand Transformation: The Eight Principles

Benjamin Franklin said: "Nothing is certain except death and taxes" (NCC Staff, 2022). We believe that bad things happening to otherwise good brands should be added to this short list. Often, the brands and their parent companies are unambiguously responsible for these transgressions as in the case of VW. Many times, they may be less or not at all responsible, as with Cadbury. *Regardless*, they need a response strategy, a roadmap to confront and address the crisis *before* it becomes a reputational, legal, and financial nightmare from which recovery may take years or become next to impossible (see Chapter 3 and the case of Dalkon Shield). This book delineates such a roadmap—a set of eight principles—that brands should use when they are perceived to have transgressed and face a resulting crisis. Each principle is outlined in a dedicated chapter and is crystallized based on a set of specific, point-in-time, and noted case studies of brands that were perceived to have transgressed and consequently were in crisis. In some of these case studies, after an initial tarnish, the brands emerged successful. These brands continue to thrive and live to tell the story. Other brands were damaged and became dinosaurs. For still others, the crisis continues to plague them as the plot is still unfolding. In each of these cases, we outline the nature of the ostensible transgression that resulted in the brand crisis, the brand's response, and the outcomes. Whether the brand succeeded in warding off extinction, there are abiding lessons that we tease apart and identify as the Eight Principles captured in brief below.

Principle 1—Do The Right Thing

Too often, brands facing allegations of transgressions respond instinctively in self-protection. Clinical psychologists working with human beings have subsumed such responses under the troika of fight, flight, or freeze. While understandable, none of these responses may be a good one in times of crisis. These responses can be seen as defensive or a denial of responsibility. In a marketplace going digital at warp speed, one of the most contagious emotions online is rage. And few things spark greater consumer outrage than a report, true or otherwise, of a brand acting in a callous, discriminatory, self-serving, irresponsible, or otherwise transgressive manner. When the transgression has caused harm, the brand needs to directly offer closure, comfort, and reassurance that victims seek. This is what we call "doing the right thing" vis-à-vis the victim. As we explain in Chapter 1 through the classic and dramatic case of "Cyanide in Tylenol," this principle suggests that the brand and its parent company should act first in victim-protection and not in self-protection. When a brand does the right thing, the path to brand transformation is set in motion. Doing the right thing involves several other steps which are explained in the remaining Seven Principles.

Principle 2—Take Accountability

Chapter 2 illustrates the nearly forgotten but dramatic case of Dalkon Shield, an intra-uterine device (IUD) invented as a birth control mechanism for women. The company's evasive and even untruthful responses to questions about the product's failure are a stark case of not taking accountability, which resulted in tens of thousands of consumer injuries and deaths, and ultimately bankruptcy for the parent company. Why is taking accountability important? In part, doing so is to disabuse the victims of the belief that it is their fault. If such disabuse is not experienced by the victims, it will only harm the brand further. In other part, this response underscores the brand's emotional maturity and lets the world know that it is willing to be accountable (even if it is not responsible), something good relationship partners do. Some may wonder, if the brand is not responsible for a crisis, why should it be accountable? Because at the end of the day, the only entity that will protect the brand from damage and help it transform is the brand itself. From such a perspective, this business of taking account-ability may sound selfish and potentially expensive but, as will become clear, taking accountability to manage a brand crisis is a necessity that has virtuous outcomes for the victims as well as the perceived perpetrator, that is, the brand. So regardless of whether the brand is responsible for the crisis, it should take accountability . . . before it is forced to.

Principle 3—Act With Lightning Speed

In Chapter 3, we describe the case of Starbucks facing a backlash for racial profiling of customers at one of its outlets in the United States in 2019. We provide a micro-level chronological unpacking of the case to highlight the company's skilled response, an awe-inspiring case of acting swiftly. High speed of response shows commitment and respect. Low speed demonstrates lethargy, lack of respect, and "delay tactics." Think about it. If you have an accident and are bleeding profusely, will you react fast? Or slow? In a situation, where the brand is perceived to have transgressed a.k.a. caused harm to its victims, it needs to place itself in the victims' shoes (as explained in Chapter 1), respond as if the harm was happening to itself, and do so at lightning speed. For sure, speed does not offset thoughtful deliberation. Indeed, the response must be carefully fleshed out, and its moving parts delineated in terms of a thorough and well-orchestrated execution strategy. But there can and should be no compromise on speed. As the saying goes, a stitch in time indeed saves nine. When it comes to managing a brand transgression, it likely saves more than nine.

Principle 4—Communicate Transparently

The world today is facing a technology tilt like never before and, in hindsight, the Internet appears to have been a mere tip of the iceberg. Artificial Intelligence (AI), machine-learning (ML) based algorithms, ChatGPT, and Metaverse are threatening to take over decision making from human beings and change lives irreversibly. It is foolhardy to think that opacity in communication, and spinning a false or incomplete narrative, can help a brand get out of trouble. The #MeToo movement, arguably precipitated with the 23 October 2017 article in *New Yorker* magazine about sexual misconduct by Hollywood mogul Harvey Weinstein, went viral within days and became a full-fledged global movement shortly thereafter. More recently, details regarding the murder of George Floyd on 25 May 2020 in Minneapolis spread like wildfire globally within a matter of hours. Ostensibly, considerations about Diversity, Equity, Inclusion, and Belonging that are now an integral part of innumerable business entities' decision making all over the world, has its roots in this event. In such an unprecedented environment, more than ever before, brands will be wise to be transparent in their communication when they come to be associated with a transgression. Disingenuous communication is often a quick road to serious brand damage, an idea we demonstrate in Chapter 4 through the case of VW's emissions scandal, what has come to be known as Dieselgate. Lies, cover-ups, half-truths . . . all lead to confusion and a compromise of trust, ultimately risking the brand and possibly the entire corporation on whose architecture it stands. Dalai Lama has said: "A lack of transparency results in distrust and a deep sense of insecurity" (Koulopoulos, 2018). Few things can be closer to the truth.

Principle 5—Choose Principle Over Profit

The story of the twin crashes of Boeing 737 MAX in many ways seems akin to VW's Dieselgate. A significant difference is that in Boeing's case, human lives were lost—346 of them. A stark commonality is that both of the companies were unsuccessful in their efforts at subverting the scandal, in large measure because of the calculus of profit first. Profit is necessary and desirable, for a host of reasons, not in the least of which is to reward a firm's shareholders. It is when the pursuit of profit becomes paramount that tradeoffs with principles might begin to taint decisions. We tease apart the Boeing case in Chapter 5 where the facts emerging from our research suggest that the profit pressure on Boeing may have played a foundational role in 737 MAX's technical glitches that led to the two crashes. The chapter also features a fascinating, and some may call counter-intuitive, story of Merck, a pharmaceutical company that chose humanistic principles even at the cost of profit . . . and profited financially.

Principle 6—Treat Each Life with Dignity

The concept of "human dignity" is crucial for companies to deeply imbibe and base their actions on—before, during, and after a transgression. Our belief is not stemming from a religious or faith-based lens but because often a brand's own dignity might depend on it. Chapter 6 lays out this promulgation through the contrasting cases of Dolce & Gabbana (D&G), the Italian luxury fashion corporate, and Ben & Jerry's (B&J's), the US-based ice cream manufacturer. D&G, once a loved brand in China, is believed to have talked down to the Chinese consumers in some of its advertising, possibly in misogynistic ways. Many perceive this to have been an action that undignified the populace in one of the largest luxury markets in the world. We juxtapose this with the case of B&J's, a brand that has built a reputation of being unconditionally devoted to shining light on socially and politically controversial issues to enhance human dignity. Beyond a clinical demonstration of its grasp of consumer thought and behavior, B&J's unwavering pursuit of its mission is exemplary in terms of how basing actions for the sake of human dignity can lead to virtuous outcomes.

Principle 7—Leadership Sets The Tone

Chapter 7 captures where the past, present, and future of a transgression reside—the leader of the corporation managing the transgressing brand. John Maxwell, an authority on leadership, has said: "A leader is one who knows the way, goes the way, and shows the way" (Leadr Team, 2019). This quote contains the essence of the chapter—that the makings of a transgression start at the top as do ways to handle it. To belabor this point—and it needs belaboring—each of the preceding six chapters carries stories where the leaders were front and center of the transgression, either as its cause or its solution. To nail this notion down more vividly, we describe the case of Fox News, the largest of the big three US new channels (along with CNN and MSNBC) and its late leader Roger Ailes. We regurgitate published evidence that led to the discovery that Ailes's toxic leadership style over decades not only drove his own egregious sexual misconduct but also that of several other senior Fox executives. Contrast this with the 26/11 terrorist attack in Mumbai, India's financial capital, which saw the murder of 166 innocent civilians and wounding of more than 300. Ten employees of Taj Mumbai, an iconic hotel and landmark on the shores of the city and one of the targets of the terrorists, also died that fateful night, most of them while trying to protect and save hotel guests. Their offering represents a culture nurtured over decades by leadership that empowers its employees and accords the highest respect to people first. Maxwell has also said: "Leadership is influence" (Maxwell, 2019). This influence begins at the top and can be bad as with Roger Ailes or good as with Taj Mumbai.

Principle 8—Build Brand Authenticity

Trust is the supreme currency in commerce. Customers, suppliers, policy makers, shareholders, employees, general public . . . all enter a relationship with a brand, or its parent corporation, based on an expectation of trust. From a brand management viewpoint, one of the most powerful and enduring ways to build trust is to imbue the brand with authenticity. Brand authenticity is more than simply "doing what you say and saying what you do." It represents the constellation of brand associations that signal to its stakeholders that the brand delivers its promise without fail—every time, with integrity, honesty, and respect. When a brand lives up to this definition of authenticity, repeatedly, month after month, year after year, decade after decade, it develops a level of trust that its competitors can only dream of or barely compete against. Its authenticity becomes a source of competitive advantage like no other. And at crunch time—as when it is perceived to have committed a transgression—the cushion of authenticity kicks in, protecting its victims as well as the brand. We talk about brand authenticity in Chapter 8 through the lens of Patagonia, a brand widely regarded in the Western world for its unwavering commitment to protecting the environment. Patagonia has promised environmental sustainability and delivered on it unerringly by creating footprints in the sand for others to follow. It has done so right from its inception to date. It has done so in thought, word, and deed. And it has done so without compromise.

The Eight Principles are listed in a summary table (Table 1) toward the end of this chapter, along with the case studies detailed in the book that illustrate each of these principles. These *point-in-time* case studies are of companies that were involved in real transgressions varying in severity and cover a span of almost 50 years (from 1969 to 2018). The brand transgressions themselves took place in ten different countries, with at least four of them with global impact. In addition, we have cited several other transgressions to illuminate a point or to buttress an argument. Capturing such a vast terrain was challenging but doing so helps sensitize the reader to some facts.

- While we have done our utmost to be thorough in our research, we sought illustration, not perfection.
- Each case study has many moving parts and most certainly it taps into more than just one principle. But we use it to focus on one and only one principle to take the reader step by step.
- It is unlikely that a brand undergoes transformation by following just one or a small subset of these principles. In most cases, the brand will need to examine its unique situation to figure out which of these principles needs what type and degree of emphasis in its specific context. More than likely, the ideal response will be to apply each of these principles in measured ways vis-à-vis each perceived transgression. Such a response will maximize the likelihood of successful brand transformation.

Table 1: Brand Transgressions and Transformation Cases

Title	Main Case	Supplemental
Introduction	Cadbury* (UK/India)	NA
Principle 1—Do The Right Thing	Tylenol (US)	Wells Fargo (US)/Snow Brand Milk (Japan)
Principle 2—Take Accountability	Dalkon Shield (US)	Nokia* (Finland/India)
Principle 3—Act With Lightning Speed	Starbucks (US)	Maggi Noodles* (Switzerland/India)
Principle 4—Communicate Transparently	Volkswagen (Germany/Global)	Stoli Vodka* (Latvia/US)
Principle 5—Choose Principle Over Profit	Boeing 737 MAX (US/Global)	Merck (US/Global)
Principle 6—Treat Each Life With Dignity	Dolce & Gabbana* (Italy/China)	Ben & Jerry's (US)
Principle 7—Leadership Sets The Tone	Fox News (US)	Taj Mumbai (India)
Principle 8—Build Brand Authenticity	Patagonia (US)	Interface Carpets (US)
Conclusion	Multiple	NA

*Location of brand transgression is different from home country of the brand.

Chapter 1
The First Principle: Do The Right Thing

Cyanide in Tylenol, Wells Fargo Banking Scandal, and Snow Brand Milk Poisoning

> "How do we protect the people?"—James E. Burke, CEO Johnson & Johnson*

Circa 1982. USA.

The year 1982 was a landmark one for our planet on several fronts. Argentina and UK got into a war over the Falkland Islands, the United States was hit by a major recession, the first CD player was sold in Japan, Steven Spielberg's classic movie *E.T. the Extra-Terrestrial* became a landmark box-office success, and a well-known Mumbai underworld operative Manohar Arjun Surve was killed by Maharashtra police in the first-ever known encounter killing. As Michael Jackson's album *Thriller* was released to worldwide acclaim, a darker kind of thriller was unfolding in the corridors of corporate America. A defining event in the annals of brand transgressions—with its epicentre located at one of the world's most successful and revered pharmaceutical companies, Johnson & Johnson (J&J)—was when its leading analgesic brand Tylenol, had been red flagged for being laced with cyanide.

Rise of Tylenol

Since its launch in 1975, Tylenol had risen meteorically to become the leader, with a market share of 37 percent and outselling the next four painkillers (Anacin, Bayer, Bufferin, and Excedrin) combined. By 1981, Tylenol was consumed by an estimated 100 million Americans and cited as one of the top 15 marketing successes by Marketing & Media Decisions, accounting for 13 percent and 33 percent of J&J's year-to-year sales and profit growth, respectively. If it had been a separate company, its profits would have placed it in the top half of the Fortune 500 (Berge, 1990). However, all this changed when the crisis hit.

---

*Dept. of Defense. (n.d.). Crises Communication Strategies. Case Study: The Johnson & Johnson Tylenol Crisis. DoD Joint Course in Communication, University of Oklahoma. *Department of Defense, USA.* Accessed on April 4, 2023, from https://www.ou.edu/deptcomm/dodjcc/groups/02C2/Johnson%20&%20Johnson.htm

https://doi.org/10.1515/9781501517334-002

Brand Transgression

On September 29, 1982, police in the Chicago area were baffled when several people, all in good health, suddenly died for reasons unknown. Mary Kellerman (age 12), Adam Janus (27), Stanley Janus (25), and Theresa Janus (19) died on the same day while Mary McFarland (31), Paula Prince (35), and Mary Reiner (27) died in the days that followed (Ganger, 2021). The first responders were dumbfounded by the string of deaths, wondering if the victims had anything in common. Medical authorities considered quarantining the entire area. The breakthrough came when Helen Jensen, a nurse from the public health department, informed authorities that in the Janus household, which had seen three deaths, there were six missing Tylenol Extra Strength pills.

Further investigation proved Jensen's hunch right. Food and Drug Administration (FDA) officials speculated that the killer bought Extra Strength Tylenol capsules over the counter (OTC), injected the red half of the capsules with potassium cyanide at 10,000 times the amount needed to be fatal, resealed the bottles, and sneaked them back on to the shelves of at least six drug and grocery stores in the Chicago area. The Illinois attorney general, on the other hand, suspected a disgruntled employee on Tylenol's factory line (Latson, 2014). At noon, local officials held a press conference and confirmed that cyanide poisoning indeed was the cause of death in all the victims. They noted that cyanide had been detected only in random capsules in the bottles of Extra Strength Tylenol found near the victims. The FDA advised that it would be prudent to avoid use of the Extra Strength Tylenol capsules until the situation becomes clear.

J&J's Chicago-based assistant public relations (PR) director first heard of cyanide in Extra Strength Tylenol capsules when a news reporter called, asking for a comment on the medical examiner's assertion that people were dying from consuming Tylenol (Dept. of Defense, n.d.). Three news broadcast networks broke the story on the same day, swiftly followed by equally damaging print media headlines. *Time* magazine called it "Poison Madness in the Midwest," *Newsweek* screamed "The Tylenol Scare," and *The Washington Post* framed it as "Tylenol, Killer or Cure." With virtually every media entity scrambling to cover "Cyanide in Tylenol," this story had ostensibly been given the widest US news coverage since the assassination of President John F. Kennedy (Berge, 1990). A post-crisis study estimated that within the first week of the crisis, more than 90 percent of the US population had heard of the seven consumer deaths from cyanide-laced Tylenol (Caesar-Gordon, 2015), a rarity in the pre-Internet era.

Impact

- **People stopped buying.** Terrified consumers nationwide either stopped purchasing Tylenol products, switched to other brands, or avoided the product category entirely. Independent surveys showed that 45 percent of existing customers were not planning to buy the brand. Many had not realized that the poisonings had involved only Tylenol capsules and not tablets (Tedlow & Smith, 2005b).

- **Retail orders affected**. Many retailers removed Tylenol from the shelves and the brand's retail orders across the country dropped by over 25 percent. Interestingly, some retailers left the shelf space open (rather than filling it with other brands), while some others put labels over shelves with Tylenol tablets indicating that those tablets were not affected; this, experts say, reflected the trade's confidence in the brand and the company (Greyser, 1982).
- **Competitors tried to cash in.** Makers of Anacin-3 worked overtime to increase production, and Bristol-Myers began offering 25 cents-off coupons for Bufferin and Excedrin in mid-October while trying not to appear malevolent (Tedlow & Smith, 2005b).
- **J&J's share price dropped.** J&J's stock plunged from more than $46 at the time of the announcement of the first death to under $19 per share (Tedlow & Smith, 2005b).
- **J&J faced lawsuits and began damage control.** One of the aggrieved families sued J&J and the Jewel Food Stores (where the affected capsule was purchased) for $15 million (UPI Archives, 1982).

Pessimism and Further Scrutiny

Several local and national government agencies initiated legislation prospectively requiring tamper-resistant packaging for over-the-counter medicines, although some—including the FDA Commissioner—expressed doubts on whether packaging could be made tamper-proof. The Proprietary Association, a group of over-the-counter drug companies, met to discuss more secure packaging for non-prescription remedies (Russell, 1982).

To J&J's relief, federal health officials, upon investigating the crime, absolved the company of wrongdoing, saying they believed the cyanide contamination was due to local tampering, and not on account of any defects at the factories (Tedlow & Smith, 2005b). However, industry experts predicted that customer anxiety might halt Tylenol's meteoric ascent. Well-known advertising guru Jerry Della Femina was quoted in *The New York Times* as saying, "On one day, every single human being in the country thought that Tylenol might kill them. I do not think there are enough advertising dollars, enough marketing men, to change that . . . . You'll not see the name Tylenol in any form within a year" (Tedlow & Smith, 2005b, p. 3). New York University marketing professor Benjamin Lipstein stated in *The Wall Street Journal*, "Johnson & Johnson is up against the most difficult problem they've ever had to face—how to dislodge the residual elements of fear. I have a headache right now, but this time I took Bayer. I have Tylenol capsules in my house, but I'll be damned if anyone is going to take them" (Tedlow & Smith, 2005b, p. 3). The long and the short of this perceived transgression was that Tylenol was facing a near-death brand crisis as its market share shrank from 37 percent pre-crisis to a minuscule 7 percent post-crisis (Tedlow & Smith, 2005b).

Many wondered what would constitute "responsible corporate behavior" in such a situation. Should J&J do a total recall? Who will bear the cost? Will the OTC market shrink? Would past Tylenol consumers return to use the brand in the future? Would this crisis impact only capsule sales, or will the brand's tablet product be affected as well? What short- to medium-term steps can J&J take to mitigate the situation? What actions can the government take? Can Tylenol ever regain its numero uno position in the market? Should companies invest in new packaging technology?

CEO James Burke Responds

Amidst all these questions and as disbelief and shock reverberated through corporate America, the immediate reaction of James Burke, the CEO of J&J, defined Tylenol's subsequent response. In internal deliberations, the first question he ostensibly asked was "How do we protect the people?" and then "How do we save this product?" (Berge, 1990). "The credo is all about the consumer," Burke said. When those seven deaths occurred, "the credo made it very clear at that point exactly what we were all about. It gave me the ammunition I needed to persuade shareholders and others to spend the $100 million on the recall. The credo helped sell it" (Knowledge@Wharton, 2012). This focus on protecting the consumer became the bedrock for the stunning brand transformation that was to unravel. To answer this question, "How do we protect the people?", J&J engaged in a series of coordinated actions—big and small— which involved the entire organization and were to become folklore.

– **Took accountability.** The company assumed accountability *and* responsibility for the crisis even though it did not occur at one of their plants. It cooperated fully and transparently with law enforcement and health authorities, as well as the media.
– **Engaged in a proactive media strategy.** Before the crisis, J&J had a perfunctory relationship with the media—its only interactions being those related to advertising and marketing. After the crisis, Burke pursued a candid and transparent communication strategy with the press. J&J received over 2,500 calls from reporters in the early weeks and it provided all available information so that the public may be informed and stay protected. Additionally, the firm established a toll-free line for the media to contact and get pre-recorded daily messages with updated declarations. Burke even met media owners and editors individually to apprise them of the situation, smoothening many a ruffled media feather.

- **Held regular press conferences.** J&J's corporate headquarters became the venue of many major press conferences. Within hours, an internal video team had set up a live broadcast feed to the New York metro region via satellite, enabling all press conferences to be broadcast nationwide. Burke featured himself in more than 50 advertisements reminding the audience not to buy Tylenol, met with heads of all the news media outlets, and appeared on *60 Minutes* and *Donahue* talk-shows to personally deliver this message to the public (Broom, 1994).
- **Alerted customers.** J&J notified customers across the country via both public relations as well as paid media to refrain from consuming any Tylenol product until the scope of the tampering could be ascertained. The company launched a toll-free hotline to field questions and allay fears to the greatest extent possible. Hundreds of calls were handled, and volunteer staff patiently provided all available information.
- **Notified the doctors.** Over 450,000 telexes were sent to physicians, hospitals, and the trade, warning against the use of Tylenol until the Chicago incident had been clarified.
- **Halted all advertising.** Advertising for all forms of Tylenol was halted indefinitely and a $100,000 reward was announced for anyone with information about the suspect (Knight, 1982).
- **Recalled all products.** Within 72 hours, in consultation with the FDA, a recall of *all* Tylenol products was initiated in the Chicago metro area. When two copycat cases occurred in California in the first week, a *nationwide* recall and destruction of 31 million bottles of Tylenol were executed despite internal resistance that doing so may be an overreaction. Production of all Tylenol products was halted indefinitely as J&J stayed firm on its credo that consumer safety was its paramount concern (Rehak, 2002).
- **Conducted an internal audit.** J&J engaged in a micro-level audit of its production, packaging, supply chain, retail, brand communication, product recall and destruction, and promotion/PR. This combined and gargantuan effort cost the company upwards of $100 million (roughly $300 million at today's prices) (Tedlow & Smith, 2005b).

Brand Transformation

On October 11, twelve days after the crisis broke out, a Tylenol Strategy Committee was formed to marshal the full force of the company to resurrect Tylenol.

Replacing Capsules with Tablets

Based on customer feedback, J&J announced a plan to exchange all Tylenol capsules for Tylenol tablets, which were perceived as more difficult to tamper with and therefore safer. This exchange was provided at substantial discounts at an additional expense of millions of dollars. The new ads debuted on October 22 with J&J sending out 61,000 "Dear Doctor" letters a few days previously, explaining the company's response to the tampering (Tedlow & Smith, 2005b).

Repackaging

Following the Tylenol poisonings there was a wave of product tamperings. Mercuric chloride was found in three bottles of Extra Strength Excedrin, rat poison in Maximum Strength Anacin, and hydrochloric acid in Visine eye drops, according to reports from Denver. Bristol-Myers Squibb, the manufacturer of Excedrin, withdrew the product from Denver merchants' shelves. American Home Products and Pfizer, the manufacturers of Anacin and Visine respectively, labeled the tamperings "isolated incidents" and took no action (Tedlow & Smith, 2005b, p. 5). It was evident that there was an urgent need for tamper-resistant packaging. However, it would cost manufacturers hundreds of millions of dollars, and there was no assurance that safer packaging would restore customer trust in OTC analgesics. Some researchers anticipated that customers would forgo OTC analgesics altogether and the industry would contract to below $1 billion (Tedlow & Smith, 2005b). The FDA issued new drug-packaging rules on November 4, requiring that, by February 1983, "tamper-susceptible" products such as capsules be placed in containers that prevented tampering, accompanied with a warning that said, "Do not use if safety seals are broken" (Communiqué PR Staff, 2017).

J&J is First Off-the-Mark

J&J responded with alacrity to the FDA order before its competitors, reintroducing Tylenol in a triple safety-sealed container on November 11, merely a week after the FDA's new mandate. The launch was broadcast live via satellite to 30 locations, where 600 journalists had assembled to cover the story. Over the next four weeks, J&J distributed 40 million coupons—each worth $2.50—as a discount to replace any discarded Tylenol product with the new triple safety-sealed packaged alternative. Customers could also obtain a voucher by dialing a toll-free number (Tedlow & Smith, 2005b). The goal was to provide thousands of consumers who had rejected Tylenol (at the company's request) with the chance to re-use the product at no cost. This packaging has since become the industry norm in many parts of the globe.

Resurgence of Brand Tylenol

According to reports, Tylenol had regained more than 55 percent of its pre-crisis market share by November end, up from October-end figures of 20 percent. These numbers only represented tablet sales because capsules, which had accounted for 40 percent of Tylenol's revenue at the time, were only recently reintroduced. By September 1984, the brand's market share had risen to 33 percent of the $1.5 billion market. By mid-1985, Tylenol still had a commanding lead in the $1.6 billion OTC analgesics industry, accounting for 35 percent of retail sales. Tylenol had regained its pre-poisoning share in a market that was now 3 percent larger (Tedlow & Smith, 2005b). Within a year of the crisis and a $100 million investment, Tylenol's sales rebounded and catapulted it back to being the nation's favorite OTC pain reliever. Consumer trust in Tylenol grew threefold compared to the pre-crisis era and its market share rose to a remarkable 48 percent 90 days after the re-launch (Hogg, 2013).

In 1983, the US Congress passed The Tylenol Bill that made tampering with consumer products a federal offence (Markel, 2014). "Many industry experts were surprised at the speed of Tylenol's comeback, *The Wall Street Journal* labeling it a marketing miracle" (Tedlow & Smith, 2005b, p. 6). The credit for this "miracle," however, cannot be accorded to marketing alone. The brand transgression leading to a crisis and ultimately ending in the brand's transformation was the outcome of a coordinated set of actions involving the entire J&J organization. Most importantly, this transformation was predicated on the first principle—Do the Right Thing vis-à-vis the consumer. By single-mindedly focusing on consumer protection, both in word and action, and being officially exonerated of any wrongdoing or negligence with respect to the contamination, the brand came to be perceived as the "victim" rather than the "perpetrator" of a dangerous crime.

In summing up the Tylenol crisis, Burke stated: "All previous managements who built this corporation handed us on a silver platter the most powerful tool you could possibly have—institutional trust . . . We got challenged by a very dramatic event of unparalleled proportions. Not only did we face up to the challenge, but we demonstrated that all of that hundred years of trust works to help solve problems, no matter how serious they may be" (Tedlow, 2006, p. 7).

The 1986 Poisoning

The horror returned in 1986, when Diane Elsroth, a 23-year-old resident of Westchester County, New York, died after ingesting cyanide-laced Extra Strength Tylenol despite the triple-sealed, tamper-resistant packaging implemented following the 1982 murders. New York's health commissioner banned sales of Tylenol capsules in that state. Again, luckily for J&J, the FDA declared that there was no obvious link between the 1982 poisonings and the current issue (Tedlow & Smith, 2005b). This time, though, the company had a template in place. A similar drill ensued: news conferences were held, contaminated bottles were recalled, broadcast notifications were issued to customers to avoid using any type of Tylenol in capsule form, and television advertising for all types of Tylenol was halted indefinitely. Burke called the poisonings an "act of terrorism pure and simple." He was candid in acknowledging that J&J had no idea how to enhance the tamper-resistant packaging it has designed. Burke stated that he would invite consumers to inform him if a recall was necessary or not through attitude surveys. Tylenol capsules accounted for approximately one-third of Tylenol sales in 1985, or $160 million. What may have worked in J&J's favor was that the business was widely seen as innocent (Tedlow & Smith 2005b, p. 11).

On February 17, Burke announced that J&J will withdraw all its OTC capsule products from the market because it could no longer ensure capsule safety at a level consistent with its standards of consumer accountability and offered to replace any that customers had purchased. He encouraged people to use Tylenol tablets instead. Consumers reacted favorably, and J&J recorded more than 200,000 responses to its offer (Tedlow & Smith, 2005b).

While Tylenol's is a story about many layers over and above that of consumer safety because of which it is considered a benchmark, there are innumerable examples of how not to respond to a crisis. We now present two such cases — Well Fargo Bank and Snow Brand Milk — highlighting the blinding contrast vis-à-vis Tylenol in terms of the focus on consumer safety, or lack thereof.

Wells Fargo Banking Scandal

For more than three decades, Wells Fargo (WF) bank's stated mission has been to "satisfy our customers' financial needs and help them succeed financially." Warren Buffet, one of the most successful investors the world has known, was a long-time investor in WF. *Fortune* magazine complimented the bank for "a history of avoiding the rest of the industry's stupidest blunders," and *American Banker* named Wells Fargo "the large bank least damaged by scandals and reputational problems (Tayan, 2019)." In 2013, it recognized WF Chairman and CEO John Stumpf as "Banker of the Year," and Carrie Tolstedt, who headed the company's large community banking division, the "Most Powerful Woman in Banking." Wells Fargo was placed seventh on Barron's 2015 list of the "Most Respected Companies" (Tayan, 2019). By the end of 2015, WF ranked first in market value among all US banks, third in terms of assets, made $22.9 billion in profits on $86.1 billion in sales, and boldly declared in its annual report that "we serve one in every three families in the United States," establishing itself as the "world's most valuable bank" (Lynch & Cutro, 2017, p. 1).

The Transgression

Then, on September 8, 2016, the WF cross-selling scandal came to light, and observers and watchdogs dug in. According to the *Los Angeles Times*, WF's internal sales culture, which was centered on exceeding unreasonable goals, resulted in employees signing up millions of clients for accounts and credit cards they didn't want, didn't need, and were often unaware of. It was revealed that certain WF workers had engaged in dubious behavior to reach their sales targets (Hiltzik, 2020). Further investigation discovered that staff opened over 2 million fake deposit accounts and more than 500,000 credit card accounts that were not approved by consumers (Lynch & Cutro, 2017), particularly vulnerable ones such as immigrants, students, and the elderly. Apparently, the bank's senior executives threatened branch managers, who in turn threatened their employees —who did everything they could to save their jobs, utilizing extraordinary techniques to cross-sell, often verging on the absurd (Tayan, 2019). "Simply put, Wells Fargo traded its hard-earned reputation for short-term profits, and harmed untold numbers of customers along the way," said U.S. Attorney Nick Hanna for the Central District of California in a US Department of Justice Statement (Comcowich, 2020).

The Response

WF's early public statement of "regret" at what occurred appeared weak and callous (ABC News, 2016). After a few weeks, the firm apologized to its customers through a full-page newspaper ad. Stumpf himself did not express remorse until he was interrogated by the Senate Banking Committee in September 2016. Instead of coming clean, the CEO shifted responsibility to the 5,300 dismissed low-level employees, "In any given year, 1,000 out of 100,000 employees didn't get it right. But I have to say, the vast majority did do it right . . . every day" (Cohan, 2016). "The 1% that did it wrong, who we fired, terminated, in no way reflects our culture nor reflects the great work the other vast majority of the people do. That is false narrative" (Glazer & Rexrode, 2016). He never acknowledged company policy or senior decision-making as the primary culprits in establishing unattainable sales targets. Even after the news surfaced, the bank was hesitant to change its sales rules. It was also revealed that managers and internal auditors had informed top executives that unrealistic sales targets were causing difficulties, with some even writing directly to Stumpf. Their concerns, however, went unheeded and were disregarded as the activities of a few low-level employees. Many of them stated that they were fired soon after making the whistleblower calls (Lynch & Cutro, 2017). This caused Warren Buffet to chastise them in a CNBC interview, stating, "The important thing is that they disregarded it when they discovered it" (Comcowich, 2020). After a protracted delay, WF fired Stumpf and elevated Timothy J. Sloan, who had worked for the bank for 29 years. After Sloan failed to resolve the issue, the bank recruited an outsider, former Bank of New York Mellon CEO

Charlie Scharf, to restore trust in the brand. Appointing an outside CEO and dismissing individuals from the Board of Directors much earlier may have shown that WF was serious about fixing its operational difficulties (Comcowich, 2020).

In 2018, the Federal Reserve slapped a $1.95 trillion asset limitation on WF, barring it from expanding beyond this limit, potentially denying it billions in profits. In 2020, the bank was fined $3 billion to settle its long-running civil and criminal investigations, representing 15 percent of its 2019 profits and reported its first quarterly loss since 2008 (Larsen, 2021). A month later, Stumpf was penalized $17.5 million and prohibited from ever working in the banking industry again (Kelly, 2020). In a recent assessment, WF was ranked the worst bank in the US based on the American Customer Satisfaction Index, a dramatic reversal from only five years back when it was viewed as the world's most valuable bank (Lynch & Cutro, 2017). And the end of its woes is not in sight as more scrutiny of its practices and culture continues.

Contamination of Snow Brand Milk

An outbreak of food poisoning is a nightmare for any food brand. Japan's premier dairy foods company, Snow Brand Milk Co. Ltd. (SBM), had to face one in July 2000 when more than 13,400 people became seriously ill after consuming three Snow Brand milk products that were contaminated with two types of toxin-producing bacteria—*staphylococcus aureus* and *cereus*. It was the worst case of food poisoning ever in Japan (Werhane et al., 2010a). The problem sourced to its production plant in Osaka was attributed to human error and oversight (Japan Times, 2000a). The production line at the factory where untreated milk was produced had come to a halt due to an industrial power outage. This dangerous substance was then carried on to the next phase of the manufacturing process without being disposed of, resulting in a poisonous skimmed milk powder. Following that, dairy products containing the deadly chemical were manufactured and sent from the Osaka facility, leading to a food poisoning outbreak. Further inquiry revealed that factory management and personnel had only a limited awareness of *enterotoxin* (the hazardous substance created by excessive bacteria build-up) and lacked fundamental food sanitation expertise, crisis management understanding, and preparedness procedures to cope with such an occurrence (Werhane et al., 2010a).

Response and Outcome

When the incident came to light, the company's first reaction was to preserve the brand rather than treat the poisoned victims. Its second reaction was to deliberately destroy evidence by replacing a part connecting a pipe with a contaminated valve just prior to inspection. Its third reaction was to resist recall as encouraged by the Osaka City Public Health Department until forced to do so. Its fourth and fifth reactions were to minimize the problem by releasing either half-truths or serious misrepresentations of the facts underlying the case (Baker, 2005). Tetsuro Ishikawa, the company's president and CEO, outraged the public when he indicated (to reporters) that "he was suffering as much as the victims as a result of the incident" (Werhane et al., 2010a). Soon after, Ishikawa resigned, followed by the entire board of directors. Because of the negative media coverage, the public believed that food poisoning was the outcome of corporate snobbery. An editorial piece in the *Japan Times* said: "Explanations by company officials as reports of illness caused by Snow Brand's products grew were not only inconsistent; they were sometimes deliberately misleading and incomplete, if not downright false" (Japan Times, 2000b).

Snow Brand was privy to transgressions in the past and had managed to recover from them. This time, however, a tipping point had been reached and something snapped with the consumers and the public at large. First, SBM products were immediately removed from store shelves across the country, even though the contaminated products and food poisoning had been limited to western Japan. Following this, eight factories were temporarily closed. Most school districts, day-care centers, and municipalities decided not to purchase Snow Brand products for at least two years. Snow Brand was also forced to pull out of a joint project to launch new coffee drinks under a single brand with two of Japan's leading beverage makers—Japan Tobacco Inc. and Key Coffee Inc. As a result, once the darling milk brand of Japanese consumers, its market share went from 45 percent to less than 10 percent within a matter of weeks after the transgression. The company dropped off the Fortune Global 500 list, whereas the previous year it had been ranked behind only Nestlé, ConAgra, Sara Lee, and Groupe Danone. Next, some of its senior executives were charged with crimes of negligence and suspended, and Snow Milk had to settle several civil suits filed by affected consumers (Werhane et al., 2010a).

Snow Milk had long been driven by the principle of *unmei kyodotai*, the belief that a business exists not for the sake of consumers or shareholders, but the benefit of its management and staff. This mindset contributed to the self-protective, self-serving behavior displayed by corporate leaders when the crisis hit. Additionally, communication was top-down, with no formal procedure to communicate negative news to senior management. The new president, Kohei Nishi, embarked on a reform and revitalization effort, including voluntarily providing additional information on product labels, launching consumer education programs on food safety and nutrition, forming a business ethics committee, adopting a code of conduct, quality assurance system based on ISO 9001, and food safety management program (Werhane et al., 2010a). Sadly, old habits do not die too soon. Having failed to learn their lesson, just two years later, Snow Brand's meat-packing unit was shut down after it was found there was deliberate mislabeling of Australian beef as Japanese to receive government subsidies in the wake of the mad cow disease outbreak in Japan. A day later the company admitted to altering expiry dates on 2,300 tons of butter (Food Navigator, n.d.). As with the earlier milk scandal, once again retailers removed Snow Brand products from store shelves. Five senior executives of the food subsidiary pleaded guilty to fraud charges for the scam that netted the company JPY 196 million (USD 1.8 million). The second scandal was a significant blow to Snow Milk, with Moody's Investors Services downgrading its credit rating to B2. It is not surprising, therefore, that, in less than three years after the original crisis, the company was merged with the National Federation of Agricultural Cooperative Associations and the National Federation of Dairy Cooperative Associations as the Nippon Milk Community Company. Ultimately, it was renamed as the Megmilk Snow Brand Company (Reuters, 2009; Werhane et al., 2010b).

Principle 1: Do The Right Thing

Milton Friedman, a well-known economist, said: "There is one and only one social responsibility of business—to use its resources and engage in activities designed to increase its profits" (Friedman, 1970). This classic capitalist school of thought was foundational to the 1980s shareholder value maximization revolution that dominates most corporate settings even today. The underlying ideological belief is that when a for-profit company maximizes shareholder value, it is acting in the best interests of its owners—the shareholders. Indeed, unless a company makes profit, it cannot reward its shareholders who have placed their trust and money in the company. It also needs profits to sustain itself, invest in expansion and other initiatives to stay competitive.

However, it is in times of crisis, like the one faced by Tylenol, when the rubber hits the road, and a brand is forced to ask the question—to what extent should it focus on saving itself and protecting its profits? The knee jerk response of minimizing damage to the brand and the company is understandable. "Stop the bleeding" is sound advice, and for good reason. Notably, J&J's response to the crisis was to stop the *consumer* bleeding versus focus on itself. When Tylenol found itself in hot water, rather than pondering how to protect its market share, sales, profit, shareholder value, competitive advantage, and/or brand equity, Burke's first, almost instinctive, response was, "How do we protect the people?" Later, in a visit to Harvard Business School, he shared: "I do know that running through my mind throughout . . . was how the hell after we'd had everybody in the world challenge the system, buy into it, and say 'Yes, we believe in it,' could we sit in our offices and say, 'Well in this case we're just not going to do it. So, we locked ourselves in . . .'" (Tedlow, 2006, p. 4). This humanistic focus on the victim—the consumer—even at the cost of the brand and profit is what we call "Doing the Right Thing."

The essence of the question, "How do we protect the people?" is the crux of this first principle. Most companies have carefully crafted and well-articulated corporate philosophies, mission statements, and credos in their marketing communications, website content, and employee training. However, when a transgression is perceived and a crisis hits, many find it challenging to act in accord with their stated values. This is where J&J was different. Long before the start of the "shareholder versus stakeholder" debate, J&J pioneered a code to guide its famed corporate culture. Penned by its scion and legendary chairman General Robert Wood Johnson II in the 1940s, the code proclaimed that J&J's "first responsibility" was to its customers followed by its employees, management, communities, and stockholders, in that order (Knowledge@-Wharton, 2012). This governing principle to act in the "public's best interest" became the driving force for Tylenol's crisis response.

Even though J&J was not at fault, it took accountability and expressed remorse rather than denial or passing the buck and decided to examine and fix the problem without fuss. The company acted with unbelievable swiftness and absorbed the $100 million recovery cost. Within a week of the first revelation of the Tylenol poisonings, all Extra Strength Tylenol stock (31 million bottles) was recalled nationally and destroyed, tamper proof packaging was developed, and customers were offered substantial discounts to replace their product with new safety-tested product. J&J had begun unconditional and transparent cooperation with FDA and the Chicago police department, and virtually the entire world was made aware of the situation in real time directly by the company. Constant and consistent communication with both internal and external stakeholders supported the "house cleaning" endeavor, and J&J treated each life with dignity rather than merely another element in a clinical cost–benefit analysis. Tylenol was likely already an authentic brand, and these actions further strengthened the foundation of confidence among its consumers. Its strong consumer safety driven culture became even more renowned for its "consumer first" principle.

Virtually every market driven economy has laws that govern a company's behavior to protect the consumer and these laws are constantly evolving in response to emerging issues. Our first principle—Doing the Right Thing—however, concerns itself with protecting the consumer even when a brand has broken no laws. "Ethics entails action; it is not just a topic to mull or debate" (Kast, 2016). Tylenol faced a transgression, managed the ensuing near-death crisis based on sound principles, took a hit, survived, and ultimately, thrived. Unfortunately, not all brands prioritize consumer protection as J&J did. And the outcomes they face as a result can be severely damaging to them, in the short as well as the long term.

We take each of these elements of J&J's response to delineate the other seven principles in the next seven chapters. Some of the stories that demonstrate these principles may land as shocking, eye-opening, even heartbreaking. Others are empowering and hope generating. Together, they spell out a clear and distinct road map from brand transgression through crisis to transformation provided a brand is willing to put its money where its principles are.

Postscript

Brands live in action, not words. As Starbucks's former chairperson and CEO Howard Schultz said, "If people believe they share values with the company, they will stay loyal with the brand" (CUB, 2018). Brand building is a constant never-ending process and just one poorly handled transgression can destroy the endeavor if the brand deviates from its core values. Since the twin crises, J&J has won numerous accolades for consumer safety and its social responsibility initiatives. The company was also ranked eleventh in *DiversityInc* magazine's "2012 DiversityInc Top 50 Companies for Diversity" list (DiversityInc, 2012). Ironically, J&J is now in the thick of another long-drawn-out crisis—its famed baby powder is under scrutiny for possibly causing cancer. And even after 40 years, who was responsible for the Tylenol murders remains an unsolved mystery.

Chapter 2
The Second Principle: Take Accountability
Death by Dalkon Shield Contraceptive and Explosive Nokia Phone Batteries

> "You have taken the bottom line as your guiding beacon and the low road as your route . . . This is corporate irresponsibility at its meanest."—Judge Miles W. Lord chastising top executives at A.H. Robins Company when hearing the Dalkon Shield case in February 1984*

Circa 1969, USA.

Loretta Ross was pregnant with her first child. But it was not a happy occasion for her: she was only 14 and a victim of rape and incest. Two years later, at 16, she was expecting her second child, again unplanned. To avoid further pregnancies, she decided to get the most well-known intrauterine device (IUD), the Dalkon Shield, implanted in her uterus. It was touted as a safer alternative to birth control pills because, at that time, there were concerns that the pill caused blood clots and increased cancer risk (Stanley, 2017). After an initial period when everything seemed fine, she started experiencing extreme pain and developed an infection. Her clueless doctor at George Washington University Hospital started treating her for a rare venereal disease. The treatment continued for six months, but Ross's pain did not subside until one horrific day when she had to be rushed to the emergency unit for a life-saving hysterectomy. Gut instinct led her to her gynecologist where she learned that several women using the Dalkon Shield were experiencing pelvic infections leading to septic abortions (Stanley, 2017).

Ross was the first of an estimated 300,000 women who sued Dalkon Shield's parent company A.H. Robins in a class action lawsuit for causing physical injuries, miscarriages, infections, emergency hysterectomies, and even deaths (Bahr, 2012). The company used all its financial and political muscle to suppress and stymie the victims and infamously refused to take accountability for its transgression, until, finally, it met its Waterloo. Justice was partially served when it went bankrupt, becoming a telling case study of what a brand should *not do* when facing a transgression driven crisis.

Dalkon Shield—The Product

The Dalkon Shield, an IUD invented in 1968 by physician Hugh Davis and electrical engineer Irwin Lerner, was created with spikes along its edges to prevent natural ex-

---

*NYT. (1984, March 2). Judge Lambastes Company in Suit on Intrauterine Device. *The New York Times*. Section B, p. 16. Accessed on November 9, 2023, from https://www.nytimes.com/1984/03/02/us/judge-lambastes-company-in-suit-on-intrauterine-device.html

https://doi.org/10.1515/9781501517334-003

pulsion from the body and contained a string that passed from the uterus into the vagina. Davis tested the new IUD on 640 inner-city women from Baltimore over 12 months. Using life-table analysis, he reported a pregnancy rate of 1.1 percent, an expulsion rate of 2.3 percent, and a net retention rate of 94 percent (Krismann, 2015). Impressed by these results, a family-owned Fortune 500 pharmaceutical company, A.H. Robins, picked up the device in 1970 for $750,000 from Davis and Lerner. The company, best known for its ChapStick lip balm and Robitussin cough syrup, had no experience manufacturing and marketing women's intimate healthcare products. It retained Davis as a consultant and modified the design of the Dalkon Shield, making it smaller in size, adding a small amount of copper salts, and a multifilament wick to aid in its removal (Krismann, 2015).

The same year, Davis published an article in the *American Journal of Obstetrics and Gynecology* describing the device as "modern," with "superior performance," and a "first-choice method"—words and phrases not normally used to annotate rigorous scientific studies. Furthermore, the company made the decision not to disclose the addition of copper salts, instead labeling it as a "confidential blending of ingredients." Disclosure of copper salts—an active substance—would categorize the device as a drug (instead of its current categorization of a medical device) and make it subject to testing and approval from the FDA (Krismann, 2015).

In 1971, the Dalkon Shield was launched in US and Puerto Rican markets with an elaborate marketing campaign that emphasized its safety vis-à-vis conventional contraceptive pills. The company aggressively targeted gynecologists, less experienced family physicians, teenagers, the underprivileged, and minority women to maximize market penetration of the Shield as a highly effective and cheaper alternative to birth or "population" control (Bahr, 2012). Over the next three years, Robins captured 60 percent of the US market, selling 2.2 million Dalkon Shields, and an additional 1.7 million in overseas markets. At its peak, about 2.8 million women used the Dalkon Shield in the United States (Connolly, 2013). The cost of producing each IUD to Robins was $0.35, which was sold to prescribing physicians for $4.35, who in turn charged $12 to patients (Roepke & Schaff, 2014), a markup of close to 3500% over cost.

Brand Transgression

Within a few months of launch, negative reviews from doctors began to surface. One gynecologist refused to offer the Dalkon Shield to her patients, calling it a "veritable instrument of torture" and a "gruesome-looking little device" with "vicious spikes" that made removal difficult for the doctor and painful for the user (Anna, 2016). Another physician wrote to Robins saying, "I have found the procedure to be the most traumatic manipulation ever perpetrated on womanhood, and I have inserted thousands of other varieties" (Bahr, 2012). Meanwhile, tens of thousands of women reported getting pregnant—casting a shadow on its efficacy as a birth control device. Ostensibly, the 1.1 percent pregnancy rate claimed by Davis was based on a small, methodologically flawed study conducted over only eight months. In new testing, the Dalkon Shield was found to have a 5.5 percent pregnancy rate over the course of a year. Moreover, 60 percent of women who got pregnant reported having miscarriages. Many others reported inflammatory pelvic infections, uterine perforations, ectopic pregnancies, emergency hysterectomies, and spontaneous septic abortions (Anna, 2016). Robins' initial response was to dismiss these pelvic infections as likely relapses of prior infections, consequences of poor insertion technique on the part of the physician, and/or poor hygiene on the part of the recipients. The company recommended the use of spermicidal agents for the first several months after insertion.

For the next three years until 1974, Robins remained silent about the increased infection rate when the first of 18 deaths associated with the use of the Dalkon Shield were reported in the United States (Miller, 1996). Congress and the FDA launched hearings and investigations. The culprit that made the Dalkon Shield dangerous was found to be the multifilament wick or string that had never been used in IUDs before. The Planned Parenthood Federation of America (PPFA) banned the Shield and recommended its removal from the bodies of those who were using it (Anna, 2016). The same year, FDA asked Robins to halt distribution of the Shield, which the company did while adding the caveat that there was "no reason to believe at this time that physicians should remove the Dalkon Shield from patients now wearing them" (Roepke & Schaff, 2014). Surprisingly, the company did not recall the devices in circulation, made no effort to educate the consumer, continued to shun accountability, and marketed the product internationally for an additional 10 months. The Centers for Disease Control (CDC) conducted research a year later that linked the Dalkon Shield to a greater risk of spontaneous abortion-related mortality than other IUDs (MMWR, 1974). In 1976, the US Congress passed federal legislation mandating that the FDA require safety and efficacy testing of all IUDs before approval (Cassidy-Brinn, 2011). According to an estimate, the Dalkon Shield had caused more than 200,0000 cases of serious uterine infections in the United States alone. And for every million dollars in profit A.H. Robins made on the Shield, victimized women had spent an estimated $20 million for medical care on problems arising from its use (Dowie et al., 1979).

Taking advantage of the inadequate medical expertise and laws in developing countries (Dowie et al., 1979), Robins found an unlikely protagonist in the United States Agency for International Development (USAID), that had $125 million at its disposal for the purchase and distribution of contraceptive devices overseas as part of its population control agenda. Robins' international marketing director wrote to USAID expressing an interest in placing "this fine product into population control programs and family planning clinics throughout the Third World." The deal was sweetened with a special 48 percent off bulk discount price for *unsterilized* devices, which were sold in the United States exclusively in sterilized packaging (Miller, 1996). In what some believed was a brazen disregard for the well-being of their consumers, Robins provided only one inserter for every 10 Shield's thus greatly increasing the probability of infection from reuse. Further, only one set of instructions was included for every 1,000 Shield's printed in three languages—English, French, and Spanish—although the devices were destined for distribution in 80 countries, primarily Asian and Muslim, making it unlikely that more than a few could read them (Dowie et al., 1979).

When USAID officials asked whether the IUDs could be safely inserted by poorly trained staff workers serving remote family planning clinics, Robins replied in the affirmative, producing a new study demonstrating that any paramedic could learn to insert the Shield in half an hour. This was in contradiction to routine reports of adverse medical reactions blamed on unqualified personnel inserting the device in the United States. Altogether, USAID purchased and shipped more than 4.5 million Dalkon Shields, to unsuspecting and low socio-economic status women in the developing world, paid for by the American taxpayer. Although there is no reliable data on the extent of the damage, it is estimated that "Shield-related PID (pelvic inflammatory disease) killed hundreds, possibly thousands of women outside of the United States" (Miller, 1996).

Impact

By October 1984, Robins had made millions from its other product lines but netted only $500,000 on the 4.5 million Dalkon Shields sold worldwide. The brand had become a legal and insurance nightmare (Kenney, 1985) with the first wave of lawsuits commencing in 1974. Leveraging their experienced lawyers and vast resources, initially the company received a series of favorable verdicts, paying out $11,000 on average per victim by attributing plaintiffs' poor personal hygiene and irresponsible sexual activity to their illness rather than a faulty IUD device (Lindenfeld, 2016). But this soon changed.

Employing a new and controversial strategy that was to become commonplace in the future, known as class action lawsuit, a few plaintiff law firms began to actively search for Dalkon Shield victims by placing full page newspaper and magazine advertisements across the United States. This advertising not only re-energized waning media interest but also led to a dramatic increase in the number of plaintiffs. In 1983, the tide turned when a growing coalition of several law firms began working together to pool their expertise and data, and secured successive multi-billion-dollar verdicts for a defective product and willful negligence (Rutchick, 1984).

It took A.H. Robins nine years after Dalkon Shield's launch and six years after the first Dalkon Shield related death, to finally acknowledge fault and send a "Dear Doctor" letter advising physicians to remove the IUD from the bodies of their patients. In 1983, the FDA also issued a similar edict (Kenney, 1985). By 1984, Robins' insurance firm had settled about 7,600 claims for an estimated $245 million. A month later, Robins launched a $4.5 million advertising campaign advising women still using the Dalkon Shield to have their doctors remove it at the company's expense. In response, Robins received more than 11,000 calls from users and 4,500 bills from doctors for removing the device (Kenney, 1985). The same year, the case took a dramatic and final twist: Roger Tuttle, the original in-house lawyer of A.H. Robins, who had left the company 10 years earlier, was now a law professor at Oral Roberts Law School in Oklahoma. He had been following the Dalkon Shield lawsuits and decided to come forward with additional information. Tuttle confirmed, for the first time, that there was an organized attempt to hide facts by Robins' executives. He produced incriminating documents that he and others had been ordered to destroy in the early 1970s, finally exposing the elaborate cover-up (Roepke & Schaff, 2014). By the end of 1985, the company was facing nearly 400,000 lawsuits from people in every state of the United States, resolved or litigated 9,500, and filed for Chapter 11 bankruptcy to prevent the filing of more lawsuits. It did, however, set up the first ever fixed-asset Trust Fund that handled 400,000 cases from more than 80 countries, and paid 170,000 claimants over $3 billion until it closed in 2000. Nearly 8 percent of American women who used the Dalkon Shield filed complaints against the company (Krismann, 2015). Unfortunately, many affected women were treated unfairly: 99,400 of the 195,000 women who were eligible for compensation picked the easiest alternative, a quick payout of $725; and 150,000 of the 195,000 cases were resolved without the assistance of lawyers. The majority of the women in the class-action complaint were awarded less than $1,000, which was insufficient to recompense those who had been harmed (Roepke & Schaff, 2014).

Brand that Failed to Transform

Right from product design to the final settlement, A.H. Robins got it wrong—showing a striking lack of remorse, empathy, compassion, humanity, integrity, ethics, leadership, or corporate responsibility.

- **Giving misinformation.** The original product was falsely reported as safe despite *inadequate testing*, the altered product was launched without *any testing*, and *deliberate mislabeling* was used to circumvent the approval process. Furthermore, when questioned during the "Pill Hearing" in 1970, Davis failed to reveal his financial conflict of interest. He falsified the product's statistics and lied under oath before the US Senate (Roepke & Schaff, 2014).
- **Stonewalling and obfuscation.** Instead of acknowledging accountability for a faulty design that had made the product potentially lethal, A.H. Robins resorted to stonewalling, denial, obfuscation, victim gaslighting, and continuing business as normal. As the number of victims continued to increase, the company went on the offensive. J.S. Templeton, medical director at A.H. Robins, wrote a letter to the *British Medical Journal* documenting awareness of the "apparent increase in the number of cases of septic abortions" including four fatalities. Yet, he distanced the company by noting: "there is no evidence of a direct cause-and-effect relationship between wearing of the Dalkon Shield and the occurrence of septicemia"

(Horwitz, 2018). Moreover, the company's strategy of shifting the blame to medical professionals' device insertion inexpertise, and the victims' poor hygiene and questionable sexual activity further antagonized and alienated both, the physicians and the customers. What was equally, and to some particularly reprehensible, was their decision to dump their flawed product on vulnerable populations in the developing world.

- **Reluctance to act.** A.H. Robins demonstrated a marked reluctance to take any action. Employee warnings that the product should be tested for safety were ignored by top management, the company waiting for several years before acknowledging that the Shield should be removed. Most alarming was the company's blatant disregard of the law—destroying incriminating evidence—and perjuring itself.
- **Litigant harassment.** As one testifying physician put it, "the (courtroom) was crawling with Robins executives. It was sickening" (Dowie et al., 1979). Even worse, litigants were subjected to invasive, embarrassing, and public questioning on personal hygiene and sexual behavior—a tactic that may have prevented more victims from coming forward. When there was no escaping responsibility, the company made it very difficult for the victims to get compensation (Taylor, 1990).
- **Refusal to take responsibility.** Robins never offered a clear, direct public apology to the victims, let alone show sympathy for reparations. US District Judge Miles Lord of Minneapolis while hearing 21 cases related to this crisis, accused Robins's executives of creating "monstrous mischief" with "an instrument of death, mutilation, and disease" (Byrne, 1985).

While Dalkon Shield failed to take accountability for its transgression and tried every trick in the book to dodge the authorities, the case of Finnish telecom major, Nokia, represents a markedly opposite stance during its 2007 battery recall crisis in India.

Nokia in India

Nokia entered the Indian mobile phone market in 1995 with a strong market network, robust supply chain and sales force, and the well-reputed HCL Infosystem as its system integration technology partner. Manufacturing of mobile phones is a complex operation requiring thousands of sub parts, not to mention that there are hundreds of variants of a single mobile model and its packaging. India posed additional logistical infrastructure challenges due to crowded airports, train stations, ports, highways, insufficient warehouse and distribution facilities, and a difficult-to-navigate tax system with considerable variation across its states and territories. In this serpentine market, Nokia established dominance within a decade over its main competitors Samsung, LG Electronics, and Motorola, cornering 76 percent of the market. Unlike many other countries where mobile phones are locked to service providers, mobile manufacturers in India sell their products directly to consumers. By 2007, Nokia India had about 5,000 employees, 130,000 sales outlets, 500 customer care centers (CCCs), and 600 Nokia priority dealers (NPDs) (Dhanaraj, Sumukadas et al., 2011).

Brand Transgression

During a routine data analysis of customer complaints in July 2007, Nokia Finland discovered that 46 million of its 300 million batteries in use (model Matsuhito BL-5C) were susceptible to overheating and dislodging upon charging (Dhanaraj, Sumukadas et al., 2011). Nokia headquarters issued a global product alert about the batteries, providing free replacements as per company policy. Customers were instructed to input their 15-digit battery code on the Nokia website, and if the firm determined that the battery was from the faulty batch, it offered a free replacement within 15 days (Dhanaraj, Mukherjee et al., 2011). While not regarded as a major safety concern worldwide, the issue exploded in Nokia's face in India.

First, India had received the major share of the defective batch. As a result, the Indian press reacted strongly to the product advisory with inflammatory headlines like, "Are you walking around with a bomb in your pocket?" This caused customers to panic and throng Nokia service centers in droves, demanding replacements even for unaffected batteries (Dhanaraj, Mukherjee et al., 2011). Second, at that time India had poor Internet penetration, and hence, Nokia's web-based resolution of the problem did not work as expected. Nokia India was bombarded with more than 150,000 phone calls and text messages within a couple of days and more than 3 million requests within a week (Dhanaraj, Sumukadas et al., 2011). Third, Indian consumers often purchase their phones independent of service providers, which made locating them and sending them the replacement battery as quickly as possible very difficult. To make matters even more complex, the BL-5C batteries were used in several different Nokia models. With no prior experience with a recall process in the Indian market, Nokia had to quickly resolve these issues before they spiraled out of control and damaged its market share, leadership position, and reputation (Dhanaraj, Sumukadas et al., 2011).

Nokia's Response

A crisis management team was set up with a two-pronged strategy: first, to deal with the belligerent media coverage, and second, to manage logistics. The press releases were kept brief, emphasizing that no major injuries or fires were caused by the faulty batteries. The Cellular Operators Association, the Indian Cellular Association, and Cellular Operators Association of India—a lobby of private Global System for Mobile Communication (GSM) cellular operators, all lobbied on Nokia's behalf (Rediff News, 2007). This was followed by a massive advertising campaign in all major mainstream publications, as well as regional and vernacular media, with clear messages on how to check and replace Nokia batteries, supplemented by press briefings in metros, sub-metros, and even small towns with limited media coverage. A toll-free telephone hot-line and short messaging service (SMS) were established to cater to the concerns of worried consumers. Supply chain management was consolidated, and a series of manual procedures were quickly arranged to comply with each state's VAT (value-added tax) laws, free of charge (FOC) invoicing, and direct-to-customer shipment. Since the company's Systems Applications and Products (SAP) system did not support zero-priced items, all documents and invoices had to be generated manually (Dhanaraj, Sumukadas et al., 2011).

Within a week of the media frenzy, battery replacements had surpassed the million mark, with the highest single delivery consisting of 70,000 pieces couriered in one day. It was made possible with the support of Nokia's responsive supply chain. DHL, the logistics provider, rented a warehouse from Nokia and sent 40 of its personnel to augment, train, and operate alongside 80 temporary Nokia workers engaged for the job. DHL compensated employees of its subcontracting courier businesses to assure delivery of the products during the festive Diwali season. Approximately 8 million batteries had been couriered before the end of four months, including batteries supplied in bulk to regional wholesalers, customer service centers, and direct-to-consumer shipping agents (Dhanaraj, Mukherjee et al., 2011). Each client receiving a new battery also received a pre-paid insulated DHL delivery bag to return their used batteries. Nokia gathered almost 100,000 old batteries through this method, as well as 300,000 from customer care centers (Dhanaraj, Mukherjee et al., 2011). This recall cost the company and Matsushita (battery manufacturer) $172 million dollars (Goldstein, 2007).

Brand Transformation

Nokia maintained its market leadership despite rising competition. Internalization of the battery crisis lessons became evident in 2009 when the company was forced to recall 14 million chargers manufactured by BYD, a Chinese manufacturer. The recall operation was conducted in the absence of any external crisis (Shepard, 2009). Given the rarity of product recalls in India, many observers believed that Nokia evaded customer wrath merely by being quick. Nokia took the prudent choice of riding the crisis generated by the media rather than retreating from it. This strategy aided in establishing the brand's reputation, dependability, and trustworthiness. Senior management responded the very same night that news outlets began hyping the recall on air. They did not wait a day, a week, a fortnight, or years as A.H. Robins did. This ensured that clients received accurate information and perspectives from the appropriate authorities, rather than depending on hearsay and disinformation.

The speed with which the crisis was managed can be credited to the effectiveness of the seamless and incident-free recall process instituted, that accounted for safety concerns associated with shipping and returning batteries, and meticulous tracking at each stage of the recall process. Nokia's goodwill with its partners and distributors, such as HCL and nodal entities in the cellular sector, who became advocates for the firm with customers and the media, helped it navigate through the crisis, recover from the disaster, and regain credibility and confidence with consumers. As a result, Nokia not only boosted its market share but was also named the "#1 Most Trusted Brand" in the 2008 Trust Brand Survey of the country's financial newspaper, *The Economic Times* (ET Bureau, 2008). "It was a Tylenol moment for me," says Nokia India CEO Shivakumar at the time. "We needed to act swiftly and aggressively, and we did just that. For a few weeks, our market position was in shambles, but we rapidly regained control. By the end of 2008, we had reclaimed our position as India's number one cellular brand" (Dhanaraj, Mukherjee et al., 2011, p. 1).

Principle 2: Take Accountability

The Dalkon Shield case exemplifies a brand whose failure to take accountability for a transgression led to its demise (after it had destroyed and taken thousands of lives). In retrospect, not only was the brand ill-fated from the day it was conceived, its owners also made one reprehensible decision after another during its life, denying that the brand had done anything wrong. When they finally acknowledged wrongdoing after many years of its launch, their actions came across as a reluctant after-thought. Tylenol acted with integrity even when it was not at fault. J&J, its parent company, responded with alacrity, transparency, authenticity, and accountability that went a long way in diffusing the crisis, helping the brand transform from the perceived transgression.

Art of Transparent and Timely Communication

Brands today are only a few X (erstwhile Twitter) characters away from being tarred and punished as customers expect to interact with organizations that espouse humanistic values and act on them (Burke, 2014). When brands face crises, even if not of their own making, transparency in communication and taking accountability are not optional, today more than ever. "When there's an elephant in the room, introduce him," advised Randy Pausch, the famed lecturer and author of *The Last Lecture* (McDowell, 2017). Tellingly, according to a Deloitte poll, more than 73 percent of board members identified reputational risk as the area they felt most vulnerable, yet only 39 percent had a plan in place to deal with a crisis (Deloitte, 2016).

It is never easy to admit a mistake, whether it's a cyber-security breach, a product flaw, a sexual harassment complaint, a government inquiry, or a viral video. As we discuss in the next chapter, speed is key in crisis response. The sooner you take accountability, the better and faster your brand is likely to recover from a transgression. When a company's most influential people demonstrate accountability through personal involvement, visibility, caring, and engagement, their actions underscore strength and excellence of leadership. Taking accountability (even when the brand is not at fault) allows for employees to be comfortable with failure, to openly express their concerns, and provide solutions.

Take Accountability Through Action

Every brand on the planet has faced or will face a crisis at some time in its existence. Its transformation, however, is in part predicated on whether its leaders take accountability . . . or pass the buck. Merriam-Webster's dictionary defines accountability as "an obligation or willingness to accept responsibility or to account for one's actions" (Merriam-Webster, 2023a). The cliché that actions speak louder than words has been captured and echoed in ancient Greek philosophy as well as modern management literature. The Greek philosopher Epictetus said: "It's not what happens to you, but how you react to it that matters" (Teach Different, 2023). Stephen Covey, the noted management thinker, has similarly stated: "What you do has a far greater impact than what you say" (Covey, 2004). Most victims of a crisis lack the bandwidth for a rational, intellectual dialogue about where the fault lies. Their need is first and foremost to be informed that it is not their fault. Next, they seek a clear plan of action as well as commitment from the presumed perpetrator(s) to address the issue. And a drop in the frequency of unfavorable front-page articles and disaffirming news headlines does not mean that the worst is over. Building trust—whether at a personal level, by a brand, or a corporation—is a never-ending process (Burke, 2014).

The opposite of taking accountability is to live life with your head in the sand. Merriam-Webster's dictionary describes this phenomenon as "unwilling to recognize or acknowledge a problem or situation" (Merriam-Webster, 2023b). McKinsey's Doug Yakola refers to such denial through the metaphor of "boiled frogs," referencing amphibians who do not notice that their native water temperature is rising until it's too late (Yakola, 2014). Indeed, for those who refuse to take accountability, all bets are off, a simple principle forgotten by A.H. Robins.

Postscript

Starting in 1933, Robins Sr. grew A.H. Robins to become one of the largest US pharmaceutical and Fortune 500 companies, which soothed millions of throats with its Robitussin cough syrup, healed dried lips with ChapStick lip balm, and generously gave to charities and higher education—$50 million to the University of Richmond (1969), the largest personal gift ever made to a private US college (Taylor, 1990). All this goodwill was ground to dust with the company's response to the Dalkon Shield transgression.

During the 1960s and 1970s, there were more than 70 brands of IUDs in the market, and about 10 percent of all women in the United States used them. However, post the Dalkon Shield crisis, IUD as a category became almost extinct in the United States. Dalkon Shield had single-handedly destroyed an entire generation's trust in IUDs and had unfairly tainted the entire category's reputation (Anna, 2016). The firm became associated with callous stinginess and hubris, displaying greed to do whatever it takes to handle a brand breach. In the process, the company went bankrupt, the brand became nothing more than a case study (albeit an important one), and millions of women and their families lived in trauma for the rest of their lives. Ironically, the Robins were never charged with criminal negligence and their roles ended when American Home Products bought out the company. Despite four and a half years of bankruptcy proceedings, they emerged with their personal fortunes intact, which *Forbes* magazine estimated at $325 million (Taylor, 1990). In a farewell letter to their employees, the father–son duo said they would remember "shared times both difficult and rewarding" and went on to say, "We have been tested, and the results achieved despite those difficult times are witness to what good people can accomplish" (Taylor, 1990).

Chapter 3
The Third Principle: Act With Lightning Speed
Racial Insensitivity at Starbucks and Maggi Noodles in a Tangle

"This is not who we are, and who we are going to be. You can and should expect more from us. We will learn from this and be better."—Kevin R. Johnson, CEO Starbucks*

Circa 2018, USA.

A balmy afternoon in April (2018) was a regular day for the half-dozen staff at a Starbucks outlet in Philadelphia. They were busy brewing coffee for their customers, ranging from businesspeople in suits to college students working on laptops to those grabbing an afternoon pick-me-up. Millions of Starbucks coffee aficionados believe that visiting a Starbucks, grabbing a corner table, using the free Wi-Fi, and then on an afterthought, heading to the counter to order a drink, is part of a normal Starbucks ritual. Waiting for several minutes before ordering is not only the "done" thing, but it's very raison d'etre. After all, that's how Howard Schultz—the former Executive Chairman and CEO of the chain—envisioned the "Starbucks experience" to be: "To inspire and nurture the human spirit, one cup, one person, one neighborhood at a time" (Gino et al., 2020, p. 1). Therefore, what happened that Thursday at this Philly outlet was not only seriously misaligned with the company's values, but it also posed a global threat to its very credo . . . and the carefully constructed Starbucks brand.

Starbucks's Ascent

Schultz's vision was to position Starbucks as a "third place" (after home and work) where customers received outstanding service, less-than-three-minute wait time, and clean, well-maintained stores (Rowe & Mark, 2019). Its transformation over three decades, from a six stores–100 employees Seattle outfit to a chain with more than 29,000 stores globally—8,000 in the United States employing 175,000 (Gino et al., 2020; Statistica, 2023)—is considered a benchmark in the "Second Wave" coffee movement, where coffee became enmeshed with consumers' lifestyle and identity rather than a commodity.

Over the years, Starbucks distinguished itself as a do-the-right-thing kind of retailer. It offered full health care and stock options to employees, embraced diversity and inclusion, created a foundation to support its communities, located stores in underserved areas, promoted certified Fairtrade products, established ethical coffee-

---

*Gino, F., Coffman, K., & Huizinga, J. (2020). Starbucks: Reaffirming Commitment to the Third Place Ideal. *Harvard Business School*, 920016, p. 9.

https://doi.org/10.1515/9781501517334-004

sourcing standards, and built farmer support centres in coffee-growing regions. Along the way, it also rewarded its investors with multiple two-for-one stock splits following its initial public offering in 1992.

Brand Transgression

While an undercurrent of racial intolerance had been present for decades in the United States, it became more pronounced in the second decade of the twenty-first century. On the afternoon of April 12, along with coffee and other drinks, a subterranean implicit racial bias was brewing at the Starbucks in Rittenhouse Square, Philadelphia. At 4.35 pm, two African American entrepreneurs, Donte Robinson and Rashon Nelson, both twenty-three years old and friends since fourth grade, entered their regular Starbucks haunt (one of them had been a customer there since he was 15 years old). They seated themselves in wait for a scheduled business meeting with an entrepreneur, Andrew Yaffe. They had not placed an order yet when Robinson went to use the restroom. He was refused access on grounds that only customers can use the facilities. When Robinson returned to his seat, a barista immediately approached him and Nelson asking for their orders. Odd, given that customers usually go up to the cash register to place their order. The two men declined, saying they will place their order once their client joined them. The barista insisted that they either make a purchase or leave. The men remained seated. And then the unthinkable happened. Within minutes, the store manager called the police to report that the two men were "trespassing." Odd again, given the "experience" that Starbucks seeks to provide its customers and that it is routine for them to wait for some time before placing an order.

The police arrived immediately and asked the two to leave. The men refused, saying they were simply waiting for a business associate and not trespassing as alleged by the store manager. The exchange lasted about four minutes, when four additional officers came in along with Yaffe (their business associate, a white man) who confirmed the appointment to the police officers. Despite objections from the two men, their associate, and other customers present in the store (DePino, 2018), the police handcuffed Nelson and Robinson and escorted them to a squad car. The two men claim the police did not ask them the reason for the altercation, did not have body cameras during the arrest, and neither of them was read their rights (ABC News, 2018). Nelson and Robinson were jailed for a few hours and during that time they were not given any information on how long they would be held or when they could contact their families or their lawyers. They were released late evening, as Starbucks did not press any charges due to lack of evidence that a crime had been committed (Associated Press, 2018a; Kamnetz, 2018). In a matter of a few consequential hours, the globally renowned brew was frothing, steaming, and spilling over.

The Fallout

Melissa DePino filmed the entire episode on her cell phone and live tweeted it to her 11,800 followers. The tweet gathered 11 million views and sparked online outrage over racial bias at Starbucks, a company that prided itself on its social agenda of racial equality and diversity. Twitterati, prominent celebrities, and public figures noted this to be simply the latest proof of America's chronic racism (Filloon, 2018) and #boycott-starbucks and #starbuckswhileblack began circulating (Zara, 2018). Along with 75 others, Asa Khalif, a Black Lives Matter activist, led a protest at the Philadelphia store demanding the manager be fired. His photograph with a bullhorn inside the store became a widely trending Twitter (now X) meme (Madej, 2018a). The following week, protests became more fervent. On Monday, about two dozen chanting protestors led by the community group Philadelphians Organized to Witness, Empower, and Rebuild filed into this Philadelphia Starbucks in the morning, holding banners reading, "End Stop and Frisk," and chanting slogans like "A whole lot of racism, a whole lot of crap, Starbucks coffee is anti-black" (Associated Press, 2018c). Before leaving the store, the crowd sang gospel songs and chanted. Speeches decried police brutality and gentrification. Camille Hymes, the regional vice president of Starbucks, attempted to meet with the demonstrators but was screamed down. Partners at stores across Philadelphia also became the focus of a lot of rage, being ejected from buses because they were wearing Starbucks hats. Family members of people of color were chastising them for working for a firm that they now considered discriminatory (Associated Press, 2018d).

Philadelphia Mayor Jim Kenney indicated in a statement published on April 14 that the business's reaction was unsatisfactory, and he asked the Philadelphia Commission on Human Relations (PCHR) to investigate Starbucks's rules and decide if the corporation might benefit from implicit bias training (Horton, 2018). Kenyatta Johnson, whose district included the Rittenhouse Square neighborhood, and other leaders from the African American community denounced the chain. They demanded an actual plan to ensure that those who visit Starbucks "are respected, and they can go to the establishment without fear of being targeted because of their skin color." They also asked that all Starbucks staff undertake sensitivity training as well as diversity and inclusion training. Demonstrators insisted that the employee who reported the men to the police be fired (McLaughlin, 2018). Making matters worse, Police Commissioner Richard Ross noted on Facebook that the arresting officers "did nothing wrong," were merely "performing a service they were called to do," and were professional in their interactions with the people, but that they "got the opposite back" (Associated Press, 2018b). The demonstrators felt otherwise. On their Facebook page titled "Shut Down Starbucks!" they iterated that the Philadelphia police "had once again proved their inherent white superiority and unwillingness to serve the black community" (McLaughlin, 2018).

Starbucks's Response

Friday, April 13
At Starbucks's Seattle headquarters, although some members of the leadership team received an email that "two men had been arrested in a Philadelphia store," it did not seem to warrant alarm because "there is always something going on," given the number of Starbucks stores in America (Gino et al., 2020, p. 7). After seeing the video trending on various social media platforms, Starbucks's response was reactive with a terse Twitter post (now X), "We are aware of the incident on Thursday in a Philadelphia store with two guests and law enforcement, resulting in their removal. We're reviewing the incident with our partners, law enforcement, and customers to determine what took place and led to this unfortunate result" (Madej et al., 2018). Starbucks's tweet, albeit swift, failed to impress. Rather, it fueled anger further as the statement was perceived as lacking in empathy, particularly towards the black community.

Saturday, April 14
Starbucks CEO Kevin Johnson realized the magnitude of the issue and the need to respond quickly. "We were accountable. And yet there is no playbook about how you handle a crisis like this," he was quoted as saying (Varma & Yamashita, 2020). He made the first of what would become a succession of public apologies, this one on the company's Twitter feed (now X): "We apologize to the two individuals and our customers, and are disappointed this led to an arrest. We take these matters seriously and have more work to do when it comes to how we handle incidents in our stores. We are reviewing our policies and will continue to engage with the community and the police department to try to ensure these types of situations never arise in any of our stores" (Gino et al., 2020, p. 8).

Sunday, April 15
Johnson flew to Philadelphia to personally meet with the two men, government officials, and community leaders. He delivered his second apology on the same day, this time through a two-minute video taking responsibility.

> "I want to begin by offering a personal apology to the two gentlemen arrested in our store. What happened and the way that incident escalated, and the outcome was nothing but reprehensible and I'm sorry. I want to apologize to the community in Philadelphia and to all my Starbucks partners, this is not who we are and it's not who we are going to be. We are going to learn from this, and we will be better for it." (Gino et al., 2020, p. 9)

Johnson went on to explain that while calls to the police are occasionally justified, this was not one of those occasions because no violent acts, threats, or disturbances had occurred. "The two men did not deserve what happened, and we are accountable," he said. He promised to look at altering store policies and providing partners with bias training. He also stated that he was hesitant to take legal action against the store management. "I own this. This is a management issue, and I am accountable" (Gino et al., 2020, p. 9). Lastly, he expressed hope of meeting the two men if they were willing and as many people of the Philadelphia community as possible in the coming two days (Gino et al., 2020).

The Starbucks CEO also posted an apology on Facebook, saying he believes "that blame is misplaced." Starbucks regional Vice President Camille Hymes' response to the call to fire the store manager was: "I know the question has come up in terms of whether or not the manager should be fired, and we take full responsibility. We put her in a position that did not allow her to be set up for success—or those two men" (Ben-Yaacov, 2018). The police and Starbucks launched separate investigations.

Monday, April 16
CEO Johnson appeared on ABC's *Good Morning America* to publicly apologize on national television where he said he did not want to "point blame" for the arrests. "My responsibility is to look not only at that individual but to look more broadly at the circumstances that set that up, to ensure that this never happens again" (6abc Philadelphia, 2018).

Tuesday, April 17
After swift but clearly thoughtful deliberation, Starbucks announced that it 1) would review the policies that led to the arrests; 2) would examine all aspects of its operations to address implicit bias and promote equity and inclusion; 3) had hired a law firm to conduct a companywide external audit; and 4) pledged to make their findings public. Nelson and Robinson were included in these discussions so that they would have a voice in Starbucks creating a more inclusive and just environment to ensure that such incidents did not happen again. Johnson also offered to serve as their mentor as they launched their entrepreneurial careers (Gino et al., 2020). Crucially, Johnson stated that the company would close all its 8,000+ US stores on May 29 so all its employees could undergo racial bias training. He noted, "Closing our stores for racial bias training is just one step in a journey that requires dedication from every level of our company and partnerships in our local communities" (Madej, 2018b).

Wednesday, April 18
Starbucks Executive Chairman Howard Schultz appeared on CBS *This Morning*, saying he was both "ashamed" and "embarrassed" with the incident (Madej, 2018b).

Wednesday, May 2
Starbucks and the City of Philadelphia reached separate agreements with Rashon Nelson and Donte Robinson. The city agreed to pay them $1 each and set up a $200,000 program for young entrepreneurs at their request (CBS News, 2018). Starbucks announced that their agreement "will include a financial settlement as well as continued listening and dialogue between the parties and specific action and opportunity"

(Starbucks, 2018) and both men were offered free online college tuition to complete their bachelor's degrees at Arizona State University (Avila et al., 2019).

Friday, May 11
Executive Chairman Schultz at the Atlantic Council (a think tank in Washington) stated: "We don't want anyone at Starbucks to feel as if we are not giving you access to the bathroom because you are less than. We want you to be more than." On May 20, Starbucks announced a change in its policy to allow anybody to sit in its stores and use its facilities, regardless of whether they make a purchase (Shane & Horowitz, 2018).

Brand Transformation

This case stands out for how an iconic brand that redefined the seemingly innocuous act of coffee drinking globally, faced a crisis of racial discrimination towards its customers, the speed with which the leadership took control of the situation, and the brand's transformation with a mix of contrition, empathy, proactiveness, and a willingness to change the company's very policies for the larger good of its customers. After its initial misstep, Starbucks has become a sterling example of implementing the gold standard of transgression management: validate the victims' concerns, take accountability, apologize, take decisive action, and control the narrative (Knowledge@Wharton, 2018). It's rare that we see, hear, or read a CEO publicly use words and phrases like "ashamed," "embarrassed," "reprehensible," "I own this," "I am accountable," and "I'm sorry" as we witnessed with Johnson (Gino et al., 2020). Crisis communication experts highlight this as a strong message of remorse, "because ordinarily when large companies find themselves in this situation, they have counsel who will advise them against" admitting they had done anything wrong. It is rarer still to have the CEO of a $16 billion company to fly across the country to personally apologize to the victims and the local community within a few days—humanizing Starbucks response (McGregor, 2018). This action continued to align with Johnson's previous apologies and commitments to become better (Gino et al., 2020).

Starbucks's response that generated the most buzz and held immense symbolism was the announcement within five days of the incident: the firm will shut down all its 8,000+ US outlets on May 29 so that all its 175,000 associates can undergo racial discrimination training led by cultural, religious, and human rights experts addressing topics such as implicit bias and conscious inclusion, and costing $16.7 million (Avila et al., 2019). Although shareholders questioned the cost, Johnson's response was, "We don't view it as an expense—we view it as an investment in our people and the long-term culture and values of Starbucks. This is what we believe we need to do as a company to provide the balance between profit and social impact" (Giammona, 2018). Academics such as Michael Useem, Wharton professor and director of the School's Center for Leadership and Change Management, averred that this training was "[a] forceful statement about the gravity of the incident." And Gabrielle Adams, a professor at the University of Virginia who studies CEO apologies, noted, "In this climate, that kind of mea culpa is what's needed" (McGregor, 2018).

As part of its commitment to be part of the solution, Starbucks also gave a formal guarantee to review the policies that led to the arrests (such as relying on partner discretion to determine who may or may not use restrooms) and in June launched another learning program for its partners, titled The Third Place Development Series, designed to encourage "empathy, community, courage, and inclusion." The company also entered into a partnership with Arizona State University to extend their curriculum on biases and their impact on society. Meanwhile, two months later, members of Starbucks's leadership team continued to spend time in Philadelphia meeting with community groups to address any remaining mistrust toward the brand (Gino et al., 2020).

In January 2019, per Starbucks's commitment, former Attorney General Eric Holder conducted an internal assessment of Starbucks's commitment to civil rights, equity, diversity, and inclusion in keeping with its long-standing efforts to be "a different kind of company." Based on recommendations of this Civil Rights Assessment, Starbucks launched programs to enhance their community engagement initiatives, advocate for issues it cares about, and foster an internal culture of equity and inclusion. Given America's controversial and long history of dealing with racism and the difficulty in understanding implicit bias, Starbucks's efforts were pioneering from a corporate standpoint. In Howard Schultz's own words, "The company's founding values are based on humanity and inclusion. We will learn from our mistakes and reaffirm our commitment to creating a safe and welcoming environment for every customer" (Davis, 2018).

After a year, the firm requested Holder to return and assess its progress toward implementing the recommendations. In his 2020 update, Holder paid glowing tributes to the steps taken by Starbucks saying that its "efforts to promote civil rights were much more than window dressing." He added, "From its CEO to the women and men who work in its cafés, Starbucks is committed to the idea that everyone should feel welcomed, respected, and safe in their stores." Holder went on to say that he "saw this commitment firsthand" while meeting with hundreds of company workers during the development of the first report and during the September Leadership Experience session, where he met with more than 12,000 store managers and field leader partners (Starbucks, 2020).

The debacle was described by the Senior VP of Public Affairs and Social Impact as "[a] profound failure to live up to our ideals and a violation of our values that jeopardized our entire sense of purpose" (Gino et al., 2020, p. 1). Interestingly, its revenues grew by 7.2 percent and customer sales increased by 3 percent in FY 2018. What is also striking is the integrity of its leaders—Schultz and Johnson—and the entire top brass who sought to douse the fire a) at warp speed b) with a consistent and transparent message of sincere contrition, c) a promise to do better over all media platforms, and d) actions that perfectly aligned with this promise. They understood the gravitas and their response was considered yet executed swiftly and also appropriate at every stage—be it toward internal stakeholders (Johnson refused to blame the store manager for the incident and took the blame on himself) or external stakeholders (changing its store policies, working with the Philadelphia community, making the racial bias training program open for other companies to access, appointing a neutral well-respected arbiter to review its policies, and making that finding public).

We now turn to the somewhat contrasting response of the Swiss food giant Nestlé in India, which faced allegations of having too much lead in its famed and much loved brand Maggi Noodles. In the words of Paul Bulcke, CEO Nestlé Corporation: "This is a case where you can be so right and yet so wrong. We were right on factual arguments and yet so wrong on arguing. It's not a matter of being right. It's a matter of engaging the right way and finding a solution" (Fry, 2016).

Nestlé's Maggi Noodles

Introduced in 1983, the concept of instant noodles took time to cook with the discerning and spicy Indian palate. It also took two "twos"—the two-rupee price point ($0.08 in 1983) and the promise of two-minute cooking time to make Maggi one of India's five most trusted brands. Heralded as "the third staple of Indian food after wheat and rice" (Synder, 2015), it ruled the instant noodle market, commanding 70 percent market share and contributing 30 percent to Nestlé India's ₹9,000 crores ($1.4 billion in 2015) annual turnover (Balakrishnan & Bapna, 2015). The brand's story, however, faced a serious twist, coming unexpectedly from the sleepy town of Barabanki (population 150,000) in what was then Uttar Pradesh (UP), one of India's largest states. UP was famous for the city of Kurukshetra where the epic war of Mahabharat (triumph of good over evil) was fought. No one saw it coming that UP would become the epicenter of a modern-day corporate Mahabharat of sorts.

The Transgression

On March 26, 2014, Sanjay Singh an inspector with the Food Safety and Standards Authority of India (FSSAI), randomly picked up a package of Maggi noodles from a grocery store and sent it for routine testing to verify the "No added MSG" claim printed on the packaging. Results that arrived a few weeks later showed that the sample had tested positive for monosodium glutamate (MSG). Perhaps, had Nestlé paid the fine of about ₹300,000 ($US 5,000 in 2014) for this relatively innocuous slip and taken subsequent action, no one would have been the wiser (Mitra, 2017). The company, however, refuted the allegations and appealed the findings. In response, in July 2014, the FSSAI sent

Maggi samples for a second testing to a different government laboratory (Fry, 2016). Results from the second test, released almost a year later, not only confirmed the presence of MSG but also indicated the presence of lead (proven to be particularly harmful to child development) at almost seven times the permitted limit (17.2 parts per million) (Ramanna & Kak, 2016).

On April 30, 2015, Nestlé India was mandated to recall its February 2014 consignment of 200,000 packages of Maggi noodles (Ramanna & Kak, 2016). On *May 21 2015*, in defiance of the legal order, Nestlé India announced that it was going to verify these results by having new tests done by independent laboratories, reiterating: "Nestlé India's current practice is to collect stock that is near the 'Best Before' date from distributors/retailers, so we are confident that these packs are no longer in the market." It also went online to reassure consumers of the safety of Maggi noodles (Ramanna & Kak, 2016, p. 6), reproducing a four-page PDF document dense with technical terminology and sans any company logo (Balakrishnan & Bapna, 2015). On *May 29, 2015*, four weeks after being asked to recall their product, Nestlé issued another statement: "We do not add MSG to Maggi noodles sold in India and this is stated on the concerned product. However, the product contains glutamate derived from hydrolyzed groundnut protein, onion powder, and wheat flour. Glutamate produces a positive test result in a test for MSG" (Ramanna & Kak, 2016, p. 6).

On *June 1, 2015*, Nestlé announced that it had shared "independent analysis" of 600 products from an undisclosed external laboratory, and their own in-house tests of 1,000 samples representing approximately 125 million packets with regulators, all of which found that lead levels were well within the limits specified by India's food regulations and that Maggi noodles were safe to eat (Ramanna & Kak, 2016). Unconvinced, the FSSAI asked each of India's 29 states to test newer Maggi samples. State governments responded in a somewhat ad hoc manner, with some banning Maggi before testing, and others banning it even after the product tested as safe. Simultaneously, a court in a different state filed a First Information Report (FIR) against Maggi brand ambassadors prompting a warning that anybody associated with "misleading" Maggi advertisements was liable for prosecution (Ramanna & Kak, 2016). Maggi lost the narrative as incessant negative media coverage over 400 TV and media outlets shaped public opinion with headlines such as "Maggi betrayal has broken our good Indian hearts," "Maggi controversy: The unpalatable truth about how lead got into your noodles," and "Maggi controversy shows Indian consumers are taken for granted." Before long there was international media coverage on protestors burning Maggi packets and photos of Maggi's celebrity ambassadors, and children holding up banners of protest. Social media outlets such as Facebook and Twitter (now X) trended #Maggiban, #Maggiinasoup, #Maggikesideeffects, and #Maggimess. According to Simplify360, a social media-monitoring group, the Maggi crisis generated 443,000 conversations on the Internet, most taking place during the first four days of June 2015, with 70 percent of them being negative (Ramanna & Kak, 2016, p. 7).

Finally, on *June 5, 2015*, Bulcke left India after two days of failed deliberations with the authorities and announced a voluntary recall of its entire Maggi stock, stating at a press conference: "Nestlé India reconfirms that Maggi noodles in India are safe. Despite that, (the company) has decided to take the product off the shelves nationwide because of recent developments and concerns around the product, which has led to an environment of confusion for the consumer. This, Nestlé believes, does not provide a conducive environment to have the product in the market, at this moment" (Ramanna & Kak, 2016b, p. 1). On *June 8, 2015*, FSSAI banned the production, processing, export, distribution, and sale of Maggi noodles, directing Nestlé India to comply with the order in three days. Five out of Nestlé's eight plants shut down and its share price in India dropped by 15 percent within a month, the lowest level it had been all year (Ramanna & Kak, 2016).

Refusing to acknowledge the crisis facing the brand, on *June 12, 2015*, Nestlé India filed a petition disputing the FSSAI's recall order at the Bombay High Court. On *August 12, 2015*, the Government of India filed a suit against Nestlé India claiming ₹640 crores ($100 million in 2015) in damages (Nair, 2016). The next day, the Bombay High Court lifted the ban noting that regulators "had not been able to substantiate its tall claim" of the food product being unsafe, slamming them for "lack of transparency" and imposing the ban in an "arbitrary manner." Nestlé was given six weeks to have its products retested at government-approved laboratories and cleared for consumption, before they could resume production and sales. The government, disagreeing with the verdict, took the case to the Supreme Court. Nestlé ultimately had its entire Maggi stock destroyed by Ambuja Cements at a cost of ₹30 crores ($5 million in 2015) between August and October 2015. Ten thousand trucks collected a mind-boggling 38,000 tons of Maggi noodles worth ₹320 crores ($52 million in 2015) from retail stores, transporting them to 10 incinerators across the country where they were crushed, mixed with fuel, and burned at an additional cost of ₹20 crores ($3.5 million in 2015) (Nair, 2016).

Impact

This transgression—which Nestlé India vehemently distanced itself from—ostensibly set the company back by an estimated ₹500 crores ($80 million in 2015). However, this was only a small part of the story. Nestlé India saw a 17.2 percent decline in its net sales, a 53 percent dip in net profit (Adilabadkar, 2020), a 42 percent drop in market share (Datta, 2018), and its first loss in three decades (Shah, 2018). The number of retail outlets selling Maggi products dropped from 5 million to 3.2 million and 400,000 wheat farmers, 15,000 spice farmers, 3,500 suppliers, and 1,600 distributors carrying Maggi products lost their business (Datta, 2018; Sinha, 2016). Internationally, governments of all countries importing Maggi Noodles from India initiated food safety testing in their respective countries including Canada, United Kingdom, Hong Kong, United States, Australia, and New Zealand, with Singapore and Nepal banning imports from India. East Africa's largest supermarket chain, Nakumatt, decided to withdraw Maggi noodles from its stores in Kenya, Rwanda, South Sudan, Tanzania, and Uganda (Sinha, 2016). In retrospect, the global repercussions rendered the immediate financial cost in India insignificant.

Delayed Brand Transformation

In hindsight, were these high-pitched, legal, long-drawn-out (March 2014 to October 2015), and contentious public duels with the Government of India, ensuing media vitriol, and loss of consumer trust in its second largest market worth it? Maggi's leadership team was widely criticized for its inconsistent response, lacking the acumen and foresight to manage the crisis, and their failure to act quickly. Despite having been in India for long, Nestlé was caught off-guard, failing to gauge the extent of the crisis or its potential implications, and to act swiftly when it mattered. Our Third Principle—Act with Lightning Speed—underscores our belief that whether brands emerge slightly burned or completely charred after a crisis depends to a great extent on how speedily they respond to the crisis. The Maggi case is reflective of a brand that took correct action only a long time after the crisis had assumed gargantuan proportions. Instead, it *allowed* a seemingly minor mislabeling issue to snowball into a full-blown crisis. We next unpack a summary from this one-of-a-kind case.

First, Nestlé India never issued an apology—ever.

Second, traditionally, companies were believed to have about a 48-hour window to respond to a crisis. However, with the advent of Web 2.0, this window has shrunk substantially. As the intuition goes, social media can make and break brands in a matter of hours or even minutes. Maggi's response was seen as slow and tepid, and when it came was one of denial and a refusal to recall the product. As noted in the Kotak Institutional Equities report: "The company's reticence in the face of mounting controversy is surprising. It's press conference came 16 days after the news broke. Sixteen days is an eternity in the age of social media" (Business Insider, 2015).

Third, their focus on the technical and regulatory aspects of the crisis while apparently neglecting public opinion, allowed control of the narrative to slip out of the company's hands. Moreover, impersonal online communication and responses did little to assuage customer and media concerns, and its patronizing reference to consumers as "confused" didn't help its case (Business Insider, 2015). Communicating primarily with the food inspectors, Nestlé did not engage with the mainstream media, the main vehicle for trusted news and information for most Indians. For a company in the consumer goods space, the company sent out text invites past midnight for its *only* media briefing on Friday at noon since the crisis broke out. Similarly, its announcement of voluntary recall was sent at 12.54 am (Bhushan, 2015).

Fourth, Nestlé pursued a crisis response approach that came across to some as arrogant, confrontational, and defiant. Importantly, the company failed to get the government on its side by doing its homework—Pandey, the government chief, had successfully tamed another food giant Britannia in 2013 in a different case (Iyer, 2015).

Fifth, Maggi failed to understand and align its activities with the macro culture of the host country. A confluence of cultural factors—a political economy that wants to be a world player despite inconsistent regulatory enforcement, a fast Westernizing urban and semi-urban populace, corporatization of the media, an activist judiciary, a deeply entrenched hierarchy based on power, and consumer activism—all colluded as external factors to create a crisis for the globally profitable Nestlé Corporation. Nestlé India—despite having many Indian executives in senior management—seems to have struggled to manage these complexities. It appeared oblivious to historical political sensitivities, treating the issue as a technical one to be sorted out with local government regulators. Legal wrangles facing multi-national corporations (MNCs) have a long history in India, with the name Union Carbide still conjuring up negative sentiments after the 1984 Bhopal gas tragedy. Even the "real thing" Coca-Cola was forced to leave India in the late 1970s due to anti-foreign sentiment.

Sixth, Nestlé's corporate culture has been characterized as exceptionally "Swiss." Nestlé India rightly took pride in its technical competence, superiority of product quality, and testing infrastructure. However, in hindsight, its choice to engage only with local government regulators might have been misplaced. As Bulcke surmised: "Perhaps, we were too fact based; perhaps we were too Swiss?" (Ramanna & Markovich, 2016, p. 4).

It took Nestle India 5 years and the personal involvement of worldwide CEO Paul Bulcke and four different country heads—from Etienne Benet, Nestlé India, and Shivani Hegde (Mother of Maggi), Nestlé Sri Lanka through Wan Ling Martello, Executive Vice-President of Asia, Oceania, and Africa to Suresh Narayanan, Nestlé Philippines—to exorcise the ghost of the Maggi crisis and regain its status in the market. In 2019, sales of the Maggi brand of products surpassed the pre-ban level of 2014, in terms of both volume and value. Like with many other brands, COVID-19 was a fortuitous event for Maggi India, generating a 20–25 percent increase in demand for Maggi's 70 products (Dutta, 2020). In many ways, this was a watershed moment for a brand that merely five years back had slid from being the king of the market to a pariah and was now back as the crown jewel of Nestlé India's portfolio.

Principle 3: Act With Lightning Speed

Jeff Bezos, founder and former CEO of Amazon, has said, "If you make customers unhappy in the physical world, they might each tell six friends. If you make customers unhappy on the Internet, they can each tell 6,000 friends" (Newman, 2015). Social media can enable and disable—all in real time. When you combine the horsepower of social media with the rise of consumer empowerment and entitlement, it becomes doubly jeopardizing, and as the cliché goes, the negative sentiment can spread "like wildfire." A huge battery of lawyers and staff will find it extremely challenging to address a situation of a nerve struck across the nation that has led to consumer angst. A brand simply cannot avoid online scrutiny in this age of transparency.

Many a brand have been burned by social media fire. When United Airlines ordered a passenger to be dragged off a flight in April 2019, officials could have predicted that the cellphone recorded video of the incident will go viral and cause significant online outrage. But instead of immediately starting to explain their position, United spokespeople initially blamed the passenger and then waited until the following day—after the video had been viewed millions of times—before commenting. By this point, the company was on the defensive and was already pegged as "the bad guys" by people around the globe (Domonoske, 2017). Consider Facebook's response to disclosures that a political research firm, Cambridge Analytica, was able to scrape personal information from 87 million user accounts without permission and sold their psychographic profiles to Donald Trump's presidential campaign. Users' trust in Facebook plunged as did its stock price—dropping $130 billion or 19 percent, in the largest single-day drop ever for a public firm. Facebook, silent for *five days*, initially denied responsibility, and then acknowledged a "leak," not a "breach" of user personal information (Kang & Frenkel, 2018). Ironically, social media messages do not have to be accurate, and the brand does not have to be at fault to be detrimental to the company. In May 2019, shares of UK's Metro Bank plunged 11 percent before it could shrug off *inaccurate* social media rumors that it was facing financial difficulties (Bown, 2019).

Denial is risky, particularly if evidence to the contrary exists. It was risky for Jeffrey Skilling who noted he was "immensely proud" of what he had accomplished at Enron and Martha Stewart who called allegations of insider trading "ridiculous." Both were proven factually wrong and had to face serious consequences (Kellerman, 2006). Stewart served five months in prison for lying about her sale of ImClone stock in 2001 (Rock, 2022) and Skilling was convicted on 19 counts of securities and wire fraud and served 12 years in prison (Stevens & Haag, 2019). After stories of Ford's fatal sport utility vehicle (SUV) rollovers equipped with Bridgestone tires were televised in 2000, the top management was inaccessible to the media for several weeks, playing down and stonewalling for months while images of crashed vehicles and reports on tragedies continued to grab media headlines. Called to testify before congress, CEO Ono finally apologized while still not admitting fault or legal liability (Kellerman, 2006). When leaders apologize and admit fault, they engage in a "secular ritual of expiation" (Tavuchis, 1991, p. x), which "enables course correction that mistakes, and wrongdoing require" (Kellerman, 2006).

Starbucks scored on innumerable dimensions vis-à-vis its superior response time. The first tweet—though ineffective—was issued on the very evening of the crisis. This was followed by an unequivocal apology on Saturday and a detailed video apology on Sunday (as opposed to a perfunctory "We're sorry if we offended anyone"). The leadership worked through the weekend to douse the fire. Add to that the speed with which Johnson decided to fly halfway across the United States to Philadelphia the next day to apologize and meet the aggrieved parties personally. "When a company is viewed as proactive and engages in two-way communication with its public, it can minimize the risk of being perceived as guilty" (Herrero & Pratt, 1996, p. 85). The speed with which Starbucks settled the matter with the victims and took the non-trivial decision to shut its stores to organize the racial training program showed the brand as caring and empathetic—quick to make decisions to serve the larger good rather than its own short run bottom line.

Forbes magazine sums up this response as follows: "Starbucks had to do something, and it had to be done fast. I believe that what it did was a perfect example of how to manage a brand crisis . . . It raised the bar on how to do what is right when something goes wrong" (Hyken, 2018). Moving forward, Starbucks racial bias training can serve as a role model for many companies. Indeed, more and more companies are engaging staff in training, including mock drills, table-top walkthroughs, crises simulations, and staged operations-based exercises. Some are strategically leveraging technology to create crisis management apps that will enable stakeholders to receive real-time in-app messages on emerging developments and crisis response. Information dissemination is democratic, quickfire, knows no boundaries, and has no off days, making the speed of response key in times of crisis. During such times, "not only is there nowhere to hide in this small world, there is also no time to even think about hiding," writes Griffin (2008, p. 34). A quick response increases the chances of the company presumed to be the perpetrator controlling the narrative and sharing the story it wants to share rather than allow idiosyncratic interpretations, conspiracy theories, and misinformation to create a new reality that adds to the crisis.

Postscript

In July 2022, Starbucks announced closure of 16 stores in the United States due to repetitive safety concerns including drug use in some of its stores. "In a letter to employees, Starbucks' senior vice presidents of operations Debbie Stroud and Denise Nelson said the company's stores aren't immune from problems like rising drug use and a growing mental health crisis" (Durbin, 2022). At the same time, Starbucks is facing the challenge of unionization, with 189 of its stores having voted to unionize since last year. In response, the company has stated that restrooms at some of its stores may necessitate closure if safety concerns continue. This statement reflects a reversal of the company's policy, which after the Philadelphia incident allowed anyone to use its restrooms.

Chapter 4
The Fourth Principle: Communicate Transparently
Volkswagen Emissions Scandal and Stoli Vodka's Russia Connection

"This is a case of deliberate, massive fraud perpetrated by Volkswagen management."—Judge Sean Cox of Federal District Court in Detroit, USA as he imposed a $2.8 billion fine[*]

Circa 2015, Germany/USA.

In a *David vs Goliath* fight, five research engineers at the University of West Virginia's Center for Alternative Fuels, Engines, and Emissions (CAFEE) took down one of the world's largest carmakers, Volkswagen (VW), by forcing it to admit that it had installed emissions-cheating 'defeat devices' in over 590,000 diesel passenger vehicles in the United States (Alter, 2015). These devices enabled vehicles to pass America's strict emission control standards during test conditions before reverting to non-compliant emissions in regular driving conditions (Leong, 2016). The company revealed that for nearly a decade, it had been programming millions of its cars around the world to foil emission tests and pollute as much as 40 times the legal limits. For these five academics, it was merely an application of the findings of a 2013 research project undertaken on a $69,000 grant from the International Council for Clean Transportation (ICCT) to study emission levels from diesel passenger vehicles in the United States. This application, however, ended up globally tarnishing the image of the 80-year-old German company and even that of the much-bandied "Made in Germany" tag (Lynch et al., 2018). Financially, the fiasco dubbed "Dieselgate" forced VW to set aside more than $35 billion to cover the costs of the crisis (Sherter, 2015). VW's case, now discussed robustly in business school classrooms, is a classic instance of how brands exacerbate crises by not communicating transparently and obfuscating facts, leading to loss of trust among customers, erosion of brand value, and prohibitive other costs.

The Volkswagen Brand

In 1937, Volkswagen (meaning "people's car") was founded in Germany when Adolf Hitler tasked Ferdinand Porsche to create an affordable car for the people. In 1945, Porsche, an unconventional thinker, and an engineering genius, designed the compact and iconic Beetle—VW's flagship car. Within four years, half of all passenger cars produced in West Germany were built by VW. The Beetle went on to surpass Ford's Model T as

[*]Ewing, J. (2017, May 17). VW Engineers Wanted O.K. From the Top for Emissions Fraud, Documents Show. *The New York Times.* https://www.nytimes.com/2017/05/17/business/volkswagen-muller-diesel-emissions.html

https://doi.org/10.1515/9781501517334-005

the highest-selling car ever built, reaching sales of more than 15 million in 1972. A global icon by 2014, VW controlled 12 brands, including passenger cars (Audi, SEAT, Škoda, Bentley, Bugatti, Lamborghini, Porsche, and Ducati) as well as commercial vehicles (Scania and MAN). With factories in 118 locations in 31 countries, it employed almost 600,000 people worldwide. Europe remained its major production hub, with 29 sites located in Germany alone (Winterkorn, 2014). In 2014, it sold 10.2 million vehicles, a 5 percent growth over 2013, had a sales revenue of €202 billion ($280 billion at 2013 exchange rates), and an operating profit of €12 billion ($16.5 billion in 2013), making it the second largest auto manufacturer after Toyota (Bowler, 2015).

Among others, two key brand levers contributed to VW's formidable position in the auto industry. First, its technological prowess. VW was one of the first companies to introduce the three-way catalytic converter, making it a "pioneer of low-emission monitoring." Second, the "Made in Germany" tag. Volkswagen's marketing tagline—"The power of German engineering"—represented a motto, a way of doing business, an organizational culture, a symbol of national pride (Noack, 2015). It stood for the status of the German industry as a center of world-class engineering and precision manufacturing where VW was perceived as reliable, successful, and innovative. These were also the factors that cushioned Germany from any significant negative impact during the 2008 global financial crisis even as US automakers were reeling and Toyota and General Motors were embroiled in safety recall predicaments (Lynch et al., 2018). In 2015, *Forbes* magazine listed VW as Germany's largest employer and public company, surpassing its nearest competitor Daimler's revenue by almost $100 billion (Forbes, 2015).

VW ruled the European market with a 50 percent market share, thanks to subsidies and tax incentives for diesel-run vehicles. In the US, however, its share was a mere 5 percent due to cheaper gasoline and significantly more stringent nitrogen oxide (NOx) diesel emission standards that were difficult to clear without sacrificing fuel efficiency or performance. Moreover, since 2000, SUVs and pro-environmental hybrid cars like the Toyota Prius had consistently remained the fastest-growing subcategories (Boston, 2015). The new CEO Winterkorn's 2008 announcement of a goal of selling 10+ million cars globally by 2018 may have been a double-edged sword for VW USA as under this top-down goal, its engineers and marketers were under a "do it or else" situation. In terms of numbers, the goal of selling 10+ million cars translated to VW needing to triple its 2007 US sales to 800,000 vehicles annually (Lynch et al., 2018).

The engineering solution was found in manipulating the software installed in cars—100 million lines of code that controlled everything—from basic operations to media to safety (Zax, 2012). The new software could control the number of pollutants it emitted by monitoring carbon monoxide and NOx emissions and then diverting pollutants to special systems that converted them into less harmful substances. Armed with its new EA189 engine, in 2009, VW announced the rollout of a new clean diesel technology called Lean NOx Trap, claiming it had solved the problem of delivering high fuel efficiency while still meeting emission standards. This was touted as another achievement of "German engineering" that competitors found difficult to replicate. Unsurprisingly, the new VW models passed the tough US emissions tests with flying colors. In 2009, its clean diesel Jetta TDI (Turbocharged Direct Injection) won the Green Car of the Year award, beating out hybrids and electric vehicles (Lynch et al., 2018). In 2014, four years earlier than expected, VW met its goal of 10 million deliveries globally. In the US, although VW sold more than 430,000 units in 2013—the highest volume for VW USA since 1973—it dropped to just 370,000 in 2014—far short of the projected 800,000, comprising only 2.2 percent of the US market (VW, 2014).

Brand Transgression

In 2012, the World Health Organization (WHO) classified diesel exhaust as a carcinogen (Gallagher, 2012). In 2013, the ICCT, an independent non-profit, noticed something unusual: diesel technologies appeared cleaner in the United States than in Europe. Searching for an explanation, it partnered with University of West Virginia's Center for Alternative Fuels, Engines, and Emissions (CAFEE) and California Air Resources Board (CARB) to perform on-road tests on several types of diesel vehicles, starting with BMW X5, VW Jetta, and VW Passat (all randomly selected). Dr. Dan Carden, director at CAFEE, and his team of four engineers started the study using a funky-looking homemade device called a Portable Emissions Measurement System (PEMS) that hung out from the back of a car's tailpipe while it navigated the road. Its purpose was to test how well diesel emissions equipment performed in a variety of driving scenarios, including on the freeway, in hilly, and in city conditions. Their data revealed that VW cars performed flawlessly in the lab, but once on the road, their emissions were 40 times the legal limit. "What the researchers accidently uncovered was that these differences were perhaps not the result of superior engineering, but rather the result of cars specifically designed to take advantage of testing environments" (Lynch et al., 2018, p. 8). Under routine driving conditions, all four wheels of a car move, and its steering oscillates while in motion and when negotiating turns. During emissions testing, however, only two of four wheels move, and the steering wheel remains stationary. Computer sensors monitoring steering and wheel movement would signal the "defeat device" to turn up the catalytic scrubber to its full power, reducing emissions, and allowing the car to pass the test. When a car returns to normal driving, the defeat device switches off and emissions return to levels far above federal regulations, while maintaining high performance (Jaffe, 2015). Both the US Environmental Protection Agency (EPA) and CARB, one of the country's toughest pollution regulators, received the report on these findings.

VW's Obfuscation Followed by a Staggered Confession

A recalcitrant VW denied any wrongdoing while discrediting the findings. After months of back-and-forth communications with the EPA, VW attributed the high NOx emission readings to "various technical issues and unexpected in-use conditions" and volunteered to recall the vehicles and do minor fixes. When VW failed to produce data on how the repairs had fixed the problem, CARB conducted more of its own testing and found the same problem. Finally, EPA's threat to withhold certification of VW's and Audi's 2016 diesel models forced VW's hand. Company officials admitted that since their US launch of the clean diesel technology in 2009, they had been installing defeat devices across 14 models (Miller, 2015). The US Justice Department described VW's deception as "one of the largest corporate fraud schemes in the history of the United States" and launched criminal investigations at the federal and state levels (Smith & McCormick, 2018 p. 16). From this point on, things went from catastrophic to apocalyptic. Share prices tumbled. Lawsuits started pouring in globally—from regulators, shareholders, and customers. Dealers demanded solutions to customers' concerns about their pollution-belching vehicles. Eco-conscious customers held picket signs at court hearings, demanding that VW buy back their cars (Smith & McCormick, 2018). The company was excoriated by the press. *The New York Times* editorialized: "What was Volkswagen thinking?" (NYT, 2015), *The Nation* wrote: "Volkswagen lied and cheated 11 million times. Will anyone go to jail for that?" (Kitman, 2015). Along with substantial financial repercussions, including back taxes, penalties, sales slumps, provisions, recalls, retrofits, and discounts for customers, VW's image and reputation took a significant hit. A brief canvassing of the timeline is instructive to realize that opaque communication and obfuscation lead to short- as well as long-term consequences, some of them irreversible.

The Dieselgate Timeline

May, 2014[1]: University of West Virginia researchers discover that certain VW diesel cars emit up to 40 times the permissible levels of harmful nitrogen oxide.

September 15, 2015: Under EPA threat of denied certification, VW admits that since their launch of the clean diesel technology, between 2009 and 2015, they had installed defeat devices on nearly 590,000 diesel vehicles across 14 models.

September 18, 2015: The EPA informs the public about VW's act of duping diesel emissions tests using "defeat devices."

September 20, 2015: VW issues video-taped public apology.

---

[1] Unless otherwise stated, most of this section is from Lynch et al. (2018).

September 22, 2015: VW admits to installing "cheat software" in 11 million diesel engines globally. VW shares plunge by 37 percent in two days wiping $20 billion off its market capitalization (Schwartz, 2018).

September 23, 2015: CEO Winterkorn, after initially refusing, steps down but insists he knew nothing of the scam.

October, 2015: In Germany, VW engineers admit to installing diesel engine cheat devices in 2008 because of irreconcilable emission limits and cost constraints. VW recalls 8.5 million cars in Europe, and discloses that it installed cheat devices in cars sold in China, its largest market. VW launches a new Compliance Department and announces further job cuts (Schuetz & Woo, 2016). In his first public admission, Michael Horn, CEO VW America, admits that he knew about the manipulation devices since 2014, saying, "Our company was dishonest with the EPA and the California Air Resources Board and with all of you. And in my German words, we have totally screwed up" (Ruddick, 2015a).

October 6, 2015: VW is delisted from the Dow Jones and later from UK's FTSE4Good Sustainability indices. Returns 3 Cars.com awards for its TDI diesel cars, Best Bet Award, and Eco-Friendly Car of the Year Award (Schuetz & Woo, 2016).

November 2, 2015: EPA issues a separate notice of violation of the Clean Air Act to Audi, Porsche, and VW for their 3-litre diesel cars, affecting a further 85,000 vehicles. VW initially expresses confusion at the allegation and subsequently admits that it had been installing defeat devices in these models since 2009.

November 4, 2015: VW admits to a third emission problem, this time in Europe. Defeat devices understate not only NOx but carbon dioxide (CO_2) emissions as well in 800,000 cars and the company sets aside €2 billion ($2.2 billion at 2015 exchange rate) to deal with the problem. None of this information is provided voluntarily; it emerges in response to probing by regulatory officials. Moody Investors Service downgrades VW debt rating. While US sales decline by 25 percent, German sales go down by only 2 percent (Schuetz & Woo, 2016). VW auto sales in China, its largest market, grows by 1.8 percent compared to the industry growth of 11.8 percent (Kottasova, 2015). Decline in sales continues for 12 consecutive months while the stock price drops by 30 percent (Vellequette, 2017).

March, 2016: Michael Horn resigns after issuing an official public apology. VW acknowledges that previous CEO Winterkorn was aware of the US investigation in May 2014 (Steitz et al., 2016). However, because past US emission violation penalties had been about $100 million, the cost–benefit calculus was deemed manageable (Schmitt, 2016).

April 22, 2016: VW announces a net loss for 2015, its first in 20 years, after setting aside billions to cover the anticipated costs of the crisis (Ewing, 2015).

June 28, 2016: VW agrees to pay $14.7 billion in buybacks, compensation, and penalties in a mammoth settlement with US authorities. The deal, which covers only 2.0-liter diesel engines, includes cash payouts to nearly 500,000 US drivers (Tabuchi & Ewing, 2016).

September 21, 2016: To meet the one-year cut-off for filing lawsuits, shareholders flood German courts with 1,400+ lawsuits demanding €8.2 billion ($9 billion in 2016) in damages for lost investments (Zacks, 2016). A similar class action suit is filed in the United States.

October, 2016: A US judge approves a final settlement that VW pay $15.3 billion. Also, affected cars need to be retrofitted with better, non-deceptive hardware and software, or bought back from customers in full. Meanwhile, a court filing claims that manipulations in emissions tests had been "an open secret" between VW and its subcontractor Bosch (Amelang & Wehrmann, 2020).

December 8, 2016: The European Commission launches legal action against seven EU nations including Germany for failing to crack down on emissions cheating (Carbonnel, 2016).

January 11, 2017: VW pleads guilty to three US charges including fraud and agrees to pay $4.3 billion in civil and criminal fines. As part of the plea deal, VW signs a "statement of facts" in which it admits that the cheating dated back to 2006 (OPA, 2017). Former CEO Winterkorn tells the German parliament that he had "no early and unequivocal notification about the testing problems," a claim refuted by Piech who tells prosecutors that Winterkorn knew about the engine manipulation long before the scandal broke (Cremer, 2017).

February 1, 2017: Car parts maker Bosch, supplier of elements of the cheat software, agrees to pay about $330 million to US car owners and dealers (Shepardson, 2017), but admits to no wrongdoing. VW says it will pay at least $1.2 billion to compensate some 80,000 US buyers of 3-litre engines as well as refitting or buying back their vehicles.

May 17, 2017: *The New York Times* reports on two "do not forward" emails showing that both Winterkorn and Matthias Müller (then head of product planning) attended a meeting on November 8, 2007, where the main agenda item was discussion of a defeat device fix—costing €270 ($400 in 2007) per car—that would allow the new engines to meet the US NOx emission standards (Ewing, 2017).

August 25, 2017: A Michigan court sentences VW engineer James Liang to 40 months in prison and a $200,000 fine (Shepardson & White, 2017).

December 6, 2017: VW executive Oliver Schmidt is arrested while on holiday in Florida and sentenced to seven years in jail (Kiley, 2017).

January 25, 2018: *The New York Times* breaks the story that in 2014 the European Research Group on Environment and Health in the Transport Sector (EUGT), a joint research group funded by BMW, Daimler, and VW, had tested the toxic effects of diesel fumes from cars with cheat devices on monkeys in the United States. While the German carmakers strongly deny the tests, saying testing on animals violates their ethical standards, a subsequent report by Stuttgarter Zeitung noted the EUGT also conducted tests on humans at the University of Aachen where, "25 young and healthy people were examined after having inhaled nitrogen dioxide in different concentrations over several hours" (Ewing, 2018a).

April 12, 2018: Herbert Diess hastily replaces CEO Matthias Mueller, after he too lands in prosecutors' sights (Bomey, 2018).

May 3, 2018: Former CEO Winterkorn is indicted in the United States, accused of trying to cover up the cheating (Shepardson & Taylor, 2018).

June 13, 2018: VW is fined €1 billion ($1.1 billion in 2018) by German prosecutors over diesel emissions cheating, bringing the total cost of the scandal to €27 billion ($29 billion in 2018) (Ewing, 2018b).

June 18, 2018: Audi CEO Rupert Stadler is arrested and charged with fraud over VW's diesel scandal (Eddy, 2019). Daimler recalls nearly 775,000 diesel cars after doubts arise over the veracity of the luxury carmaker's claim that its vehicles never had emissions-cheating devices (Reuters, 2018a).

August 2018: Gasoline (petrol) cars represent 62 percent and diesel cars 33 percent of all new registrations in Germany. Porsche announces that it will no longer produce cars with diesel engines, and instead focus on expanding its product range with electric or hybrid vehicles (Liptak, 2018).

September 10, 2018: Shareholders' case against VW claiming €9 billion ($10 billion in 2018) in damages opens in Brunswick, Germany (Reuters, 2018b).

October 16, 2018: Audi agrees to pay a fine of €800 million ($900 million at 2018 exchange rates) (Reuters, 2018c).

April 15, 2019: Winterkorn and four other managers are charged with "serious fraud," unfair competition, and breach of trust. Though Winterkorn may never be prosecuted in the United States since he is a German citizen, and Germany only extradites its nationals to other EU countries, all could be tried in a German court (Burger & Martin, 2019).

May 7, 2019: Bosch is fined €90 million ($95 million at 2019 exchange rates) for "negligently infringing its quality control obligations," according to investigators in Stuttgart (Reuters, 2019).

July 31, 2019: Stadler and three former Audi managers are charged with fraud (Eddy, 2019).

September 24, 2019: CEO Herbert Diess, supervisory board chairman Hans Dieter Poetsch, and former CEO Winterkorn are charged with market manipulation (Telford, 2019).

April 2020: VW reaches settlements totaling €620 million (U$630 million at 2020 exchange rates) with 200,000 of the 260,000 claimants participating in a class action lawsuit brought by German consumer group VZBV over the carmaker's rigging of diesel emissions tests (Reuters, 2020a).

May 25, 2020: The German Federal Court of Justice (Bundesgerichtshof—BGH) in a precedent-setting ruling says VW car owners are entitled to damages and can return their cars for price paid minus usage (Amelang & Wehrmann, 2020).

September 6, 2020: A German court rules former CEO Winterkorn to stand trial on charges of simple fraud and organized commercial fraud over his alleged involvement in "Dieselgate." The charges come after VW had already paid an estimated $34.69 billion in total legal costs with expectations that outflows will continue in 2021 (Reuters, 2020b).

September 15, 2020: VW announces completion of a three-year review by independent monitor Larry Thompson (as part of a plea deal with the US Department of Justice) on the design and implementation of compliance programs—such as a uniform code of conduct, an expanded whistleblower system, and establishment of a top-level compliance committee—to prevent future behavior evidenced through the scandal (Sun, 2020).

September 24, 2020: A German court opens proceedings against Winterkorn on charges of market manipulation as part of the emissions scandal.

September 28, 2020: Former Audi boss Rupert Stadler becomes *the first to stand trial in Germany over the "Dieselgate" scandal five years after VW first admitted responsibility* (Reuters, 2023).

VW's Crisis Response

The Dieselgate scandal was an unprecedented display of how a titan of the German automobile industry went to great lengths to not only approve wrongdoing but also repeatedly cover it up by communicating opaquely and falsely. VW did not come clean when the scandal broke and even when newer transgressions kept surfacing. This behavior reached the top echelons of the company resulting in allegations of cheating, lying, displaying arrogance, misleading, and obfuscating facts, throwing the entire diesel car industry out of gear.

Apology

VW's first public statement came on *September 20, 2015, five days after* they admitted to installing cheat devices and that too via a video-taped apology from then-CEO Martin Winterkorn saying he regretted breaking the public's trust. He iterated VW's commitment to cooperate with regulators, conduct an internal probe, and "do everything necessary to reverse the damage this has caused . . . with the greatest openness and transparency." In this first video, he defended VW by saying: "It would be wrong to cast suspicion on the honest hard work of so many because of the terrible mistakes of only a few. Our team doesn't deserve that." VW also was silent on its social media accounts bursting at their seams and used its global Twitter (now X) account only for broadcast—never once replying to a tweet (Schuetz & Woo, 2016, p. 9).

Internal Restructuring and Investigations

Despite being under pressure to step down, CEO Winterkorn insisted he was the best person to conduct the investigation. On *September 23, 2015*, Winterkorn finally stepped down as CEO while retaining his other positions within the VW group, expressing shock at the extent of the misconduct, and stressing that he was personally unaware of any wrongdoing. Apologies from other VW executives and communication in corporate ads echoed the same themes, of minimizing the company's responsibility, and obfuscating the problem. The new CEO Mathias Muller and the person made in charge of the internal investigation were both long-time insiders close to the Porsche family. The group launched a whistle blower program and gave employees until *November 30, 2015* to provide information on the scandal, with promise of protection from dismissal and damages but not from prosecution (Lynch et al., 2018).

On *December 10, 2015*, VW Group held a press conference to report their findings from interviewing 87 staff, seizing 1,500 computers belonging to 400 employees and studying data equivalent to 50 million books. Nine managers were suspended, not fired. None was named nor was their seniority disclosed. The company stated that a "chain of errors" within the company rather than the action of a few engineers caused the scandal (Ruddick, 2015b).

Reparation

Only when VW stock plunged 20 percent two days after (September 21) did they order dealers to halt sales of all its 2.0 litre four-cylinder diesel cars. On *September 27, 2015*, 9 days after the scandal broke, VW launched an official website to provide customers with basic information about models affected, a toll-free number, and an email for further inquiries. No information was provided on the impact of the falsification of the emissions: environmental, performance after repairs, and value of their vehicles (Davis, 2015). The new CEO publicly announced that all affected vehicles in Europe would be fixed by 2016 but did not make a comparable commitment for its US customers. Instead, they were offered a $2,000 loyalty bonus from *October 7 through November 2, 2015*, to purchase or lease any VW gasoline or hybrid model (Lynch et al., 2018). Considering that $2,000 discounts are routine in the US auto market, to some, this offer appeared like VW's effort to sell even more of its cars rather than repair the damage. On *November 9, 2015*, VW issued a "Goodwill Package" to the affected 2.0L vehicle owners and extended it two months later to 3.0L vehicle owners that included a $500 VW prepaid visa card, $500 credit for VW dealer services or products, and 24-hour roadside assistance for three years (Lynch et al., 2018). Expectedly, even as lawsuits were being filed, the German newspaper *Süddeutsche Zeitung* reported that the company was engaged in tactics to delay verdicts to obfuscate their role in the scandal (Ewing, 2016). As a result, several thousand consumers chose to settle and were denied the full benefit of the rulings.

Differential Response to Legal Challenges

VW's response varied by country: in the US, it paid out $23 billion in fines and settlements covering customer compensation ($10,000 each), dealer compensation, environmental settlements, support for research to lower diesel emissions, civil penalties, and additional funds for the repair and buyback of vehicles. In Canada, the government and consumers received substantially less compensation, roughly CAD $2 billion. In Europe, VW refused to settle with governments or consumers in Germany, Ireland, Italy, Netherlands, Spain, Switzerland, and the UK. However, later court rulings in Germany forced the company to respond. In developing countries, such as Brazil, China, and India (where it was fined $1.7 billion), VW did not take any substantial action barring contesting the claim. This differential response strategy may appear to be "market-driven" but was questioned on considerations of treating customers equitably, particularly because it stemmed from a severe global crisis (Jung & Sharon, 2019).

Has the Brand Transformed?

Why would an environmental and industry leader concoct such a scam? What about the management and corporate culture that allowed for a crisis of such magnitude? What actions has the company taken to ensure that the probability of a similar crisis happening in the future is minimized?

Corporate Governance Structure

While brand Volkswagen continued to make solid inroads in world markets, it was run somewhat peculiarly. The board was composed of major shareholders from the Porsche family (50 percent), the state government of Lower Saxony (20 percent), Qatar's sovereign wealth fund (17 percent), and independent shareholders (13 percent). Of the twenty-member supervisory board responsible for management oversight, ten were union officials representing employees, five (including two women) were family members, and two each represented Lower Saxony and Qatar. The composition lacked diversity (primarily male, 17 German and Austrian) and independence (1), and ongoing power struggle between the Piëch and Porsche families hampered the board in its ability to fulfill its oversight function and hold management accountable. The fact that both the new CEO and person in charge of overseeing the scandal were long-time insiders and close to the family makes one curious as to what and how much may have changed on this front (Lynch et al., 2018).

Over-Ambitious Goal Setting and Culture of Anticipatory Obedience

In cohort with this board, a domineering, top-down management culture of "anticipatory obedience" compromised employees' ability and motivation to flag concerns. Winterkorn was known to have an aggressive "failure-is-not-an-option" leadership style. He announced that within a decade (by 2018), VW would not only be the highest-selling carmaker in the world, but also the most profitable (pretax margins of 8 percent compared to 2006). In like vein, he announced at an auto show in 2012 that VW's CO_2 emissions would be 30 percent lower by 2015 compared to its 2006 levels, goals that were seen by many engineers as impossible within the bounds of existing regulations. However, VW's prevailing "yes" culture led engineers to find multiple ways to doctor emissions—such as coming up with cheat devices, using artificially high tire pressure, and mixing diesel with engine oil to improve fuel economy numbers. The mandatory Code of Conduct review by all employees was a smokescreen behind which these activities occurred (Lynch et al., 2018). How much of the ingrained obsequiousness in the VW's employees' DNA has changed remains to be seen.

As *Automotive News* put it: "Compared with other run-ins between the EPA and automakers, VW's alleged violation stands out in its brazenness" (ATE, 2015). In light of this assessment, that VW would rebound from this transgression quickly was unfathomable. VW commissioned the law firm Jones Day to do an internal investigation and promised to publish the findings. But the company later reneged on its promise citing "unacceptable risks." The company also refused to turn over internal emails to state attorney general's in the United States citing German privacy laws (Bruce, 2016). Similarly, investigators trying to get to the bottom of who knew about the cheat devices inside the company, got little help from VW. The company defended its actions by arguing that installing defeat devices to protect diesel engines from undue harm was standard and legal industry practice in Europe (Schmitt, 2016).

In 2016, just a year after the scandal, while the Dieselgate fire was still raging, VW overtook Toyota and General Motors to retake the crown of the leading car manufacturer in the world selling 10.3 million cars. *It holds that position to date even as it continues to fight lawsuits—both criminal and civil—pay fines, and compensate consumers across the world for its 2015 fiasco.* In 2018, after record sales in the previous year, VW roared back to profit (Jung & Sharon, 2019).

What led to this unexpected recovery? The news that other German (BMW, Daimler) and American (Fiat Chrysler, GM) automobile manufacturers had practised similar deceptive behaviors may have helped "normalize" VW's transgression and divert the attention paid to it. Further, other automobile scandals, both before and after the VW debacle, might have inured consumers to distressing business news. These included Toyota's recall over problems with its accelerators in 2010 and GM's recall over ignition switch defects in 2014, both of which were related to customer safety issues (Jung & Sharon, 2019). The automobile category, in and of itself, may also have something to do with it. Customers consider automobiles as a symbol of freedom and are reluctant to jeopardize this freedom. The transgression (cheating on emissions reporting) itself, too may have been perceived by customers, as not a big deal since it did not harm their lives in any meaningful way. Finally, the humongous financial penalty VW had to pay (and continues to pay) might have been viewed as adequate punishment by many customers.

VW did undergo a four-step process of replace, restructure, redevelop, and rebrand. Muller replaced seven out of the ten top VW executives and restructured the company's hierarchy by halving the number of top managers reporting to him to enable the company to make more efficient, timely, and smarter decisions. He also cut the compensation of the remaining senior executives by 37 percent in his first year as CEO and redeveloped VW strategy of open resistance and criticism of electric vehicle (EV) technology, by embracing a shift in that direction with a goal of launching 30 models by 2025. VW used this shift to create a new image built on electric vehicles, shared mobility, self-driving technology, and called for an end to governmental subsidies for diesel vehicles (Welch, 2019). As Muller told the *Financial Times* in an interview in 2018, "(the crisis) actually acted as a kind of accelerator to address issues that, previously were unable to be addressed" (McGee, 2018).

Next we contrast VW's staggered and delayed response to its transgression with Stoli's vodka response to a crisis of misunderstood identity.

Stoli Vodka

On *July 23, 2013*, John Esposito, incoming President of the Stoli Group USA, was alarmed to learn that one of his company's most popular products—Stoli Vodka—had received a vehement boycott call on social media. The hashtags #DumpStoli and #DumpRussianVodka, coined by Dan Savage, a prominent gay rights activist, went viral overnight after he published an article in Seattle's independent newspaper *The Stranger* titled "Why I'm Boycotting Russian Vodka" (Savage, 2013). Savage felt that Stoli Vodka, along with all other Russian-made products, should be boycotted because of their heritage and many discriminatory laws passed by the Vladimir Putin led Russian government, including a ban on adoption by gay parents and state-sanctioned violence, bullying, persecutions, and unwarranted arrests against the lesbian, gay, bisexual, transexual, queer/questioning plus (LGBTQ+) community (HRW, 2018). Such a boycott would demonstrate solidarity with the gay community.

Transgression by Association

Stoli Vodka's parent, the SPI Group, valued at $1.6 billion in the United States (Quittner, 2013), is not a Russian company though its original creator Yuri Shefler was formerly Russian. Further, although the grains for Stoli Vodka did originally come from Russia, the company was headquartered in Luxembourg and operated manufacturing facilities in Riga, Latvia (Bell, 2020). Add to that, when Putin made it illegal to ship alcohol or its components in bulk outside of Russia in 2010, Stoli no longer had any Russian roots though its bottles still said, "Russian Vodka." This was not known to the public and those calling for a boycott (Odell, 2015). As a result, despite not being Russian and not having engaged in a transgression, overnight Stoli Vodka became the symbol of American outrage simply because of its perceived association with Russia. The timing could not be worse as Stoli was preparing to launch Stoli USA to better market the spirit and ramp up sales.

Stoli is one of the most popular vodka brands among the gay community, who tend to spend a lot of money in bars, and the boycott represented millions of dollars in lost revenue. Ironically, Stoli had long been a supporter of the LGBTQ+ community, continuously advertising to them, supporting pride events globally, and producing short "documentaries" about the problems and accomplishments of "regular" LGBTQ+ people. The backlash on social media was powerful and swift with "Dump Stoli" celebrations being held at bars across the country and hundreds of pubs in large and small cities no longer selling Stoli Vodka (Odell, 2015). Competitors exploited the opportunity, taking over Stoli's shelf space and spreading anti-Stoli misinformation.

Stoli's Response

Val Mendeleev, the CEO of SPI Group, wrote an open letter in support of the LGBTQ+ community on July 25, criticizing the Russian government's "dreadful" actions that the company firmly opposes and is outraged by. "Stolichnaya Vodka has always been, and continues to be, an ardent supporter and friend to the LGBTQ+ community," (Quittner, 2013). "SPI is based in Luxembourg, makes its vodka in Latvia, and employs Russian ingredients (wheat, rye, and raw alcohol) combined with clean artesian well water at our historic distillery and bottling facilities in Riga, Latvia," the letter continued. The SPI Group also recruited Edelman, a public relations agency, to help it navigate the problem and not spiral out of control. The public relations team interactions with *CNN*, *The Huffington Post*, *The Advocate*, *The New York Times*, *SiriusXM*, *BuzzFeed*, and *NPR* helped change the tide in Stoli's favor. A reporter from *The New York Times* even went to Latvia to verify the production process (Odell, 2015).

Mendeleev traveled to the United States, appeared on radio shows, and granted interviews with the press. He described himself as "ex-Russian," having left the country 20 years ago. To further distance the brand from Russia, he reiterated that the SPI Group was not allowed to sell its products within Russia. In a *New York Times* article, he stated, "Stolichnaya . . . is no more a proxy for the Russian state than Google, whose co-founder Sergey Brin was born in Moscow" (Higgins, 2013). Esposito said, "Hurting Stoli in the US is probably going to make the Russian government happy, given that they've been fighting us for the last thirteen years. They're probably going to be sitting there chuckling" (Dodds, 2013). Several employees working in Stoli's Riga production facility, along with Latvia's small LGBTQ+ community, also wrote an open letter to US consumers saying "if the boycott works, Latvians will lose their jobs. Who are they going to blame? Putin? No, they are going to blame gays" (Shah et al., 2016, p. 10).

Simultaneously, the Stoli team went after bar owners' accounts and spoke with distributors one-on-one to clarify the tale, as well as holding focus groups. They assessed analytics daily to gain insight into the volume of activity as well as the sentiment of reporters who were reflecting on and commenting on the #DumpStoli message. Stoli felt it was critical to keep lines of communication open with distributors, the media, and their PR agency. Social media engagement peaked within the first 15 days of the crisis and Stoli addressed all negative comments within 6 hours and put out written responses within 24 hours (Shah et al., 2016).

The Association of LGBTQ+ Journalists and CenterLink, a network that supports the construction of LGBTQ+ community centers, met with Stoli President Esposito and requested assistance in terms of community resources and bullying prevention (Odell, 2015). Following this, patrons of Chicago's Sidetracks bar once again toasted "Vashe Zdorovie!", which is Russian for "Bottoms up!" with a Stoli Vodka cocktail. A prohibition on the brand was lifted by the owners of the renowned club. Dan Savage, the man who began the boycott in the first place, changed his mind, saying, "The key thing is to help Russian homosexuals and lesbians who are currently being persecuted in Russia . . . It is the correct thing to do to send 100 per cent of monies raised to groups operating in Russia, which is why I support the Russia Freedom Fund" (GayCities, 2014).

The word "Russian" is no longer on the Stoli label, with "Stoli the Vodka" appearing in its place. Print ads include the copy "All People are Equal. All Vodkas are Not"

(Odell, 2015). Stoli's case like all others is a multi-layered one. What is striking about Stoli's response is how transparently and firmly it supported the LGBTQ+ community, a group that has faced persecution for centuries and supporting whom is perceived to be risky in many parts of the world even today.

Principle 4: Communicate Transparently

Customers and the public often judge an organization more by how it handles a problem rather than how it got into the problem in the first place. However, there are some factors that got VW into trouble to begin with that cannot be overlooked.

Volkswagen made this crisis much worse than it needed to be by not coming clean from the start—a violation of our Fourth Principle—and the consequences showed. The lack of preparation was revealed in its initial responses that often were ill-considered and obfuscating. As Hans-Gerd Bode, VW's communication chief at that time, said, "A crisis like this, the company was not prepared for" (Hakim, 2016). Their drip-drip revelations and concomitant reparation, the frequent revision of data on numbers of cars and models affected, downplaying the magnitude of the transgression, delayed in-person public apologies that only came when they were caught, the defensive media responses denying knowledge of any wrongdoing, lying, and proclamations that the problem was more technical than ethical only to retract them later—complicated an already difficult situation and did not signal remorse or a commitment to repair the damage done.

A firm's ability to manage its relationships with its stakeholders (in this case customers) in a crisis is crucial. Research has shown that accuracy, clarity, and disclosure are not only concepts that constitute organizational transparency but also key message features in firm communication with its stakeholders (Holland et al., 2018). Holland and colleagues found that the use of transparent messages contributed to higher perceived credibility when a rebuilding or denial strategy was used in response to a preventable crisis (Holland et al., 2021). Empathy, transparency, and authenticity are key to effective communication, particularly when considering the long-term health of the company (Erickson, 2021). During a crisis, any breakdown in communication tends to be magnified and failure to deliver on stated promises damages a firm's reputation more than if no apology or commitment were made in the first place (Halperin et al., 2019). Moreover, 20 years of research examining organizational crises confirms that brand transgressions or other firm misdeeds are heavily scrutinized by the public and a firm's stakeholders (Cheng et al., 2022). VW's shifty and reactive, rather than consistent and proactive strategy, in its restitution made it billions of Euros poorer and the end is not yet in sight. Stoli was targeted by association with no apparent transgression, yet it faced the threat of a more severe crisis. Recognizing this, the brand went above and beyond in displaying its empathy, authenticity, and transparency in communication with US distributors, bar-owners, and customers—particularly of the LGBTQ+ community.

In today's business climate, brands need to level with the fact that information—fake or otherwise—goes viral at breakneck speed, a development we call "ultra-rapid information dissemination." This trend is now more than a decade in the making and companies simply cannot take shelter in calling their ignorance of it as an "oops" moment. Opacity in communication is an option only for those brands and firms that are willing to risk their existence. The question facing such entities is not, "Will we be found out?" but rather, "When will we be found out?" To reframe a saying, the light at the end of tunnel may well be that of a "full throttle ahead" freight train heading towards the transgressing brand.

Postscript

On May 24, 2022, VW agreed to pay $193 million to 91,000 claimants in England and Wales because of the Dieselgate emissions scandal. This amount is in addition to VW having to pay legal and other costs that the claimants incurred. The verdicts in Scotland and Northern Ireland are awaited. The company "did not admit any wrongdoing as part of the settlement. In a press release it said settlement was the 'prudent course of action commercially' to avoid the legal cost of a six-month trial and possible appeals. The company believes too much time has passed since the scandal emerged in 2015 for other owners to bring claims, although there are two other UK claims in the early stages of litigation" (Jolly, 2022).

Chapter 5
The Fifth Principle—Choose Principle Over Profit
Boeing 737 MAX Twin Crashes and Merck and River Blindness

> "We don't 'sell' safety, that's not our business model."*—Denis Muilenburg, CEO Boeing at the 737 MAX Congressional Hearing, planes that were grounded for more than two years after two deadly crashes.

Circa 2018, USA.

The past few years have seen Boeing—which held the title of the world's largest aircraft maker until recently—go into bit of a tailspin. The crashes of two Boeing 737 MAX passenger aircraft a mere five months apart in late 2018 and early 2019, that killed a total of 346 passengers forced it to ground its entire fleet of 737 MAX jets worldwide. Layer that with the 2019 pandemic crushing air travel, and history saw Boeing lose its market leading position and reputation in what is the biggest crisis in its mostly glorious 106-year existence.

The McDonnell Douglas Takeover

The twin catastrophes turned the global spotlight on how Boeing's culture had changed since its 1997 acquisition of McDonnell Douglas for $13.3 billion. Pre-acquisition, Boeing was known as an engineering-first company that spoke the language of safety before that of finance (Useem, 2000, 2019). The acquisition was dubbed as a reverse takeover and "the fatal fault line" (Irving quoted in Ebbs, 2020; Frost, 2020) because McDonnell's employees, culture, and strategy dominated the amalgamated firm. Apparently, the joke was that "McDonnell Douglas bought Boeing with Boeing's money" (Useem, 2000), and the company ostensibly adopted a cut-throat culture that upgraded current models for cost-effectiveness (Frost, 2020). In the words of then-CEO Harry Stonecipher, a disciple of Jack Welch, "When people say I changed the culture of Boeing, that was the intent, so that it was run like a business rather than a great engineering firm . . . It is a great engineering firm, but people invest in a company because they want to make money" (Callahan, 2004). The full impact of this cultural change likely manifested 20 years later with the twin crashes (Frost, 2020).

---

*Kelly, J. (2019, October 30). When A Company Prioritizes Profit Over People: Boeing CEO Tells Congress That Safety Is 'Not Our Business Model.' *Forbes*. https://www.forbes.com/sites/jackkelly/2019/10/30/when-companies-prioritize-profits-over-employee-and-consumer-safety-after-fatal-boeing-737-max-crashes-ceo-tells-congress-that-safety-is-not-our-business-model/?sh=286af7c4151a

https://doi.org/10.1515/9781501517334-006

About Boeing

Established in 1916, Boeing designs, manufactures, sells, and delivers military and commercial airplanes, rotorcraft, rockets, missiles, satellite, electronic and defense systems, advanced information and communication systems, and performance–based logistics and training programs. Its popular range of commercial aircraft includes the 737, 747, 757, 767, 777, and the 787 Dreamliner. Boeing had a monopoly on the global market until 1974 when the Airbus Group (a European consortium established in 1970) launched its first commercial airplane, and the resulting duopoly has dominated the global aircraft industry, accounting for approximately 91 percent of the market. In 2016, with more than 10,000 aircraft (half the world's fleet) in service in 150 countries, Boeing had a 31.5 percent market share compared to Airbus's 27 percent and held the position of being the largest US exporter and global manufacturer of commercial aircraft. In 2017, it employed 140,000 people in 165 countries, had earnings of $9 billion, increased share repurchases to $18 billion, and increased dividends by 20 percent (Boeing, 2018a). In 2018, its revenue exceeded $100 billion (Sheetz & Macias, 2019).

Boeing 737

Launched in 1967, the 737 became one of the most successful aircraft designs of all time, evolving over four generations with different variants. Boeing began to develop a major redesign of the 737 and debuted the 737 Classic series in the late 1980s and early 1990s (737-300, -400, and -500; Slotnick, 2019). Purportedly, the 737's success was largely due to its economical two-engine design with a wider fuselage and easier maintenance compared to its earlier four- and three-engine versions in the 707 and 727 (Hayward, 2020).

The Airbus Challenge

In the 1980s, Airbus launched its A320 series and several Boeing customers, including Lufthansa and United Airlines, switched to it. This prompted Boeing to upgrade the 737 to the 737 Next Generation (NG) series with improved fuel efficiency, range, and capacity as its distinguishing features, while retaining important commonalities with the Classic so that upgrading or operating mixed fleets would be easier and more cost-effective (Slotnick, 2019). In 2010, Airbus launched the A320NEO family, a redesigned and more efficient version of the A320. Boeing's plan to build a new plane rather than further redesign its 737 changed rapidly when news broke that their long-time client American Airlines was about to close a deal on 260 Airbus aircraft, including 130 A320NEOs. In a drive to win the order, Boeing dumped the financially costly and time consuming idea of designing an entirely new airplane and pivoted instead to retrofitting the 737 to create a new generation of aircraft, a quicker and vastly less expensive effort (German, 2021). Moreover, Boeing's existing customers favored a modified 737 so they would not need to restock spare-part inventories and pilots could easily make the switch without needing simulator training costing approximately $2,000 per pilot (Paur, 2011).

In 2011, Boeing announced the 737 MAX family of three differently sized models—MAX 7, MAX 8, and MAX 9—that would enter service in 2017. Touted as the next generation of a tried-and-tested mainstay of consumer aviation, 737 MAX would have more fuel-efficient engines, a lower carbon footprint, updated avionics and cabins, longer range, lower operating cost, and sufficient overlap with previous models so pilots could switch back and forth with ease. By November that year, Boeing announced it had 700 commitments (Reuters, 2011), and in December, Southwest Airlines became the first 737 MAX customer, placing an order for 150 aircraft—the largest in Boeing's history (Boeing, 2011; Casadesus-Masanell & Elterman, 2019a).

Brand Transgression

Apparently, competitive and cost-cutting pressures led Boeing's decision-makers to make some controversial choices while minimizing or dismissing any concerns raised. First, according to reports, "Engineers were pushed to submit technical drawings and designs at roughly double the normal pace . . . It was go, go, go" (Beresnevicius, 2020b; Gelles et al., 2019). The 737–100's original frame was stretched from 29 meters (94 feet; 124 passenger capacity) to 43.8 meters (143.8 feet; 230 passenger capacity). Like the Airbus A320NEO, the 737 MAX used the larger and more fuel-efficient CFM Leap-1 engines that were 40 percent wider and twice as heavy compared to previously used 737 engines, requiring a longer and heavier airframe and wider wingspan (Tkacik, 2019). However, the MAX could not be taller than its predecessors given that Boeing was intending to seek an amendment to its original 1968 certification rather than one for a new plane (Langewiesche, 2019). Therefore, in 2015, a decision was made to mount the engines further forward and higher up on the wings. This change created a shift in the plane's center of gravity causing it to have unusual stall characteristics (Tkacik, 2019). Second, rather than redesign the plane, Boeing chose to create a new software patch to fix this problem. The plane has two external sensors that monitor the angle between the plane's wings and oncoming airflow, or angle of attack (AOA). When this angle was too large, the plane would stall, pitch its nose up, and have a rapid loss in altitude. When the external sensors detected that the AOA was at a critical level, the maneuvering characteristics augmentation system (MCAS) would be activated to rapidly lower the angle of the plane's nose and restore the AOA to a safe level (Langewiesche, 2019). Third, in December 2015, it was found that the MCAS activated when only one of the plane's two AOA sensors reported an issue and did not require confirmation between the sensors which was of concern to engineers. When deliveries of MAX began in 2017, Boeing's engineers were aware that the AOA indicator designed to warn pilots when the two AOA sensors disagreed was not working as intended. In two separate press releases, Boeing deemed that the alert was not crucial for safe operation. However, it was made available as an upgrade at an extra charge. Fourth, reasoning that the software would work in the background, Boeing decided not to disclose the existence of MCAS in the flight manuals as doing so would require time-consuming Federal Aviation Administration (FAA) approvals and additional simulator training for pilots (Nicas et al., 2019). Instead, pilots were only required to take a one-hour tablet-based course (Beresnevicius, 2020a). According to some reports, in 2017, Lion Air wanted its pilots to receive simulator training before flying the 737 MAX. However, Boeing convinced them it was unnecessary (Beene et al., 2020). Rather, they sold the 737 MAX to Southwest Airlines with a $1 million per plane rebate guarantee if simulator training was needed (CNN, 2019). Fifth, the pace of production led an employee on the 737 MAX team to write to his general manager, "Frankly, right now all my internal warning bells are going off . . . And for the first time in my life, I'm sorry to say that I'm hesitant about putting my family on a Boeing airplane" (McFadden et al., 2019). Sixth, given its limited resources to hire and retain qualified personnel, the FAA relied primarily on Boeing's engineers for expertise and input, resulting in Boeing certifying 96 percent of its own production (Kitroeff et al., 2019).

Boeing applied for an amended re-certification of the 737 MAX in January 2012, received approval in March 2017 (Johnson, 2020), and began commercial service on Lion Air subsidiary Malindo Air in May 2018. Before the end of the year, 230 737 MAX planes had been delivered to customers globally (Boghani, 2021), of which 130 were in service with 28 different airlines, having flown 42,000 flights, and moved about 6.5 million passengers (Slotnick, 2019).

The Twin Crashes

On October 26 and 28, 2018, the same Lion Air 737 MAX aircraft experienced altitude and airspeed sensor malfunction, where pilots—who knew nothing of the MCAS—could not understand why the plane's nose was repeatedly and automatically driving down. Both landed safely and were kept in service (Langewiesche, 2019). The next day, *October 29, 2018*, two and a half minutes after takeoff from Jakarta, Lion Air 737 MAX Flight 510 went into a 700-feet nosedive, flying unusually fast (Langewiesche, 2019). The pilots asked to return to Jakarta, citing an unknown "flight control problem." Eleven minutes in the air, the pilots reported that the plane's indicators were showing different altitude readings. Subsequent investigations found that the plane dove sharply 22 times, before crashing into the ocean at a speed of 10,000 to 30,000 feet per minute or 340 mph (Gates, 2018), killing all 189 people on board. Indonesia's Transportation Ministry ordered emergency inspections of all 737 MAX aircrafts in the country—all were determined to be airworthy within two days. Some country governments ordered grounding of the 737 MAX aircraft while the FAA publicly affirmed the airworthiness of the 737

MAX, and Boeing's then CEO Muilenburg persuaded then US President Donald Trump not to ground the aircraft (Zhang, 2019). Meanwhile, several airlines around the world continued flying the 737 MAX, and Boeing continued to successfully market it, with 248 new orders and 386 deliveries of $120 million each, including its first delivery to China—a landmark event (Beresnevicius, 2020a; Slotnick, 2020).

In December 2018, Ethiopian Airlines' pilots experienced flight control problems on four separate occasions within a span of seven days, including erratic altitude, vertical speed, and involuntary rolling to the right (Beresnevicius, 2020a). Within five months of the Lion Air crash, on *March 10, 2019*, Ethiopian Airlines 737 MAX Flight 302 took off from Addis Ababa enroute to Nairobi. Within a minute of takeoff, the pilots reported a flight control issue. A further minute later, the MCAS activated and pitched the nose downward four undirected times. The pilots were unable to recover the plane to normal flying conditions even though ostensibly, they followed all the procedures highlighted in the Operations Manual Bulletin (OMB). One minute later, the plane slammed into the ground at 700 miles per hour. All 157 people on board were killed (Czarnecki, 2019).

When black box data from the planes pointed out bad engineering practices and simple design errors as having contributed to both the calamities (Peterson, 2019), it forced Trump's hand to reverse the FAA's decision and bar all 737 MAX aircraft from flying in American airspace. Soon all 371 737 MAX aircraft, serving 8,600 flights per week for 59 airlines were grounded (Pandey, 2020). Not left with many options, Boeing issued a statement saying it was doing so "out of an excess of caution" (Boeing, 2019). Analysts and customers were quick to note that the company took this stand only after its hand was forced by the authorities. The ban lasted until November 2020, making it the longest ever grounding of a US airliner.

Boeing's Response

Boeing's overall responses left consumers confused, worried, sceptical, and distrustful, as they demonstrated "no contrition, no soul searching" (MacGillis, 2019), and were scripted and tardy, scarcely indicating any assurance or promise of reparation. Boeing issued its first public statement ten hours after the first crash in Indonesia over its Twitter (now X) feed: "We are deeply saddened by the loss of Lion Air Flight JT 610. We express our concern for those on board and extend heartfelt sympathies to their families and loved ones" (@BoeingAirplanes). The tweet linked to a statement that added: "Boeing stands ready to provide technical assistance to the accident investigation. In accordance with international protocol, all inquiries about aviation accident investigations must be directed to Indonesia's National Transport Safety Commission" (Boeing, 2018b).

A full week after the crash, Boeing issued a second statement informing the public of their continued technical assistance and expressing its "deepest sympathies" to victim families. The press release included a single sentence on the fatalities and a paragraph defending the safety of the planes and laying blame on the pilots, noting that "the appropriate procedure to address unintended horizontal stabilizer movement and how to override it" was contained in the relevant flight manuals and that it was not clear if the pilots followed them (PRNewswire, 2019).

Eleven days after the crash, Boeing updated the Operations Manual Bulletin (OMB) and provided the *first* detailed description of the MCAS to every airline that operated the 737 MAX (Boeing, 2018c; FOX, 2019). One month after the first crash, the Indonesian government shared black box data findings that the 20° difference between the left and right AOA sensors pushed the plane's nose down and caused it to crash (Beresnevicius, 2020a). Boeing, however, continued to call out pilot performance, highlighting maintenance issues, and continued deliberating on whether to launch an MCAS software upgrade that would allow pilots to override it manually. Meanwhile, the 737 MAX continued to be ordered, manufactured, delivered, and flown.

After the second crash, Boeing's stock price dropped 11.5 percent in its *"worst day since 9/11"* (Czarnecki, 2019) with public opinion appearing to be in steady freefall. Questions emerged as to why the second crash occurred if Boeing had provided all 737 MAX operators with OMB instructions on how to deal with MCAS issues. Boeing, however, stayed consistent with alleging that the problem lay with Ethiopian Airlines' standard of operations, inadequate pilot training, and insufficient pilot experience, even as the MAX remained airborne.

Nine days later, Boeing's CEO wrote an open letter informing the public that a software update and pilot training would be available within a few weeks, even though no approvals had been obtained. Even after receiving their first cancellation of 49 MAX aircraft worth $5 billion from Indonesia, Boeing executives continued to defend its safety and rejected calls to investigate their relationship with the FAA. The Ethiopian Investigation Bureau's preliminary report (April 4, 2019) provided the strongest link to date that faulty AOA sensors were at the heart of both fatal crashes. The next day, 26 days after the second crash, CEO Muilenburg posted a video on Twitter (now X), saying Boeing was "sorry for the lives lost." He acknowledged that it was "apparent that in both flights, the MCAS activated in response to erroneous angle of attack information. We own it," vowing that a software update meant similar accidents would "never happen again" (Onyanga-Omara et al., 2019). However, he continued to defend the plane's design saying: "The history of our industry shows most accidents are caused by a chain of events. This again is the case here, and we know we can break one of those chain links in these two accidents" (Boeing, 2018b). The video was limited mostly to social media and any mainstream media that quoted from it. Even as protestors gathered outside a shareholder's meeting in Chicago (April 29, 2019), he defended Boeing's safety record, saying a software fix would make Boeing's 737 MAX jets "one of the safest airplanes ever to fly," and insisted the two crashes were caused not by "any single item." In his most direct acknowledgment of responsibility until then, Muilenburg told reporters that his company made a "mistake" by failing to communicate the problems it was having with software aboard its 737 MAX aircraft and that it was "unacceptable" that Boeing was not more transparent with aviation authorities and the global traveling public (Cava, 2019).

Impact

The Boeing 737 MAX crashes and mandatory groundings not only had a seismic impact on the company, but they also caused turbulence in the aviation industry, which in turn affected the US economy.

- **Market position**. Boeing lost its market leader status to Airbus (McCarthy, 2019).
- **Compensation**. In July 2019, Boeing announced that it would allocate $100 million to assist victims' families with their education and hardship living expenses, as well as for community programs and economic development (Gates & Miletich, 2019). Several families were critical for not being consulted and the plan being "too vague." By March 2020, Boeing had spent $18.6 billion (Bushey & Meyer, 2020) on compensation to airlines and victims' families, lost business, and legal fees.
- **Boeing stock**. By December 2020, Boeing's shares had fallen roughly 23 percent, erasing nearly $55 billion from the company's market capitalization (Reinicke, 2019).
- **Production**. During the grounding, no airline took delivery of the 737 MAX. Boeing reduced MAX production to just 42 aircraft per month (Slotnick, 2019), and with 400 aircraft awaiting certification and delivery (January 2020), it suspended MAX production and shuttered its manufacturing plants in Seattle, Columbus, Philadelphia, and Charleston until May 2020 (Wolfe, 2020). Within two days of the announcement, Boeing lost $11 billion in market value (Reinicke, 2019).
- **Order cancellations**. By June 2020, nearly 600 orders had been cancelled by airlines and leasing companies (Josephs, 2021a).
- **Supply chain**. Boeing's extensive supply chain manufacturing aircraft components and flight simulators also suffered similar losses, as did the aircraft services industry, which included crew training, aftermarket, and aviation insurance.
- **Layoffs**. Boeing announced job cuts to prune its employee count by 20 percent to 130,000 by the end of 2021 (BBC, 2020).
- **Economic loss**. The company reported a $2.4 billion quarterly loss in August 2020 (Wattles, 2020), with the commercial aircraft division revenue falling by 65 percent year on year (Josephs, 2021b). With Boeing's first full year loss in more than 20 years, the Treasury Secretary noted that the grounding could reduce the country's gross domestic product (GDP) by half a point in 2020 (Martin & Slotnik, 2020).

- **Legal wrangles**. Boeing had to face more than 100 lawsuits in the US District Court in Chicago (Casadesus-Masanell & Elterman, 2019b). One of them brought on behalf of Lion Air passengers alleged that Boeing's sensors and control systems were defective, and that the corporation was negligent in its design. In July 2020, claims for 171 of the 189 victims were entirely or partially settled. Reuters speculated that certain Lion Air cases may have been settled for about $1.2 million per claim (Singh, 2019). Boeing shareholders filed a class action lawsuit questioning the effectiveness of its board oversight and control (Volkov, 2020) and Southwest Airlines passengers sued Boeing for conspiring to hide "the defect in this model, and to assure the public that the 737 MAX 8 was safe (it was not), and later that it was fixed (it was not)" (Beresnevicius, 2020b).
- **Reputational damage**. Media investigations released several internal emails where Boeing executives mocked the FAA, airline customers, and joked about 737 MAX's safety concerns. For example, "This airplane is designed by clowns who in turn are supervised by monkeys," and "I still haven't been forgiven by God for the covering up I did last year" (Leggett, 2020). Boeing's average reputation score was discovered to be -71 on a scale of 0–100 with 0 being neutral. While the long-term impact on its brand is unknown, according to the company's research, 40 percent of regular travelers were not ready to fly on the 737 MAX (Willis, 2020).

Investigations

As federal agencies, Congress, Senate, and the press investigated the crisis from all angles, the House Transportation and Infrastructure Committee (T&I) 2020 report provided the most scathing account of the catastrophe. "The MAX crashes were not the result of a singular failure, technical mistake, or mismanaged event. They were the horrific culmination of a series of faulty technical assumptions by Boeing's engineers, a lack of transparency on the part of Boeing's management, and grossly insufficient oversight by the FAA" (FAA Report, 2020). The report cited five primary reasons for the crashes:

1. Internal pressure to update the 737's design quickly and inexpensively.
   - Boeing had outsourced the development of MCAS and coding of the AOA Disagree Alert to software engineers from developing countries earning $9 per hour (Wasson, 2019).
2. Wrong assumptions about the design and pilot performance.
3. Boeing's culture of concealment.
   - It failed to inform US regulators for one year that it inadvertently made the alarm alerting pilots to a mismatch of flight data optional on the 737 MAX, instead of standard as on earlier 737s.

- Pilots and airlines received the OMB update with a detailed description of the MCAS for the first time after the Indonesian crash (FOX, 2019).
4. Inherent conflicts of interest with regards to workflow, where Boeing employees were deputized to act on behalf of the government.
5. The company's influence over top FAA managers.

On the one-year anniversary of the Lion Air crash, during his testimony with the US Senate Commerce Committee, CEO Muilenburg said: "Before we start today, I'd like to speak directly to the families of the victims who are here with us. On behalf of myself and the Boeing Company, we're sorry, deeply, and truly sorry . . . I want to convey our absolute commitment to safety and commitment to rebuilding the public's confidence in what we do to prevent accidents like this from ever happening again. We will never forget and that's our commitment going forward" (Gunerigok, 2019).

The Senate in rare bi-partisan agreement called out Boeing for caring more about profits than the safety of its passengers, its "culture of concealment," blatant conflict of interest, and willful negligence (Beresnevicius, 2020a). Its December 2020 report found that FAA's relationship with Boeing allowed the 737 MAX to go to the market before adequate testing and covering up information that may have contributed to the crashes. For example, although an internal FAA analysis showed a 15 times higher likelihood of future crashes over the 30–40 years life of the 737 MAX, the FAA allowed the airplane to keep flying. The agency was accused of giving Boeing too much control over the certification process, being "inappropriately coached" by Boeing to reach a desired outcome during recertification, and performing tests on simulators that were not equipped to re-create the same conditions as the crashes (FAA Report, 2020). Senator Blumenthal accused Boeing of putting passengers in "flying coffins as a result of Boeing deciding to conceal MCAS from pilots." Senator Cruz asked, "How come your team didn't come to you with their hair on fire, saying, 'We've got a real problem here'? What does that say about Boeing? Why did you not act before 346 people died?" Senator Duckworth scolded Muilenburg, saying, "You set those pilots up for failure" (FAA Report, 2020).

The National Transportation Safety Board (NTSB) noted that Boeing failed to adequately assess the consequences of MCAS failure and made incorrect assumptions about flight crew response. The US Inspector General said Boeing deliberately misrepresented MCAS to avoid scrutiny. The House of Representatives blamed the FAA's delegation of authority to Boeing for engineering defects, mismanagement, cover-up, and oversight lapses. Consequently, FAA revoked Boeing's authority to issue airworthiness certificates for individual MAX airplanes and imposed a fine for exerting "undue pressure" on its designated aircraft inspectors (Levin, 2020).

Boeing's Lacklustre Transformation

It was evident that the road to retribution for Boeing was going to be a long one. With the MAX, Boeing damaged its relationship with three main pillars that keep the aviation industry together—airlines, crew, and passengers. The stakeholders responsible for oversight, Boeing's board did not convene for nearly a month after the first crash and formed an interim airplane safety committee only after the second crash. Although this committee met multiple times, very few board members were present at each meeting. It took the board more than two years to fire Boeing's then-CEO Dennis Mullenburg (January 2020) despite overwhelming evidence of his failure to deliver truthful reports about the cause of the crashes (Feeley, 2021). Their appointment of David Colhoun as CEO, an old board hand, was seen by some as a recipe for the status quo rather than independent appraisal and change.

In a memo to employees, Calhoun said that Boeing is "engaging in a full-scale enterprise transformation effort, evaluating every aspect of our business for opportunities to improve" (Sharma, 2020). It started working on submitting software updates, a pilot training plan, and completed multiple certification flights for the 737 MAX to resume flying again. With Boeing $39 billion in debt, he started his tenure looking for funds to deal not just with the impact of the coronavirus epidemic on air travel, but also with the prolonged grounding of the 737 MAX (Duguid et al., 2020). Pointing out that the credit market was "essentially closed" to Boeing, the company actively lobbied, was allocated $17 billion as a federal stimulus package (Tangel & Cameron, 2020), and then rejected it as it involved giving government a stake in Boeing. Instead, it announced a bond issue to raise $25 billion, and engaged in cost-cutting measures by offering 170 mid-level executives buyout offers, reducing research and development (R&D) spending, and putting on hold a flight research center scheduled to open in Boston (Johnsson, 2020). FAA recertified 737 MAX to fly again in November 2020, ending a 20-month grounding, and clearing the runway for take-off. It has since delivered 450 and had orders for nearly 4,000 (Corliss, 2023).

While it may be true that a for-profit company is in business to create value (aka profit) for its shareholders, companies that prioritize their core ethical philosophies are strongly positioned for a win. A case in point is the pharma giant Merck, who chanced upon a cure for onchocerciasis or river blindness and chose to invest billions in a drug they knew would generate no returns.

Merck and the Cure for River Blindness

The world's largest producer of prescription drugs, headquartered in New Jersey, with more than 70,000 employees, Merck sells products and services in about 150 countries, is worth $46 billion, and has been ranked as one of the best companies to work for. Merck is known for its strong ethical values and leadership—a thought process that was established by its founder, George W. Merck (1894–1957) who had stated, "We try to remember that medicine is for the patient. We try never to forget that medicine is for the people. It is not for profits. The profits follow, and if we have remembered that, they have never failed to appear. The better we have remembered it, the larger they have been" (Vagelos & Galambos, 2006, p. 171). These words have since been the foundation of Merck's overall corporate philosophy. The company has deliberately fashioned a corporate culture to nurture creative and fruitful research, with their scientists among the best paid in the industry and given great latitude to pursue intriguing leads. Inspired to think of their work as a quest to alleviate human suffering, each potential research lead is extensively reviewed and analyzed based on the likelihood of success, the existing market, competition, potential safety problems, manufacturing feasibility, and patent status before deciding on whether to allocate funds for continued experimentation (Betz & De Paoli, n.d.).

In the late 1970s, the patent protection for two of its best-selling drugs was about to expire and there was no new drug on the anvil. In 1975, Merck scientists discovered a compound that killed animal parasites and Merck launched *Ivermectin* in 1981 for deworming dogs, cattle, sheep, and pigs. An instant bestseller, researchers felt it might hold the key to treating onchocerciasis or river blindness in humans. River blindness, affecting about 75 million people in more than 35 developing countries in Africa, Middle East, and Latin America, was labeled by the World Health Organization (WHO) as a public health and socioeconomic problem of considerable magnitude. The cause: a parasitic worm that lives only in humans. People are infected by the worm's tiny, immature larvae when bitten by black flies that breed along fast-moving rivers. These larvae settle in tissue near the bite and can live for 7 to 18 years mating and releasing thousands of larvae that generate an unbearable itch that drives some to suicide. Eventually, the parasite moves to the eyes causing blindness. It is believed that the breeding cycle needs to be suppressed for 14 years to stop reinfections. No treatment for river blindness existed and critics noted that big pharma ignored these tropical diseases to focus on drugs for rich nations (Steiner & Steiner, 2012, pp. 121–123).

The Choice

Merck had a decision to make. Should it invest about $200 million to produce a safe, effective drug suitable for the community-wide treatment of river blindness? Innumerable challenges existed. Even if it did succeed, the monetary returns would likely be close to zero because neither the recipients nor their governments could afford the drug even if it were to be sold at cost. Also, given the patients' remote locations, distribution would be expensive, even if possible. They could also not rule out isolated instances of improper use and unintended consequences in developing country settings. Importantly, the drug would have to undergo expensive clinical trials to prove its efficacy and if the new derivative proved harmful to humans, Merck's best-selling animal drug and its reputation could both suffer (Gates, 2014). There was also a real possibility that no international organization, government, or foundation may buy and distribute the drug. Indeed, Merck approached many agencies, from WHO to USAID, to find a way to distribute the drug, but none were interested. Finally, at a press conference on *October 27, 1987,* Merck announced that it would manufacture and ship Mectizan at no cost to whomever or wherever it was needed, for as long it was needed to control river blindness. It partnered with local governments and private agencies for distribution. This was a landmark event in the history of global health as Merck showed the courage to place social need over profits.

Since 1987, Merck has manufactured and shipped more than 2.5 billion tablets of Mectizan at no charge, in 37 countries at a cost of $3.9 billion. It is estimated that this has prevented 40,000 cases of blindness annually, returned to use 62 million acres of farmland, and added 7.5 million years of productive adult labor to national workforces (Merck, 2022). According to one study, two areas in Africa have gained an estimated $573 million in net benefits over a 40-year period (Waters et al., 2004, p. A16). Merck expanded the Mectizan Donation Program to include the prevention of elephantiasis (lymphatic filariasis) in African countries where the disease coexists with river blindness. Today, the Merck Mectizan Donation Program includes partnerships with numerous non-governmental and governmental organizations, private foundations, WHO, the World Bank, United Nations Children's Fund (UNICEF), and the United Nations Development Programme (UNDP). The United Nations reports that river blindness may soon be eradicated.

Merck, in its actions of helping develop a new drug and giving it away for free, believed that despite the substantial cost, placing principle over profit vindicates their decision, which was grounded in its core values—that its business is preserving and improving human life and doing it with the highest standards of ethics and integrity. This remarkable story has its genesis in Japan where in the late 1970s, Satoshi Omura of Tokyo's Kitasato Institute developed a soil-dwelling bacteria called Streptomyces that was extremely successful at killing parasites. He sold this culture to Merck, USA, who bought it to treat Japanese citizens plagued by tuberculosis after World War II. Merck did not make any money from this venture, and it is likely no accident that Merck is the largest US pharma company in Japan today. "The long-term consequences of acts of goodwill are not always clear, but somehow I think they always pay off" (The Business Enterprise Trust et al., 1991). In his blog, Bill Gates makes an interesting observation about a metal sculpture commissioned by John Moore (a warrior in the battle against onchocerciasis) in Merck's lobby. It depicts a small boy, investing in the future of his African village by guiding a blind man with a stick. "It does not highlight the cleverest product of Merck, the most profitable product, or the most scientifically advanced example of the company. Instead, it is a monument to human and corporate decency—one that highlights how a company that chooses principle over profit wins in the end" (Gates, 2014).

Principle 5: Choose Principle Over Profit

Human beings are creatures with reason. Reason depends on respect for rules. As creatures with reason, we are 'duty-bound' to follow logical, ethical principles and avoid contradiction (IEP, n.d.). These words of the eighteenth-century philosopher Immanuel Kant are now associated with the field of deontology, which contends that each of us has an obligation to others and that certain universal rules apply to every situation and bind us to these obligations. As we have seen throughout this book, businesses that place profit before principle are businesses at risk. They are at risk of suffering a loss of reputation with their internal and external environment, loss at the bourses, loss of consumer confidence, and loss of employee trust. On the other hand, as found by a Bentley University study, "a values-based culture generates benefits in the form of increased awareness of ethical issues, commitment to the organization, employee integrity, improved decision making, willingness to communicate openly about problems, to report an ethics violation to management, to seek advice about ethical issues, and reduced unethical conduct" (Driscoll, 2017).

A company is often assumed to conduct its business operations under applicable regulations, statutes, and laws. To us, this represents a baseline minimum. We are making the case for a company to go beyond, based on values-driven voluntary thought, word, and action. Merck's culture was built on the ethic of serving humanity, a philosophy fed into the corporate DNA by the founder himself. Ditto with Johnson & Johnson, whose credo guided James Burke when the Cyanide in Tylenol case erupted. For many years, Toyota was content to sell its cars at a slight loss in the United States because it was accomplishing a key business purpose—it was trying to establish a long-term relationship of trust with the US customers. Some justifiably call this a market share grab. However, that may not be the entire story. The US regulators have relentlessly pursued the creation of an economic environment of open competition, customers being sufficiently well-informed, and the existence of a strong and actionable legal framework to address corporate wrongdoing. In such an unforgiving business climate, Toyota's effort at grabbing market share would have backfired if its products were fundamentally flawed. Another aspect of Toyota's strategy was that it was attempting to disabuse US consumers of their belief that items made in Japan were cheap and unreliable. Perhaps a low price was hurting Toyota in this pursuit, but the company accomplished both goals—trust and market share—by patiently playing out "The Toyota Way," a specific emphasis on long-term business goals, even at the expense of short-term profit. Today, we teach this "Japanese" principle in classrooms all over the world.

There were other dimensions to the unfortunate and yet evolving story of the 737 MAX. Boeing ostensibly played into its transgression deeper, particularly by choosing not to take accountability and choosing not to *communicate* about the disasters. A crisis creates a vacuum, an informational void that gets filled one way or another. As discussed in the last chapter, the longer a company is perceived to have transgressed and delays communication, the more likely it is that this void will be filled by critics.

Boeing's initial strategy appeared to be "the less said the better." Irv Schenkler, a management professor at NYU's Stern School of Business, opines that this strategy created a vacuum in which the media stepped in and reported details on meetings and messages that contradicted company statements. Boeing converted an operational crisis into a reputational mega-crisis—driven by poor messaging from the start, creating concern and fear (Baker, 2019).

Many saw Boeing's approach as defensive, passive, and slow, implying a lack of remorse at the loss of human life, empathy with those affected by the crisis, transparency, and willingness to take accountability. Its haste to produce a new aircraft that accounted for about a third of its revenue revealed an overriding emphasis on profit. Timothy Coombs, a crisis communications expert, argues that three features define corporate openness—availability to the media, willingness to disclose information, and honesty. It is an open empirical question how Boeing performed on each of these three features (Matthews, 2019). A *PR Week* article observed: "Boeing lost control of the public narrative and appeared to be reacting to public pressure rather than putting the safety of passengers first" (Hickman, 2019). Forbes further reported: "(The public) noticed a seemingly complete lack of urgency, a lack of responsibility taken for the crashes, and the deflection of blame. They noticed immediate silence from the top. And of course, they noticed that Boeing had to be forced to ground their 737 MAX 8 fleet—and that they did not offer to do so in the first place" (Temin, 2019).

Boeing was Different Earlier

Boeing is more than 100 years old, a magnificent brand, and an industry leader, feats near impossible unless it was supremely well-managed. Indeed, since the start of the jet age, Boeing had been less a business and more, as writer Jerry Useem noted in a *Fortune* article (2000), "an association of engineers devoted to building amazing flying machines" (Frost, 2020). For a long time, this perspective served it well: *build a great airplane, whatever the cost.* Employees were well paid and enjoyed watertight contracts, thanks to an assertive, family-like union, and a commitment that put design and quality in aviation above all else. In the process, it produced some of the world's greatest planes. The company's philosophy was described as "go-for-it-and-damn-the-expenses—but not damn the quality" (Frost, 2020). As we have outlined earlier in this chapter, the inflection point seems to be when Boeing took over McDonnell Douglas in 1997, in the country's tenth-largest merger and the shift in its headquarters from Seattle to Chicago in 2001, that somewhere the emphasis shifted to returns on investment first.

Postscript

A company that set the standard for jet-age manufacturing is now continuing to deal with a transgression that goes to the very heart of its identity. Ironically, its own dictum states, "[W]e value human life and well-being above all else and take action accordingly . . . . by committing to safety first, we advance our goals for quality, cost, and schedule" (Boeing, n.d.). The 737 MAX crashes were devastating, but there is too much riding on the company for its stakeholders, the US, and the global economy. To quote Warren Buffett: "Boeing has already had a strong safety record. And the 737 crashes were a glaring exception to that safety record. Boeing is not going anywhere" (Josephs, 2019). The company's cost-cutters may have led it down the path towards its most egregious transgression in its 106-year-old history. Surprisingly, as if the MAX twin crashes were not enough, on *January 5, 2024,* the door of another Boeing 737 MAX aircraft being used by Alaska Airlines accidentally flew open mid-flight. No one was injured this time around and the flight landed safely. FAA has started its inquiry stating: "This investigation is a result of an incident on a Boeing Model 737–9 MAX where it lost a 'plug' type passenger door and additional discrepancies... Boeing's manufacturing practices need to comply with the high safety standards they're legally accountable to meet" (Blackman & Romero, 2024). The company's leadership's and engineers' hope to help the brand fly into greatness seems to be facing rough winds yet again.

Chapter 6
Sixth Principle: Treat Each Life With Dignity

Dolce & Gabbana in China and Ben & Jerry's Ice Cream

"People don't care how much you know until they know how much you care."*—Theodore Roosevelt, former US President.

Circa 2018. China.

A Chinese saying goes: "Water can hold the boat up, but it can also capsize it." Italian luxury major Dolce & Gabbana (D&G) found this out the hard way when promoting its first-ever fashion show in China. As it turns out, it might have tried too hard to be humorous without understanding the nuances and sensibilities of the local culture. The Chinese were irate, and D&G faced a backlash, ripples of which continue to be felt by the brand. And five years later, D&G is still trying to win back China and paying for their mistake—of not treating their customers with dignity.

D&G in China

China is the world's most populous nation, with the largest number of luxury goods buyers of any country on the planet. In 2005, D&G lucked out when it became the first fashion house to obtain a license to operate in mainland China without a local joint venture partner. In 2017, roughly 30 percent of D&G's $1.3 billion revenue came from the Asia–Pacific and many Chinese celebrities came to be associated with the D&G label. By 2018, the company had opened 58 boutiques in 12 cities—a number larger than in any other region in the world (Stevenson, 2020). To develop a stronger foothold, in November 2018, D&G organized a multi-million dollar Euro fashion show in Shanghai titled *The Great Show* that boasted an invitation list of 1,500 guests and featured 350 models and 40 celebrities on the catwalk (Zhou, 2018).

Brand Transgression

Three days before the event, D&G released three short promotional videos titled *Eating with Chopsticks* on Instagram, Facebook, Twitter (now X), and Sina Weibo. Intending to bridge the gap between its own Italian roots and the Chinese culture of its target customers, the advertisements depicted a gorgeous Chinese woman bedecked

*TR Center (n.d.). Theordore Roosevelt Quotes. *Theordore Roosevelt Center*. Accessed on November 7, 2023, from https://www.theodoreroooseveltcenter.org/Learn-About-TR/TR-Quotes?page=112

https://doi.org/10.1515/9781501517334-007

in D&G jewelry awkwardly eating Italian food staples—pizza, spaghetti, and an enormous cannoli dessert—with chopsticks as the announcer asked the sometimes embarrassed, sometimes giggly actress in Chinese, "Is it too huge for you?" (Adegeest, 2018). The woman was also depicted as using chopsticks somewhat clumsily. The pizza was described as the "GREAT traditional Pizza Margherita" while the chopsticks were termed "stick shaped cutlery." The humor (if intended) fell horribly flat. The Chinese were outraged and saw the ads as inappropriate, misogynistic, and racist, fueling an online debate.

Diet Prada, the fashion industry watchdog on Instagram, called out the brand for its "offensive videos on the usage of chopsticks and false stereotype of a people lacking refinement to understand how to eat foreign foods" (Adegeest, 2018). Social media users filmed themselves destroying D&G products and a Gartner report revealed that mentions of the brand, most of them negative, surged 2,512 percent on the Chinese platform Weibo. Within 24 hours, D&G was forced to remove the videos from Weibo and went dark for three months, although they still appeared on Instagram, Facebook, and Twitter (now X), which were not accessible to most mainland Chinese due to Internet censorship (Hills, 2021). Many Chinese citizens demanded an apology from D&G, numerous Chinese celebrities who were endorsing D&G cut ties with the brand and dropped out of the event, two D&G brand ambassadors terminated their contracts with the company, and the luxury fashion house faced protests worldwide. To make matters worse, in an ill-thought-out Instagram message on an American fashion blog, D&G co-founder Stefano Gabbana expressed his displeasure over the videos' removal, calling China "ignorant dirty smelling mafia," (Krishna, 2018) and a "country of shit," claiming that the Chinese ate dogs (Northman, 2018). As screenshots of these derogatory Instagram statements about China emerged, the fury . . . well . . . escalated.

D&G's Response and the Fallout

Subsequently, in its weak defense, D&G issued a statement that their account, as well as the accounts of its designers, had been hacked. Not only was this explanation too late by then, it also lacked credibility. D&G had no choice but to cancel the fashion show at the last minute. Five days after the release of the three videos, the two founders, Domenico Dolce and Stefano Gabbana, issued a video apology saying in Mandarin, "Dui Bu Qi!" ("We apologize!") (Zhou, 2018). Symbolic of China's powerful cancel culture, retailers in the Asian market, including Alibaba, Jindong, and Suning pulled the brand's products from their shelves (Dalton, 2018). In 2021, Japanese cosmetics giant Shiseido revoked its global license with D&G, with France being an exception. Sales dropped 98 percent from the same period the previous year (Bain, 2019), and the brand's Asia–Pacific market shrank from 25 to 22 percent of its total turnover (Cristoferi, 2019), all because of three promotional and ill-advised videos that indignified the Chinese customer and the poorly construed response to the transgression. A contrasting story is that of the much-loved ice cream brand Ben & Jerry's that challenges business convention through its almost obsessive emphasis on human dignity.

Ben & Jerry's Ice Cream

When co-founders and childhood friends Bennett Cohen and Jerry Greenfield started Ben & Jerry's (B&J's) in 1978 out of a renovated gas station in Burlington, Vermont they just wanted to make good ice cream. However, they grew to believe that the company should aim to have a socially beneficial impact beyond its product and chose to prioritize progressive principles of equality and sustainability as integral to their mission. And over its almost 45 years of existence, the company has shown time and time again what treating each life with dignity means and the positive outcomes this dictum brings.

Ben & Jerry's Raison d'Etre: Political and Social Activism

The first time B&J's (now a Unilever company) linked its product with a social cause (political activism) was in 1988 when it used the wrapping of its new chocolate covered ice cream the "Peace Pop" as a signal for the US federal government to divert 1 percent of its defense budget to peace-building initiatives. This was a direct challenge to the billions of dollars spent on nuclear weapons by the Reagan government when one in five children in the United States were poor. Business in those days rarely took a stance on social issues, and certainly not on matters that were not directly related to their operations. Internally, staff worried that customers would perceive condemning government policy as "unpatriotic." Externally experts warned that such "controversial" positions would hurt their bottom-line. The co-founders, however, stood their ground (Solis, 2020).

B&J's has since taken a position on almost every significant social issue to emerge in the previous three decades, with CEO Matthew McCarthy noting, "When it comes to social activism, no topic is off-limits for Ben & Jerry's" (Quiroz-Gutierrez, 2021). The company speaks out—with provocatively named and self-described "euphoric" ice cream flavors—that have become its signature branding strategy. Here are some notable examples that tell the story better than words possibly can:

– "Fossil Fuel" to protest drilling in Alaska (2005)
– "Truth or Clone-sequences" to oppose Food and Drug Administration (FDA) approval of animal cloning (2007)
– "Food Fight Fudge Brownie" to demand genetically modified organism (GMO) labeling (2014)
– "Scoop Ice Cream Not the Reef" to raise awareness about the Great Barrier Reef (2014)

- "Hubby Hubby" (2009) and "Apple-Y Ever After" (2012) in support of same sex unions; "I Dough I Dough" to commemorate the Supreme Court's decision to legalize homosexual marriage (2015)
- "Empower Mint" to protest erosion of voting rights (2016)
- "Home Sweet Honeycomb" to support legislation to resettle refugees in Europe (2017)
- "One Sweet World" to promote economic and racial justice (2017)
- "Pecan Resist," "Orange Impeachment," and "White Macadamia Nut Privilege" in remonstration of Trump (2018)
- "Justice ReMix'd" to advocate for criminal justice reform (2019)
- "Change the Whirled" demanding racial equality (2021)
- "Change Is Brewing" to curb police violence (2021)

The company has a separate division (independent of Unilever) that focuses exclusively on activism overseeing its social mission, both through dollar donations and developing long-term relationships with grassroots organizations. It comprises of social activists, non-profits, policy experts, and policy advocates that use the company's corporate muscle to amplify their activism, and connect with and sell ideas directly to B&J's customers. Holding a rare position in corporate America, Chris Miller, as B&J's Corporate Activism Manager, notes, "We use all the tools we have to sell ice cream and put them in service of grassroots activists . . . We do make donations to support our groups, but we're also experts at framing, communication, buying media, using digital, and running social channels" (Solis, 2020).

Ben & Jerry's: Walking the Talk

Is it all talk and no walk? Apparently, B&J's lives the values it espouses. Entry-level positions in Vermont receive $18.13 an hour — $7.17 above the state's minimum wage — and employees can take home three pints of ice cream every day. Since 2015, it has also stopped asking applicants about their criminal history, in support of a national campaign to reassimilate those with criminal records. While acknowledging they have more work to do, B&J's is a poster child of how to use your product to create progressive change, in addition to generating profit. "Ice cream is not 'just ice', it is JUSTICE . . . and cream. Our ice creams are sweet, but the love for fighting oppression tastes even sweeter; it's our secret ingredient!" remarked co-founder Ben Cohen. "Ben and I have been reading up on Freud and the idea of the subconscious recently, and we realized over the years that the fastest way to dismantle the heart of white supremacy is through the stomach," added Jerry Greenfield, the other co-founder. Indeed, "Justice is a dish best served cold" (Watarastaporn, 2020). Experts concur. Emily Barman, Sociology professor at Boston University, believes, "As far as capitalism goes, they're doing a pretty good job." Americus Reed, a marketing professor at Wharton School of Business notes, "To me, Ben & Jerry's are basically activists who happen to sell ice cream. When people say, 'I'm a Ben & Jerry's customer,' they're not just saying, 'I like the ice cream' — they're saying, 'I believe in those values'" (Solis, 2020). Stephanie Creary, a Wharton management professor specializing in identity and diversity notes, "I think Ben & Jerry's is probably the most prominent . . . for-profit corporation that has such an active and strong stance on racial justice. They set the bar really high, that's the reality" (Solis, 2020).

On January 7, 2021, following the uprising at the US Capitol, the corporation responded swiftly with social media messages condemning the "failed coup" and calling for President Trump's impeachment. In July 2021, it sparked outrage by announcing that it will "stop selling our ice cream in the Occupied Palestinian Territory," (B&J, 2021) prompting swift anti-Semitic backlash from Israeli politicians and criticism from the Anti-Defamation League. Israel's Prime Minister Naftali Bennett called the company's actions a "boycott of Israel," and vowed to "act aggressively" against Unilever. A key aspect of CEO McCarthy motivation, though, is that the ice cream company's actions are not "cause marketing," but rather business activism. McCarthy claims that the firm does not consider whether social justice action or cause can help sell more products when making decisions. He notes, "We don't do the things we do to sell more ice cream. When people know what you stand for, you're clear about what your values are, and put your actions consistently behind your values, you're going to create more loyalty with your fans" (Quiroz-Gutierrez, 2021). Part of Unilever's acquisition agreement when it bought out B&J's in 2000 was that it would spend a minimum of $1.1 million per year on activism (Bahler, 2019). Thirty years after the launch of Peace Pop, B&J's is still engaged in advocacy . . . and prospering—it was the highest selling ice cream brand in the United States in the 52 weeks preceding November 2020, with about $863.1 million in sales (Wunsch, 2021).

Ben & Jerry's Registers as B Corporation

A "B Corporation" is a nonprofit accreditation program that demands US businesses demonstrate that they provide value for all stakeholders, not just their investors. A "B Corp" Certification is a designation that a business is meeting high standards of verified performance, accountability, and transparency on factors ranging from employee benefits and charitable giving to supply chain practices and input materials. To achieve certification, a company must:

– **Demonstrate high social and environmental performance** by achieving a B Impact Assessment score of 80 or above and passing a risk review. Multinational corporations must also meet baseline requirement standards.
– **Make a legal commitment by changing their corporate governance structure** to be accountable to all stakeholders, not just shareholders, and achieve benefit corporation status if available in their jurisdiction.

– **Exhibit transparency** by allowing information about their performance measured against B Lab's standards to be publicly available on their B Corp profile on B Lab's website (B Corp, 2023).

When B&J's became a B Corporation in 2012, it formalized the concept of valuing social and environmental impact on equal footing with profit. As a B Corp, B&J's is committed to ensuring that the businesses with whom it partners adhere to the same set of standards. It refers to this way of conducting business as "connected prosperity" (Michalak, 2019), a notion that everyone involved in the production process, from staff to suppliers to customers, should profit.

Principle 6: Treat Each Life With Dignity

In pursuit of positive financial outcomes, businesses aspire for satisfied and loyal consumers. They develop products, processes, systems, and services while keeping this aspiration in mind. The United Nations Guiding Principles on Business and Human Rights (UNGPs) require enterprises to declare a public commitment to respect human rights, conduct due diligence on human rights, and provide a remedy when things go wrong (EHRC, 2019). Whether a corporation adopts this advice or disregards it is determined by its values, where it sees the firm is headed, and what it is doing to get there.

A corporate culture that respects its employees will likely translate into a more rewarding customer service philosophy. GM fostered a claustrophobic workspace and it showed in the way the employees treated their customers (Darmstadter, 2016). Ditto with United Airlines (Romero et al., 2017). One year after its fiasco, which went viral overnight, United sent its staff on a four-day training program to instill a sense of compassion, ensure safe and efficient operation (on-time departures), and to do it all with a smile (Josephs, 2018). Compared to 59 percent of employees at a typical US company, 91 percent at Patagonia (see Chapter 8) feel it's a great place to work.

Jerry Fritz perfectly encapsulates why businesses should prioritize customer service training, "Products and prices can be duplicated, but a strong customer service culture can't be copied" (Lucas, 2022). Tom Rieger, author of *Breaking the Fear Barrier*, notes:

> "Putting the subtle differences between these metrics aside, focusing on just a "happy metric" of customer service ignores perhaps the most critical role of a service representative. Yes, reps are customer advocates, but they are much more than that. They often have to be the parent, the coach, or the referee who says "no." Customer service reps are not just customer advocates. They are defenders of your brand" (Reiger, 2012).

The sobering fact is that customer satisfaction works both ways. "When customers feel mistreated or misled, they give what they got," according to Reichheld, a leading expert on customer and employee loyalty. "They leave—if they can—and complain if they can't. They demoralize your employees. And they badmouth your company, alienating your prospects. They're costly . . . Each time you live up to the Golden Rule (treat others as you would like to be treated yourself), your reputation is enhanced; each time you fail, it is diminished" (Hayden, 2016). The "negativity looms larger" principle suggests that people are considerably more inclined to complain about a negative experience than they are to share a pleasant one. The negative word about poor customer service reaches more than twice as many people as the positive news about exceptional customer service, and a staggering 91 percent of dissatisfied consumers will leave and never return (Hayden, 2016). A study done by marketing professional Dan Kennedy noted that 68 percent of customers who choose to leave a brand and do business with one of its competitors in the marketplace do so because of the attitude of indifference they experience (ERC, 2017).

Technology entrepreneurs used to create and sell devices. Today, they create and sell platforms for human behavior like social media. In other words, technology is now in the behavior business (Keen, 2015). The more technologically connected and closer people become, the more important values and principled behavior become. In an age of constant technological disruption, treating each life with dignity is more important than it has ever been. D&G suffered because it perceptibly (and likely inadvertently) indignified its customers. One of the consequences of being treated with indignity is moral indignation and a desire to punish the transgressor. At the core of such thought process is a summary experience with the brand: "You did not respect me or treat me with dignity." Dignity is not dished out by what is clinically called "good customer service." It has an emotional, situational, and experiential core that must be carefully developed for a "dignity paradigm" to become part of a brand's DNA (Reiger, 2012).

Postscript

Five years later, D&G's China fiasco has yet to be forgiven or forgotten. The brand's website displays just 47 outlets in China (down from 58), with stores more recently shutting in Beijing, Shanghai, and Chengdu (Hills, 2021). D&G is more or less nonexistent on the main Chinese e-commerce sites Tmall and JD.com, who according to Shaun Rein, founder of China Market Research Group, are "terrified of these nationalistic consumers" and are unlikely to carry the brand soon (Hills, 2021). D&G is also having difficulty gaining traction on Chinese social media and has not signed a major mainland Chinese celebrity since the event. While hiring Chinese celebrity ambassadors and influencers may appear to be the way to re-establish confidence in the nation, Rein feels it will be "career suicide" for the celebrity/influencer. D&G though is not giving up. At the 80th Golden Globe Awards earlier in 2023, Chinese American actress Li Jun Li (playing the role of Anna May Wong in the movie *Babylon*) donned a shimmering silver D&G dress. Contrastingly, Michelle Yeoh, winner of the Best Actress

Oscar for her performance in *Everything Everywhere All at Once* and a bigger name than Li chose Armani Privé. D&G's effort at wooing China was also reflected in its New Year campaign for the Year of the Rabbit featuring relatively low-profile Asian models. Will these acts of deference change D&G's fortunes in China? At one time, Stefano Gabbana called the Kardashians, America's reality TV superstars, "the most cheap people in the world" (Ap, 2023). Yet the family used the brand heavily at the wedding of Kourtney Kardashian. So, there may still be hope for D&G to recover from its Chinese misadventure even though its revival in China looks like a prospect it may have to work very hard at (Hills, 2021) . . . and do so by espousing dignity.

Chapter 7
Seventh Principle: Leadership Sets The Tone

Sexual Harassment at Fox News and the Ultimate Sacrifice at Taj Hotel Mumbai

> "Inherently, having privilege isn't bad, but it's how you use it, and you have to use it in the service of other people."*—Tarana Burke, founder of the #MeToo movement.

Circa 2016. USA.

On July 6, 2016, former Fox News anchor Gretchen Carlson filed a sexual harassment lawsuit against her former boss and Fox News's powerful leader, Roger Ailes, sparking an internal inquiry that resulted in a flood of sexual harassment charges against him from more than 20 female employees. It turns out that Ailes, a bombastic, imposing man, had perpetrated sexual harassment of female employees at Fox for more than 25 years and through his behavior as a leader had created a culture of misogyny and entitlement in one of United States's top-ranked news channels.

Fox News and Roger Ailes

Roger Ailes established his reputation as a conservative "kingmaker" after successfully leading the political campaigns of Republican candidates Richard Nixon (1968), Ronald Reagan (1984), George H.W. Bush (1988), and later Donald Trump (2016) (Dockterman, 2019). He was hired by Rupert Murdoch in 1996 to set up Fox News as a counterpoint to CNN's "left wing slant" (Dickinson, 2011). As Fox News chairman, he shaped the network into a 24/7 political campaign, allowing the Grand Old Party (GOP, used interchangeably with the Republican party in the United States) to sidestep skeptical reporters and conduct a 24-hour assault on public opinion. Designed to replicate the appearance and feel of a news setup, it ostensibly couched political propaganda as independent journalism, blurring the boundaries between journalism and politics (Dickinson, 2011). The formula rocked the American political and media landscape, with Fox surpassing CNN as the most popular cable news network reaching more than 90 million households (Stanglin, 2017). Fox News profits were estimated to be $816 million in 2010, about a sixth of Murdoch's overall earnings, while employing one-third the number of people and with 30 fewer outposts than CNN (Dickinson, 2011). Besides his much-heralded success with making Fox the leading news channel,

---

*Brockes, E. (2018, January 15). #MeToo founder Tarana Burke: 'You have to use your privilege to serve other people.' *The Guardian*. https://www.theguardian.com/world/2018/jan/15/me-too-founder-tarana-burke-women-sexual-assault

https://doi.org/10.1515/9781501517334-008

Roger Ailes was the classic example of unhindered power residing in leadership gone haywire. The network's enormous success gave Ailes carte blanche to mold it in his image—Ailes was Fox News and vice versa. The news channel projected his vision. It reflected *him*. He decided the agenda and hired people specifically to motormouth his worldview. He was purportedly a dictator at work, instilling fear in his colleagues, rewarding loyal employees and punishing those who strayed. Ailes insisted on absolute allegiance. "I only understand friendship or scorched earth" (Dickinson, 2011). Employees believed he was invulnerable. At the heart of his control were the nondisclosure agreements (NDAs) that all employees were required to sign. The purpose of these NDAs was to conceal and privately settle widespread sexual harassment cases and deny employees access to the judicial system. Even when women took risks with their careers by reporting abuse, these legal maneuvers ensured that harmful behaviors remained hidden, allowing offenders to retain power (Dockterman, 2019).

Brand Transgression

Apparently, within Fox, Ailes's behavior was well-known. New female hires were welcomed by Ailes's infamous words, "Turn around and give me a spin." He is rumored to have reportedly questioned a female executive, "Does Rupert know you're more than a hot blonde?" Commenting on another woman during her pregnancy, he said, "I could tell. Do you know how I could tell? Because your breasts look big." He was alleged to routinely promise quid pro quo promotions in exchange for sexual favors (Ellison, 2016). Ailes was notorious for hand-picking blonde, slender ladies for on-camera shows, and requiring their workstations to be see-through to allow viewers to see their legs. Women at Fox were also encouraged to wear skirts rather than pants (Dockterman, 2019). These women employees worked in fear that coming forward would result in being maligned publicly and privately within the company, as the Fox PR Department would leak the most damaging personal stories about employees who were on Ailes's bad side (Gross, 2016).

Brand Crisis

The lid was first lifted in 2014 when *The New Yorker* magazine published an article on Roges Ailes, titled "The Loudest Voice in the Room." In this story, an anonymous former female producer at NBC alleged that Ailes offered her an additional $100 per week in exchange for agreeing to "have sex with him anytime he pleased" (Dockterman, 2019). Two years later, former *Fox & Friends* co-host Gretchen Carlson accused Ailes of "severe sexual harassment" and of jeopardizing her career by reducing her pay and rescheduling her shows to lower-profile timeslots after she declined his advances. Carlson said in her suit that when she confronted Ailes about his treatment of her, he responded, "I think you and I should have had a sexual relationship a long time ago and then you'd be good and better and I'd be good and better" (Crockett, 2016). Eventually, she was fired. Her lawyer, however, found a way to circumvent the NDA by filing a lawsuit against Roger Ailes, not Fox News or its corporate parent, 21st Century Fox, though the latter ultimately ended up paying for her settlement (Parloff, 2016).

The lawsuit stunned everyone at Fox and the media world as it was the first time anyone at Fox News ventured to challenge Ailes. Ailes hired Rudy Giuliani, New York City's ex-mayor and Trump's ex-attorney, for his legal defense and rejected Carlson's charges, stating instead that he terminated Carlson's employment owing to her show's low ratings, even enlisting four female staff members to vouch for him (Dockterman, 2019). However, the dam had broken, and a landslide was impending. James and Lachlan Murdoch hired an external law firm—Paul Weiss—to conduct an internal investigation on Ailes (Chenoweth, 2016), uncovering proof of wrongdoing from the more than 20 female staff who came forward with their harassment experiences at the hands of Ailes. According to one woman, Ailes videotaped her and then used the footage to blackmail her into pressing other women to place themselves in situations where Ailes could harass them. Andrea Tantaros, another employee, alleged that Ailes made her feel uncomfortable by making weight-related comments, inquiring about her personal life, and wanting a hug. Nothing was done in response to her complaint and, instead, she was advised by Fox News Senior Vice President Bill Shine, "Roger is a very powerful man. You should not fight this" (Crockett, 2016). Kellie Boyle, a marketing consultant who met Ailes while interviewing for a job, recalls Ailes telling her, "If you want to play with the big boys, you have to lay with the big boys." Without completely falling for the hook, she inquired as to what his desire would entail—would he be her only big boy? "You may have to give a few blowjobs here and there, but everyone will know you're with me," Ailes responded (Kenny, 2018). Victims from the 1960s, 1980s . . . came forward with similar stories of sexual harassment, sexual assault, threats of job loss for not cooperating, and being fired (Crockett, 2016).

On July 21, 2016, after lengthy talks, Ailes eventually relinquished control of Fox News. However, he did not leave empty-handed: he was paid $40 million, $20 million of which was based on his previous year of work, and the remaining $20 million was the severance payout guaranteed in his contract, regardless of whether he was dismissed for cause or decided to quit (Ellison, 2016). He was not, however, granted an honorable exit as he had requested: he was just locked out of Fox News. In September 2016, 21st Century Fox reached a $20 million settlement with Carlson on Ailes's behalf. He did not contribute to the settlement (Stelter, 2016).

The Fallout

The rot at Fox began at the top with Ailes, but did not stop there. Other individuals accused of sexual misconduct were fired in the months that followed, including Ailes's assistant Bill Shine and the 8 p.m. star Bill O'Reilly. Fox News had settled a sexual harassment suit against O'Reilly for $32 million—and then renewed his contract (Garrahan, 2017). By mid-2017, 21st Century Fox had spent $110 million on sexual harassment complaints in the previous nine months (Shugerman, 2017). In June 2021, Fox News agreed to pay a record $1 million to resolve a New York City Commission on Human Rights investigation into what the commission described as a "culture of pervasive sexual harassment and retaliation at the network" (Byers, 2021). This settlement was the "first of its kind against a major news network by a civil rights enforcement agency in the country," according to the commission. As part of the deal, Fox agreed to waive mandatory arbitration clauses in employee contracts for four years.

Did Fox News Transform?

The Murdochs implemented some visible changes. New human resource management. A workplace council to address sexual harassment. A new complaint mechanism for sexual harassment. A 24-hour helpline. And a redesigned newsroom replacing Ailes's bunker. However, complaints about the sexualized Fox environment continued well after Ailes was fired. Lisa Bloom, alluding to a 2019 complaint she filed against Fox commentator Britt McHenry alleging misconduct and retaliation, noted, "They give lip service to the idea that they have improved but they have not. This is the fifth client I'm representing against Fox News. Nothing has changed" (Stelter, 2020). Fox News host Ed Henry was fired in 2020 after being accused of sexual misconduct and rape by Jennifer Eckhart, a former Fox Business Network producer (Stelter, 2020). CNN's *New Day* co-anchor Alisyn Camerota, who had worked for Fox for many years, stated in 2020, "I guess it is rotten to the core . . . unless you get rid of and stamp out the predators, then of course, the culture will still be rotten" (Stelter, 2020).

Meanwhile, although Gretchen Carlson has not resumed her broadcast journalism career, she has been the most visible and vocal advocate who has successfully lobbied Congress in passing the game-changing *Ending Forced Arbitration of Sexual Assault and Sexual Harassment Act* (2022). This act bars the use of clauses in employment contracts that force victims of misconduct into private arbitration often used to shield perpetrators (Bowman, 2022). She has also co-founded Lift Our Voices, a nonprofit organization dedicated to the elimination of non-disclosure agreements and mandatory arbitration clauses in employment contracts relating to toxic workplace situations (Aurthur, 2021). Roger Ailes died in 2017 due to a bathtub fall at the age of 77 (Stanglin, 2017). His death marked the end of what some would call a brilliant career that went horribly wrong because of leadership gone amok.

The Taj Mahal Palace Hotel Mumbai

"Athithi Devo Bhavah" goes the Sanskrit saying, meaning, "Treat your guest as God." This teaching has been part of India's tradition and culture since ancient times. A part of corporate India has adopted it as well—a guiding customer service principle—with the employees of Indian Hotels Company Limited (IHCL) Taj Mahal Palace in Mumbai (Taj Mumbai) being exemplars. On November 26, 2008, when ten terrorists attacked the city of Mumbai, one of the targets they chose was IHCL flagship seven-star luxury property, the Taj Mumbai in the city's heavily frequented downtown area. As many as 31 people died on the premises, of which one-third were employees, many of whom sacrificed their lives in the call of duty because, at the Taj, the customer is God.

The Taj Mumbai, was established in 1903 and draws its roots from the patriotic movement to free India from colonial rule. Its founder, Jamshedji Tata, was denied entry into the Royal Navy Yacht Club, pointing to a sign that said, "No Entry for Indians and Dogs." He vowed to create a hotel the likes of which the British had never seen (TATA, n.d.). Today, IHCL, a $20 billion conglomerate has 200 properties in 12 countries and 80 cities spanning four continents (IHCL, 2020). The *Condé Nast Traveller* ranks Taj Mumbai as the 20th best hotel globally, noted for its high standards of quality, willingness to go above and beyond to delight guests, and well-trained personnel who take pride in being a part of the Tata culture (Condé Nast Traveller, 2021). Their training program is so comprehensive that every employee has a deep understanding of regular guests and can safely go about their job knowing that all efforts taken to care for the consumer will be fully supported by management.

The Taj awed and pleased when it first opened its doors and not just because of its magnificent facade. It was Mumbai's first electric structure. It housed the first ice-making machine. The first soda producer. The first elevator. The first generator. The first automatic laundry machine. The first polishing machine in the world. It was a modern wonder, a tantalizing glimpse into the future for many who had never traveled outside of India. Above all, it was a hotel that promised treatment based on decency and respect (TATA, n.d.). And then a horrendous tragedy struck that would have severely tested the most principled entities.

The November 26 Terrorist Attacks

At dusk, ten heavily armed Pakistani militants arrived by sea on the shores of Mumbai, India's thriving financial and entertainment hub, divided into groups, seized vehicles, and attacked heavily populated targets, including a prominent train station, a busy restaurant, two luxury hotels (one being the Taj Mumbai), a Jewish culture center, and a hospital. Their 60-hour siege of the city killed 166 and injured more than 300 (Biswas, 2018). The synchronized and indiscriminate destruction that occurred during the attack, known as 26/11, wounded the nation's psyche by revealing the country's vulnerability to terrorism. Much like 9/11, the abiding images of Taj Mumbai's burning domes and spires, which remained ablaze for two days and three nights, will forever be symbolic of these tragic events. The nightmare ended when nine terrorists were killed and one apprehended.

The Exemplary Heroes of the Taj

When four terrorists entered the Taj at 9.30 p.m. on that fateful day, the hotel had an estimated 1,200–1,500 patrons in their rooms, restaurants, and milling in its iconic lobby. Two entered the hotel's main lobby and shot 20 people. The other two came in through another door, firing randomly and throwing grenades. The four then proceeded to the hotel's sixth level, where they murdered anyone they saw, and set fire to a section of the hotel. Many people had locked themselves in rooms and were being held prisoner in various parts of the hotel, creating a hostage situation. Despite having no manuals, policies, or extensive training on handling this type of crisis, the Taj's staff rose to the occasion, with Karambir Singh Kang, the hotel's general manager (GM), rushing back from a conference at another property to coordinate and lead the evacuation from the front. The GM and his family traditionally lived in a suite on the sixth floor of the hotel. Kang was unable to establish contact with his wife and two children. Even when he received news that the sixth floor had been set on fire and there was no hope of anyone surviving, Kang continued to work until noon the next day. Only then did he call his parents and inform them of the awful news. On hearing it, his father a retired general said to him, "Son, do your duty. Do not desert your post." To which Kang responded, "If it (the hotel) goes down, I will be the last man out" (Deshpande & Raina, 2011).

The top brass of Unilever was participating in a banquet to send off and welcome their outgoing and incoming CEOs on the second floor, for which 35 Taj employees were assigned under the leadership of a 24-year-old banquet manager, Mallika Jagad. When the attack occurred, the staff locked doors, turned out lights, separated husbands from wives to reduce risk to families, offered water and assistance, and evacuated them the next morning through windows with the assistance of the fire brigade. Jagad later said, "It was my responsibility . . . I may have been the youngest person in the room, but I was still doing my job." Elsewhere in the hotel, Thomas Varghese, the 48-year-old senior waiter at Wasabi, an upmarket Japanese restaurant, asked guests to crouch under the tables and refrain from using cellphones, and his workers to form a human cordon around the restaurant's 50-odd guests. He was able to evacuate all the visitors and members of his staff, but he sadly perished in the process. There were numerous other instances of heroism, including telephone operators remaining at their posts and alerting guests on status and safety, and staff refusing to leave guests due to their close relationship with them, having served them for years. Later, the group's then-chairman, Ratan Tata, personally visited the families of all 80 employees killed or injured in the attack. Expecting to be met with rage and grief, during one such visit, he met with a widow who stated, "My children had no idea their father was a hero" (Deshpande & Raina, 2011).

The Taj Culture: Lessons in Leadership and Customer Care

What explains this "extreme customer-centric culture" demonstrated by employee after employee at the Taj who placed their own lives at risk to save the lives of their guests? Serendipitously, on the very same day of the attack, Rohit Deshpande, a Harvard Business School (HBS) professor, was interviewing Ratan Tata for a case study on crisis management at the Taj. The events prompted him and his co-author Anjali Raina to probe deeper into the organization's human resource (HR) practices and publish a pivotal article on how the Taj creates this type of employee culture. While conceding that India's traditional culture of hospitality and the values of the House of Tata may have played a role, the authors submit that it is the culture at the Taj that has been created, practiced, nurtured, and polished over generations to the point that it operates on autopilot without much supervision or mandates. It has its roots in the Taj's recruitment strategy that prioritizes character over academics, and their training of the organization culture — "Taj way of doing things" through empowerment, mentoring, and real-time recognition of employees (Deshpande & Raina, 2011).

While corporations routinely recruit high-performing students from well-known universities, the Taj Group hires trainees from smaller cities (Pune, Chandigarh, Dehradun, Haldia, Mysore, and Coimbatore), lesser-known second- and third-tier institutions, and even straight from high school through campus-connect programs, where traditional collectivistic values such as respect towards elders, concern for others, humility, discipline, and honesty are still believed to hold sway. Rather than talent and skills, Taj recruiters evaluate candidate motivations (beyond compensation), such as integrity, desire to make a difference, conscientiousness, going above and beyond the call of duty, independent thinking, working effectively under pressure, and loyalty. New recruits undergo a mandatory 18-month skills certification program (industry standard is 12 months) led by incumbent managers (vs outside consultants) who pass on tacit knowledge. In addition to domain specific skills, they receive customer engagement training in grooming, hygiene factors, personality, language, and listening. Given that 70–80 percent of employee interactions with guests are likely to be unsupervised, trainees are taught not to go by the book but to improvise and maximize customer delight in spur-of-the-moment decision-making. Furthermore, based on the notion that happy employees lead to happy customers, customer delight is linked to employee benefits through a powerful rewards program called Special Thanks and Recognition System (STARS). Outside experts found that service standards and customer retention rates spiked after the launch of STARS and even won the hotel the best Human Resource Innovation Hermes award (2002) in the global hospitality industry (Deshpande & Raina, 2011).

A key "counterintuitive" strategy is that employees are expected to act as customer ambassadors as opposed to corporate ambassadors. Employees know that for any action, reaction, and behavior that is aimed at delighting the customer, the entire organization will stand behind them unconditionally. This shift in perspective alters how they engage with and respond to the needs of guests. For instance, when an irate guest swore never to stay at another Taj property due to an air-condition malfunction, a trainee manager without consultation or approval from any supervisor or subsequent justification for the additional cost of his decision offered the guest free breakfast, a complimentary ride to the airport, and a pick up from Taj in the new city he was traveling to (Deshpande & Raina, 2011). The Taj group's exceptional hiring, training, and employee recognition methods have led to several Gallup's Great Workplace awards and employees pursuing long-term careers with the company due to aligned values and a deep-rooted customer-centric culture.

Principle 7: Leadership Sets The Tone

Does an intimidating leadership style help in yanking a lethargic workforce out of its drudgery, something that empathy may not manage effectively? Does compassion have a place in today's corporate work culture? Or more importantly, does compassionate leadership lead to a better bottom line? Howard Gardner, the articulator of the theory of multiple intelligences, suggests that social intelligence is what makes some leaders adept at extracting maximum performance from subordinates by using interpersonal skills based on empathy (Cherry, 2021). Political intelligence, which lies at the opposite end of the spectrum, subscribes to intimidation or the need for "scary leaders to steer you through" and "creatively pushing followers to overperform."

While some may justify intimidation linked to a larger objective (Motorola's Ed Zander's abrasive style got the sluggish company to post a 26 percent sales increase in 2004; Kramer, 2006), as the Fox case shows, there is often a thin line separating intimidation and abuse. With success and intellectual brilliance, the ego may assume control, hubris could take hold, entitlement might creep in, and the company's culture may spiral out of control. Given that leadership has traditionally been a male purview in most arenas, women often end up as victims of this entitlement driven intimidation, abuse, and retaliation. Also, members of the "dominant" group are prone to two additional pitfalls: first, they acquire empathy deficits that prevent them from understanding perspectives other than their own; second, they act rashly and breach workplace ethics (Keltner, 2017). Research is robust in its finding that powerful men overestimate their own sexual attractiveness, sexualize their profession by seeking opportunities for sexual trysts, and end up transgressing (Keltner, 2017). In a culture marked by fear-based leadership, employees tend to be preoccupied with avoiding or concealing mistakes rather than providing creative suggestions on improving process, productivity, or customer care. Even Nike, voted the ninth greatest place to work for millennial women by Mogul, a women-only technology platform, for decades perpetuated sexual harassment and gender discrimination (Agnihotri & Bhattacharya, 2018).

In this age (we call it the age of transparency), change is appearing at warp speed. Values-driven millennials and Gen Z are emerging as the opinion leaders in the workforce and the customer base. In such an environment, an organization can thrive only through leadership based on empathy. This empathic leadership needs to be translated into every thread that binds the organization together. However, few companies have been successful in instilling this empathy—a quality that stood out in the Taj Mumbai case. The Taj employees exhibited this level of empathy because of the collectivistic nature of the company's culture. A Gallup poll reveals that 61 percent of workers feel disengaged at work, resulting in a significant negative impact on productivity. A lack of workplace bonding also increases psychological distress, whereas positive workplace social interactions promote employee health by lowering blood pressure and heart rate, and boosting the immune system (Harter, 2021). Every manager should be accountable for fostering a positive workplace culture that will result in superior customer care, increased productivity, social connection, loyalty, and engagement.

Postscript

The Ailes story served as a precursor to the exposure of sexual harassment in the workplace. However, it took a year before *The New York Times* published a story shining light on another entertainment industry heavyweight, Hollywood biggie Harvey Weinstein and producer of several Oscar winning movies. This story exposed Weinstein's three-decade-long predatory behavior and sexual assaults on women, many of them established film stars. The case went viral, precipitating the #MeToo movement globally that dismantled the taboo and silence surrounding sexual misconduct by those in power. A study by Temin & Co, a New York-based crisis consulting firm, examining the scope of the #MeToo movement's influence, found that it has led to the removal of at least 417 high-profile executives and staff in 18 months in the United States. All but 7 of the 417 defendants were men, and just 8 were in a consensual relationship with the people who brought the charges against them (Nicolaou & Smith, 2019). Jason Mollica, a digital media expert and professor at American University in Washington DC, noted that the speed and reach of "Twitter and Facebook allowed the #MeToo movement to gain worldwide visibility and put names and faces to those harassed and/or assaulted." Using data from October 10 through December 17, 2017, from the social media analytics platform Talkwalker, he found that #MeToo was mentioned 312,000 times with a total reach of 1.1 billion (Rogers, 2017). #MeToo may also have helped lessen gender preconceptions and other barriers that frequently prevent women from working on projects that are historically dominated by men (Luo &

Zhang, 2021). The movement brought to sharp focus how a leader's behavior can trickle down to the very nooks and crannies of the entire corporate environment. In 2009, *Hotel Mumbai*, an Indian-Australian-American co-produced movie, first showed the horrors of 26/11 to the world. In 2019, *Bombshell*, a Hollywood movie starring Charlize Theron, Margot Robbie, Kate Mckinnon, and Nicole Kidman, revealed the sexual harassment accounts of women at Fox. Both were released to critical acclaim.

Chapter 8
Eighth Principle: Build Brand Authenticity
The Cases of Patagonia and Interface Carpets

"Everything man creates does more harm than good. We have to accept that fact and not delude ourselves into thinking something is sustainable. Then you can try to achieve a situation where you're causing the least amount of harm possible."*—Yvon Chouinard, Founder, Patagonia.

"Titans like me have been fueling the human species' overconsumption for the past 100 hundred years. We needed to do something to stop this . . . Our civilization was chewing up resources faster than the earth could renew them. I stood indicted as a plunderer, a destroyer of the earth, a thief, stealing my own grandchildren's future. And I thought, My God someday what I do here will be illegal. Some day they will send people like me to jail."**—Ray Anderson, Founder, Interface.

Circa 1973.

The need for our last principle—build brand authenticity—has likely been at play since marketing began but is only now becoming a well-researched cornerstone of good brand management. As illustrated through many of the case studies in the preceding chapters, brands that did not handle their transgressions appropriately, suffered. This is in part because these brands failed to a) recognize, b) own, and c) act upon this principle. Indeed, this principle is not as observable as the others, and therefore, is also not easy to act upon. These challenges, however, do not absolve the transgressing brands from ignoring it. Indeed, unless a brand is making a committed effort to live up to this principle, that is, to being authentic, and keeping tabs on its own performance, all bets are off. It is no surprise that all the transgressing brands that fared poorly—Snow Brand Milk, Volkswagen, Dalkon Shield, Wells Fargo, Boeing—somewhere forgot to live up to being authentic in their thoughts, words, and deeds.

So, what is brand authenticity? To unpeel this final notion, we have structured this chapter differently by diving right into carving out the anatomy of a "good brand doing great." We think this structure will offer insights into brand authenticity more compellingly and vividly through an exemplar that has built itself through a sustained and committed set of actions over virtually the entire period of its existence. The brand in focus is a moderate sized US entity that in our consideration is among the most authentic brands in the world—Patagonia.

---

*Beer, J. (2019, October 16). Patagonia Founder Yvon Chouinard Talks About the Sustainability Myth, the Problem with the Amazon—and Why its not Too Late to Save the Planet. *Fast Company.* Accessed on November 8, 2023, from https://www.fastcompany.com/90411397/exclusive-patagonia-founder-yvon-chouinard-talks-about-the-sustainability-myth-the-problem-with-amazon-and-why-its-not-too-late-to-save-the-planet

**Anderson, R. C., & White, R. (2009). *Confessions of a Radical Industrialist: Profits, People, Purpose—Doing Business by Respecting the Earth.* New York, NY: St. Martins Press (pp. 10–16).

https://doi.org/10.1515/9781501517334-009

Rise of Patagonia

Patagonia's story starts with its leader (yes, as we saw in the last chapter). In the 1960s, Yvon Chouinard was well-known in mountaineering circles as a keen outdoorsman who enjoyed falconry, kayaking, and fishing (Hoffman, 2012). The environmentalist in him, however, was searching for some crucial answers. Rock climbers' iron pitons (pegs or spikes driven into a rock or crevice to support a climber or a rope) were littering rock surfaces, which disturbed Chouinard. He decided to learn blacksmithing and launch his own business to produce high-quality, reusable steel pitons for climbs in places like Yosemite. The demand for his gear rose, and in 1966, the back-of-the-car business became Chouinard Equipment, a partnership he created with his climbing buddies, Tom and Doreen Frost. By 1970, it had become the top provider of climbing equipment in the United States (Hoffman, 2012). Even when everything was going smoothly, Chouinard was disturbed by the fact that the reusable steel pitons, which had to be pounded in, were causing damage to the granite surface. He came up with a solution: reusable metal pitons that could be inserted by hand rather than being hammered so they left no trace on the rock's surface. Chouinard Equipment's apparel line was introduced in 1973 under the name Patagonia, a mountainous region shared by Chile and Argentina. This unplanned shift to garments led Chouinard to realize that the apparel industry was contributing to the environmental catastrophe much more than his pitons. He had to come up with a new answer yet again.

A Different Approach to Business

In his best-selling book *Let My People Go Surfing: The Education of a Reluctant Businessman,* Chouinard shares his business philosophy of being willing to abandon the sale of best-selling products if they are harmful to the environment. Laying blame for most of the world's economic, social, and environmental issues on commerce, he pivoted from following the "regular rules of business" and instead sought to use business as a driver of positive change. Patagonia became an "experiment" in his quest to "challenge conventional wisdom and present a new style of responsible business." He believed that the Zen philosophy provided "perfect" insight on how to run a business, explaining: "In Zen archery . . . you forget about the goal—hitting the bull's eye—and instead focus on all the individual movements involved in shooting an arrow . . . If you have perfected all the elements, you can't help but hit the center of the target." This philosophy veered Patagonia away from focusing on profit and towards "being authentic" and "doing things right" (Chouinard, 2006, pp. 74–75).

With Patagonia's growth and expansion came challenges. The company was reorganized several times, and after the 1991 recession, it cut costs, dumped and merged inventories, consolidated sales, and eliminated several layers of management while laying off 20 percent of the workforce (Hoffman, 2012). Chouinard learned his lesson of sustainable growth through this experience—that of modest borrowing and controlled growth with a hard focus on doing what is good for the planet—a vision that got firmly entrenched in the company's DNA including its employees and suppliers. As the firm's 30-year milestone approached and its revenues increased to $270 million, Patagonia was seen as a successful business model based on being environmentally and socially responsible. In his aforementioned book, Chouinard laid out the two pillars of this blueprint: a) Patagonia spends less than 1 percent of its revenues on marketing (Reinhardt et al., 2010), and b) when it does, it connects its products to their environmental footprint. There were several other moving parts of his strategy to be authentic, which we piece meal next.

Social and Environmental Responsibility and Activism

Patagonia's stated goal is: "Build the best product, create no extra harm, utilise business to inspire and implement solutions to the environmental crisis." Environmental stewardship guided all corporate decisions even if they were more costly, difficult, and time-consuming. This was eventually expanded a few years later to include "Patagonia is in business to save our home planet" (Patagonia, 2020).

Employees

Consistent with one of Peter Drucker's classic statements, "Culture eats strategy for breakfast" (Foreman, 2016), Patagonia recruited environmentally conscious employees as their enthusiasm and shared vocabulary made communication between team members simpler, allowed for faster problem solving, and made them effective drivers of change. This human resource strategy that aligned with Patagonia's corporate goals was reflected in the use of recycled paper for catalogues, solar energy in offices, recycled fiber carpets, and developing polyester from recycled soda bottles (Hoffman, 2012). Employees in Salt Lake City turned their parking lot into Utah's first recycling station, protesting and defeating the government's construction plan, which would have endangered the Ventura River.

Suppliers

Patagonia was part of President Bill Clinton's Apparel Task Force in the mid-1990s (Danao, 2018), which was instrumental in the creation of the Fair Labor Association (FLA), an organization that Patagonia helped found. In 2014, Patagonia became a Fair-Trade Certified Company that ensured fair salaries and safe working conditions in its supply chain benefitting more than 72,000 workers in 10 countries worldwide (Patagonia, 2014). Taking this a step further, Patagonia collaborated with its Fair Trade worker committees to jointly determine distribution of profits (Danao, 2018), choosing its suppliers based on shared values of quality, and social and environmental responsibility, rather than commercial efficiency. Executives opined that their selection process contributed to lower fault rates of their products.

Raw Materials—Organic Cotton

In 1993, after an independent environmental impact analysis of four of its most-used products, Patagonia discovered that cotton from industrial farming, which accounted for 20 percent of the company's sales, was harmful to the environment as its production required a variety of toxic chemicals (Szekely & Dossa, 2019). In 1994, Chouinard gave his team 18 months to produce its cotton sportswear with 100 percent organic materials (Gunther, 2017). Despite innumerable financial and supply chain challenges, Chouinard's commitment was firm: "Do it, or we never use cotton again." Patagonia succeeded in going fully organic but it came at a cost: the company paid 300 percent more for cotton in 1996 than a year earlier, went a year without making a profit on its cotton products, and had to decrease its cotton-based product line from 91 to 66 styles (Szekely & Dossa, 2019). Patagonia's cotton sales grew 25 percent, but more importantly, the company established an organic cotton industry as a prototype for better known peers such as Nike, Timberland, and Walmart to follow (Hoffman, 2012). As an extension to this initiative, Patagonia raised the bar by experimenting with recycled cotton and founded the Sustainable Apparel Coalition with a mission to "build the best product, cause no unnecessary harm, and use business to inspire and implement solutions to the environmental crisis" (Wolfe, 2023).

Product Lifecycle Initiative and Common Threads Recycling Program

In addition to creating the industry standard of offering a 100 percent satisfaction guarantee on its products, Patagonia went the extra mile by repairing or replacing any product that failed to meet customer expectations. As a result, its wholesale return rate was assessed at 2.6 percent and its direct return rate at 12.9 percent, both of which were substantially lower than their respective sector averages (Reinhardt et al., 2010). Further, to demonstrate its commitment to the environment, and to make future changes based on public feedback, it launched *The Footprint Chronicles* in 2007—an interactive feature on the company's website that allowed customers to track the environmental impact of their purchases. The effort would go so far as to advise shoppers to spend less and think twice before purchasing an item of clothing (Reinhardt et al., 2010).

The Common Threads Recycling Program was a natural extension of the Product Lifecycle Initiative reflecting Patagonia's efforts to take full responsibility for the items it manufactured, "from birth through death and then beyond death, back to re-birth." It signified a comprehensive commitment to extend each product's life and re-duce landfill trash, with a focus on the four Rs—Reduce, Repair, Recycle, and Reuse (Bardelline, 2010). It also helped reduce the number of products purchased by Patago-nia customers through a two-fold process. First, customers were persuaded to repair damaged garments as many times as possible to increase their lifespan—through company produced "do-it-yourself" guidelines. Those unable or unwilling to do so themselves were charged a reasonable fee by Patagonia to do it for them. Second, Pa-tagonia partnered with eBay to create a secondary online market for customers to sell clothing that no longer fit or was used (Szekely & Dossa, 2019). Patagonia organized retail swap events or encouraged donation of still usable products to non-profits and environmentalists to support reuse. Finally, when an item was no longer usable and all other possibilities had been exhausted, buyers were encouraged to return those to Patagonia in postage paid envelopes so that they could be dismantled and repurposed responsibly (Reinhardt et al., 2010).

In 2011, the program was rebranded with a fifth R—Reimagine—to encourage a "world where we take only what nature can replace" and renamed the Common Threads Initiative (Patagonia, 2011a). As an extension to the program, the brand hosted "Worn Wear" events across the country where customers could come to repair or have their products fixed for free. Social media was flooded with thousands of images and videos from customers across the world showing their patched-up Patagonia apparel to showcase the initiative. While most firms encourage customers to buy from them re-peatedly, Patagonia and its customers took satisfaction in their zero-waste purchases. Patagonia has since set up 70 global repair centers that repair more than 100,000 pieces of clothing a year (Ryan, 2020). An estimated 60,000 people have pledged to eliminate excessive consumption and the company has recycled more than 13,000 pounds of gar-ments (Patagonia, 2009).

These initiatives were by no means costless. Repair and recycling came with a capacity expansion cost of about $350,000 per year and often times customers were offered replacements to cut down on repair wait times (Reinhardt et al., 2010). Choui-nard, however, also knew that being environmentally responsible was not enough: "If we want to lead corporate America by example, we have to be profitable. No company will respect us if we are not profitable, no matter how much money we give away or how much publicity we receive for being one of the '100 Best Companies'. It's okay to be eccentric as long as you are rich, otherwise, you are just crazy" (Chouinard, 2006, p. 160).

"Don't Buy This Jacket"

In the United States, the last Friday in November is branded Black Friday and has traditionally seen the highest retail spending than any other day of the year. While most major retailers continue heavy discounting of their merchandise on this day to attract price-conscious buyers, Patagonia chose to highlight its efforts to reduce consumption and environmental waste. As a result, it ran the classic "Don't Buy This Jacket" ad during this period. The advertisement highlighted the environmental impact of one of Patagonia's best-selling "R2" fleece jackets and encouraged people to think twice before purchasing one, and instead opt to buy a used Patagonia product (Patagonia, 2011b). Few businesses had the courage to tell customers to think twice about their purchases and spend less. Even fewer went into depth about a particular product's negative environmental impact.

Despite, or perhaps because of this, the company's revenues increased by 30 percent to $543 million in 2012, followed by another 5 percent increase in 2013. The pitch aided in the production of $158 million worth new clothes (Falk, 2013). By 2017, the corporation had reached a revenue of $1 billion (Thangavelu, 2020). In 2019, it generated an estimated $800 million in income, and Chouinard's net worth was projected to be $1.2 billion by Forbes, nearly all of which was based on the value of his business (Au-Yeung, 2020). "I know that sounds weird, but every time I have made a decision that is best for the planet, I have made money," Chouinard has been quoted as saying (Greenlee, 2021).

Customers now look forward to Patagonia's Black Friday attention-grabbing sustainability campaign, encouraging them to do the exact opposite of what most other brands want them to do. In 2016, it donated 100 percent of profits from Black Friday sales to environmental groups and in 2019, Patagonia Action Works matched all donations made to environmental groups (Howland, 2018). In 2020, it introduced a new campaign called "Buy Less, Demand More," sharing research on how "Buying a used garment extends the life of the item by an average of 2.2 years, which reduces its carbon, waste, and water footprint by 73 per cent" (Weaver, 2020). Notably, Patagonia is the first brand that allows buyers to compare new and used products through its "browse used" link on its website and educate customers on demanding three things from the textile industry: regenerative organic cotton, fair trade manufacturing processes, and recycled fibers (AC, 2021). Patagonia recently announced that it will no longer be adding its logo to new products as attaching a non-removable logo to a garment diminishes its life expectancy by several years. Further, it has started collecting and recycling busted but well-loved Patagonia clothing, into new jackets, shirts, vests, and hand-sewn bags that are selling brilliantly (Joe, 2021).

Impact on the Apparel Industry

Research has found that buying used instead of new clothing can reduce an individual's carbon footprint by up to 60 percent. This has led to a new trend in retail: secondhand clothing, and Patagonia has played a significant role in it. According to ThredUp, a San Francisco–based online consignment company, secondhand products are a $28 billion sector that is predicted to more than quadruple by 2024 (Thomas, 2020). It is also where the next generation of consumers might congregate: most Gen Z consumers regard buying used apparel, shoes, or accessories as having no stigma, and 40 percent have done so, more than twice as many as Gen X and Boomers. With the global clothing industry on track to account for more than 25 percent of the world's annual carbon footprint by 2050, Patagonia's initiatives like Worn Wear are more than just a fad—they are crucial to our planet's health (Batten, 2020) and their success has prompted other companies to undertake "recommerce."

Certified B Corporation

Patagonia became a Certified B Corporation in 2011. Businesses that view the Earth as a stakeholder and certifiably demonstrate this in their values, mission, policies, and procedures are awarded this certification. Quality, Integrity, Environmentalism, and Innovation are its four basic values and are described by Chouinard in his book as "[l]ead an examined life, clean up our own life, do our penance, support civil democracy, and influence other companies" (Chouinard, 2006, p. 200).

One Percent for the Planet

Patagonia has donated 1 percent of its annual sales to grassroots environmental groups since 1985, and in 2002, Chouinard and Craig Mathews of Blue Ribbon Files founded One Percent for the Planet, an international organization with the goal of "building, supporting, and activating an alliance of businesses financially committed to creating a healthy planet." To date, it has enlisted the help of more than 5,400 business partners and raised approximately $530 million in certified donations across 100 countries (1% for the Planet, n.d.).

Activism

The company has uniquely blended business and politics for more than 45 years, priding itself for its activism, which it believes does not run contrary to running a successful business (Howland, 2018). In Alaska, Patagonia has backed efforts to keep waste from mining operations out of the Bristol Bay, which is home to a thriving salmon fishery. It has campaigned to safeguard grizzly bears in Yellowstone National Park (Patagonia, 2016), fought for forest preservation in Poland, gotten involved in national politics opposing the North American Free Trade Agreement and the Trans-Pacific Partnership, and has produced feature-length documentaries, such as *DamNation*, about the dangers of damming rivers (Horn, 2014).

Not surprisingly, it has been targeted by developers, the fossil fuel industry, and lawmakers. In 2016, President Obama established the Bears Ears National Monument to honor the "extraordinary archaeological and cultural record" as well as the land's "profoundly sacred" value to numerous Native American tribes (Fox et al., 2019). Eleven months later, President Trump reduced Bears Ears by 85 percent and Grand Staircase-Escalante National Monument by 45 percent via an Executive Order. While archaeologists, conservationists, and tribes challenged this legally, Patagonia has been at the forefront of the protest as well (Gonzales et al., 2017). Within an hour of the order, in its first run-in with a president, Patagonia claimed on its home page: "The President Stole Your Land," filed a lawsuit (DuBois, 2018), and Chouinard went on national television (CNN) calling the Trump administration "evil" (Miller, 2018). The Trump administration retaliated by accusing Patagonia of playing politics to sell more garments, and the hashtag #BoycottPatagonia began to circulate on Twitter (now X) (Schnell & Azzolini, 2019).

In 2018, Patagonia announced that it will donate $10 million to help fight climate change, the precise amount Patagonia saved with the 2017 Trump corporate tax-break from 35 to 21 percent (Business at the Bay, 2018) that the company believed were "irresponsible" cuts (Folley, 2018). Other companies like Ben & Jerry's also spoke out against this tax break. However, none gave their tax dollars away (Robertson, n.d.).

Walking the talk of supporting civil democracy, Patagonia gave its employees four days paid leave to work as poll workers during the Presidential election and encouraged people to vote for climate leaders. Referring to climate and science deniers whose election coffers were filled with money from fossil fuel companies, Chouinard went so far as to add "Vote the Assholes Out" on some of Patagonia's garment tags (The Drum, 2020). The brand's fight against the establishment through direct and powerful messaging turned out to be a windfall, setting sales records in each of the Trump presidency's first three years and on the verge of hitting the $1 billion mark (Bhasin, 2020). Patagonia was named a 2019 UN Champion of the Earth in the "Outstanding Entrepreneurial Vision" category (UNEP, 2019). The Axios/Harris 2021 poll ranking placed Patagonia at #1 among the top 100 brands (The Harris Poll, 2021) with 66 percent of outerwear consumers' expenditure going to the brand (Huckabay, n.d.). In a public opinion poll by GlobeScan and global think tank SustainAbility, Patagonia was also ranked among the top five in terms of sustainability, alongside Unilever, IKEA, Interface, and Natura & Co. (GlobeScan, 2021).

Patagonia continues to be a resistance brand, even in the Biden era. By engaging in activities that most companies wouldn't even contemplate, it has proven to customers that its environmentally friendly branding isn't just rhetoric. For all its success, Chouinard acknowledges: "There's no such thing as sustainability. There are just levels of it. It's a process, not a real goal. All you can do is work toward it . . . I keep at it because it's the right thing to do." *Fortune* magazine summarized the Patagonia phenomenon as follows: "[Patagonia] is business conducted upside down and inside-out. Everything about it flies in the face of consultants' recommendations about How to Maximize Profits and Cut Costs. Simply put, it's radical. Which is exactly how Patagonia's founder, Yvon Chouinard, likes it" (Casey, 2007).

Interface Carpets—Mid-Course Correction to Become a Prototypical Company of the 21st Century

When Ray Anderson founded Interface in 1973, a modular carpet and commercial broadloom company, he had never heard the term sustainability. Within two decades it had become the world's largest "carpet tile" manufacturer, touching $1 billion in sales. In 1994, a colleague handed him a hand-written note saying, "Some customers are asking what Interface does for the environment. How should we answer? . . . When it comes to the environment some customers believe that Interface does not get it." Anderson's first reaction was, "Don't get what? Making carpet tiles demands so many petroleum-derived chemicals that we aren't just dependent on oil companies, we are like an extension of them. We haven't broken a single environmental rule. Not even bent one. We were legal, in compliance—100 percent" (Anderson & White, 2009, p. 9). To respond in an authentic manner, he established an internal environmental task force and agreed to give the opening speech at its first meeting. Describing his struggle on the days leading up to the event he wrote, "At the time, I hadn't given one thought to the environment; all I was concerned with was dollars and cents. How could I possibly speak passionately about a topic about which I was neither an expert nor cared a great deal about?"

His "spear in the chest" epiphany came when reading Paul Hawken's *The Ecology of Commerce* whose key premise was that "our living systems were in decline and the biggest culprit was the industrial system . . . The problem is with the way we make stuff, digging up the Earth, turning it into products that quickly become waste in the landfill or incinerator. It's the fundamental mindset that says, 'Use it, take it, it's all yours'" (Posner, 2009, p. 48). Hawkens was speaking directly to people like Anderson, arguing that neither individuals (lacking collective power) nor government (mostly reactive) had the capacity to provide transformational change, and that only capitalist businesses were "large enough, wealthy enough, and pervasive and powerful enough to lead humankind out of the mess we are making" (Anderson & White, 2009, p. 14).

Hence began Anderson's journey to transform Interface into not merely a sustainable—but a regenerative—enterprise. He began his speech by saying, "I hear some of you think I've gone around the bend. That's my job, to go around the corner and see what's on the other side." After finishing his speech, he posed two questions to his stunned employees, "What if Interface were to be the first industrial company in the world to become sustainable? What would a restorative company look like?" The reaction within the company and industry was one of shock. Bob Shaw, owner of Shaw Industries, one of the world's largest carpet manufacturers, said to Anderson, "You're a dreamer. It's OK to be a dreamer and lose your money. But you're going to take the whole company down with you" (Posner, 2009, p. 48). This was a risky move for a multibillion-dollar carpet tile company that had never considered the environment before.

Mission Zero

In 1995, he gave Interface a moonshot goal: "To be the first company that, by its deeds, shows the entire industrial world what sustainability is in all its dimensions: People, process, product, place and profits—by 2020—and in doing so we will become restorative through the power of influence" (Interface, n.d.). Interface recognized it had to completely transform its entire business model to achieve Mission Zero. It created its Eco Dream Team and enlisted experts steeped in environmental issues to help ascertain the most critical areas of change needed. Anderson challenged his employees to join him in ascending the seven fronts (later named faces) of Mount Sustainability: zero waste, benign emissions, renewable energy, closed loop recycling, resource efficient transportation, stakeholder sensitization and cooperation, and redesigning commerce (Anderson & White, 2009, p. 41).

The QUEST (Quality Utilizing Employees' Suggestions and Teamwork) program invited employees to identify, measure, and eliminate traditional and nonrenewable energy waste—defined as any cost that did not add value for customers. Between 1995 and 2009, QUEST was able to save $433 million in waste expenses (Rothaermel & Janovec, 2012, p. 4). The ReEntry® Reclamation and Recycling program, involved collecting and recycling post-consumer vinyl-backed carpet tiles (even from competitors!) to create backing material (GlassBacRE), producing nontoxic adhesives (TacTiles) and textiles, leveraging nature's designs for products, and experimenting with leasing "flooring services" as an alternative to selling carpets (Interface, n.d.). Interface began working with suppliers to incorporate recycled and bio-based materials and renewable energy and process efficiencies. In 2003, it began offering carbon-neutral flooring across North and South America and then expanded it globally (UNFCCC, 2020). The Carbon Neutral Floors Program sought to recognize customers' carbon reduction and Facebook, Apple, and Starbucks were some of the earlier customers.

Not all new strategies were successful, however. Anderson credited "the marketplace's goodwill based on what we're doing," for being able to recover from the dot. com crash that slashed Interface's revenue by 30 percent (Makower, 2016). Their proudest contribution was developing the world's first biomimetic carpet tile inspired by the forest floor—Entropy where no two tiles are alike but blend into each other no matter their age or direction of installation—that evolved into accounting for about 40 percent of Interface's annual sales. Between 1996 and 2008, Interface had increased sales by 66 percent and more than doubled its earnings, primarily due to reduced energy and water usage as opposed to raw materials savings (Rothaermel & Javovec, 2012). Collectively, these initiatives resulted in reducing the company's carbon footprint by 1 million metric tonnes (Interface, n.d.).

Impact

Interface's course-corrected business model piqued Walmart US CEO Mike Duke's (later to become CEO Walmart) interest, who self-invited himself and his team to visit Interface for a walk-through. The success of the visit led Interface to draw on 20 in-house experts to launch InterfaceRAISE, a sustainability consultancy unit to help other companies transform the way they viewed and implemented sustainability though immersion workshops, coaching/mentoring, current-state assessments, and strategy formulation. Interface was also the recipient of several global ethics and environmental accolades with *Fortune* magazine naming it one of the "100 Best Companies to Work For" in 1997 and *Time* magazine placing Ray Anderson on its 2007 "Heroes of the Environment" list (Rothaermel & Javovec, 2012). Anderson would later comment, "We unconsciously injected a sense of purpose, a higher purpose in our workforce, and it had a galvanizing effect" (Posner, 2009, p. 48). Further,

> "Sustainability has given my company a competitive edge in more ways than one. It has proven to be the most powerful differentiator I have known in my long career. Our costs are down, our profits are up, and our products are the best they have ever been. Sustainable design has provided an unexpected wellspring of innovation, people are galvanized around a shared higher purpose, better people are applying, the best people are staying and working with a purpose, the goodwill in the marketplace generated by our focus on sustainability far exceeds that which any amount of advertising or marketing expenditure could have generated—this company believes it has found a better way to get bigger and more legitimate profit—a better business model." (Anderson & White, 2009, p. 167)

Anderson passed away in 2011 but his team has continued the mission. Over the last 25 years, Interface has become a leader in sustainability by establishing rigorous sustainability targets and making outstanding progress in reducing its carbon footprint, emissions, water consumption, and trash to landfills. In a watershed moment, as manufacturing circularity pioneer for more than 25 years, Interface launched its first carbon-negative flooring product in 2020. Since 2016, Interface has been pursuing a new mission—"Climate Take Back"—to reverse global warming and become carbon negative by 2040, and has released a blueprint "Lessons for the Future Report" for themselves and others to follow. Looking to not just reduce negative impact but also generate positive impact, Interface is collaborating with Biomimicry 3.8 on a pilot project called "Factory as a Forest" to examine how a factory can be made to deliver the same services and positive impact as an ecosystem, including water filtration and carbon sequestration (King, 2015). It is also looking to copyright and license its secret sustainability recipe so other businesses can scale up their sustainability agendas. In addition to collaborating with groups like LEEDS and Green Building Council to develop market standards for green buildings, Interface has also launched a Materials Carbon Action Network program with industry peers like Gensler, CertainTeed, Armstrong, and others to decarbonize the construction sector (Building Transparency, 2020). In terms of attracting talent, Nigel Stansfield, Interface's vice president, sums it up well: "If you talk to the 25-year-olds now in the job marketplace and ask, 'Would you like to come work for a carpet-tile company?' I don't imagine many would say yes. But when you ask, 'Do you want to come work for one of the world's most sustainable manufacturing businesses?' It's a very different conversation to have" (Makower, 2016).

Principle 8: Build Brand Authenticity

A 2019 study by Stackla found that 90 percent of consumers—especially millennials and Generation X—said that authenticity was important to them. Interestingly, the same study also reported that consumers were 2.4 times more likely to say user-generated content (UGC) was more authentic compared to brand-created content. Ironically, marketers were 2.1 times more likely to say brand-created content was more authentic (Stackla Survey, 2019). It seems that either some marketers have blinders on, or they simply do not understand their customers. Both these suppositions are a recipe for a marketer's fast tracking on a downhill slope. *As abstract a concept as it might be, brand authenticity isn't difficult to grasp; it is simply about a brand delivering purposefully on its promise unfailingly, transparently, and even obsessively, without deception, disrespect, or sleight of hand. And if the brand missteps—as any brand will do a number of times in its life—it corrects itself without fuss and with lightning speed.* We live in confusing times touched by information explosion and fakery. Add to this discomforting mix customers seeking ways to connect with brands based on more than a clinical cost–benefit analysis, and authenticity begins to seem like a good, even critical, pursuit.

What is an Authentic Brand?

– **Authentic brands are trustworthy, genuine, and inspiring**. They are committed to the customers' success, resulting in higher levels of loyalty and profit accorded to them. Not all authentic brands are built on an obsessive pursuit of sustainability as Patagonia but for sure, they are sensitive to the consequences of their actions on the planet at large and do not shy away from taking action to minimize the negatives. The UK based Body Shop brand was built on perceived promises of being cruelty free and 'no animal testing.' In 2006, the company faced a consumer boycott after it was sold for $850 million to L'Oreal, a company prone to animal testing at the time of the sale. Consider the case of Dove, on the other hand. Dove turned itself from a soap with one-third moisturizer to a brand with a higher order vision when it launched its Campaign for Real Beauty in 2004 (now the Dove Self-Esteem Project). "Beauty should be a source of confidence, not anxiety" might read like a positioning statement but it goes deeper and ultimately has become the brand's new purpose. By aligning its marketing efforts with its purpose, Dove has now come to be authentically associated as a brand that supports empowerment of all women, not just those who look cosmetically beautiful. Dove's redefinition of beauty and its own promise has led to an upward spike in its perceived trustworthiness (Sunrise, 2021). Sure, the brand committed a transgression when it pitched fair skin as superior to dark skin, but it quickly backtracked, apologized sincerely, and came out of the mess (Dua, 2017).

– **Authentic brands have a purpose beyond profit**. Patagonia is authentic because it is purpose-driven, its purpose being not merely selling clothes but to "save the home planet" while doing so. Ben & Jerry's purpose is to advance human rights and enhance the dignity of every human being. Tylenol's purpose, as revealed in Chapter 1, was to save the customers first even if it meant taking a massive profit hit. Chouinard as quoted in *Beloved Brands* notes, "Purpose is not a strategy. You can't reverse into a mission and values through marketing. The organisations that are struggling with this are probably the ones that are thinking about marketing first. The role of marketing is to authentically elevate that mission and purpose and engage people in it . . ." (Robertson, n.d.). For the skeptics, here is an interesting piece of hard data: studies conducted by Deloitte show unambiguously that purpose-driven companies witness higher market share gains and grow three times faster on average than their competitors, all while achieving superior customer satisfaction (O'Brien et al., 2019). Such businesses establish stronger connections with customers, do more for their communities, attract and retain superior talent, and achieve better results and impact. Those that lack purpose may survive and even thrive in the short term, but eventually run into problems if a purpose vacuum continues to plague them.

– **Authentic brands are propelled by the passion of their creators, who instill this drive in all their stakeholders**. Chouinard and Anderson both believed that by improving people's lives, they were improving the world. Their brands reflected that approach at a micro-level. They understood that to achieve their purpose, the business had to be financially lucrative, yet they were more driven by their desire to help their consumers' lives become better. This focus on enhancing lives versus enhancing profit is probably the most important difference between companies that do authenticity right and companies that don't. Chouinard echoes this: "Most public corporations operate to maximize profits for the shareholders. Decisions are made for the short-term health and growth of the company. At Patagonia, we make our important decisions based on wanting to be here 100 years from now. We know that if all is going well with our work, the profits are bound to come" (Chouinard, 2019, p. 151).

– **Authentic brands are better cushioned against transgressions, both before and after the transgression**. Stakeholders will more readily forgive an authentic brand gone rogue, because an authentic brand missions itself towards something bigger than profit or a share of the customer's wallet. That "something bigger" is a selfless dedication to creating an empowering ecosystem for its customers. Authenticity is about purpose with passion, and only then profit.

Postscript

Patagonia's founder and his family, instead of selling or going public, have transferred their ownership of the company, estimated at $3 billion, to a climate focused trust and a non-profit organization. They did so to ensure that all its profits—approximately $100 million per year—are used to fight global climate change. The firm's official statement noted, "[E]very dollar that is not reinvested back into Patagonia will be distributed as dividends to protect the planet" (Gelles, 2022).

Conclusion

Tying the Eight Principles Together

Circa, 2023.

Our beautiful planet's history over the past three years reads as follows:

- COVID spun the world around and the resulting supply chain disruption aggravated matters.
- Digitalization has replaced more traditional ways of doing business in a hurry.
- Artificial intelligence (AI), ChatGPT, Metaverse, and other technological innovations are knocking on our doors to create a new, uncertain, and ever evolving status quo.
- Robots have become a visible part of our lives.
- Russia invaded Ukraine, reminding us of how a localized war can have disastrous global consequences.
- Energy crisis and rising cost of living are looming like a large shadow.
- Diversity, equity, inclusion, and belonging have become topics of difficult conversations that companies never had to deal with before.

Little wonder then that the world seems like a confusing and sometimes scary place. Now, consider the following, fortuitously concomitant events, that have come to light within the last year:

- Joseph Sullivan (JS), the former chief security officer (CSO) of Uber and now the CSO of CloudShare, was convicted for obstructing proceedings of the Federal Trade Commission (FTC) and an attempted cover-up of a 2016 hack of Uber, involving theft of about 57 million Uber user records and 600,000 driver license numbers. His transgression included paying the hackers in exchange for them signing an agreement not to disclose the hack. Investigators were also misled into believing that the hackers did not take or store any data. On its part, Uber disclosed the incident only after a new CEO, Dara Khosrowshahi, took over in 2017. Joseph Sullivan was recently sentenced to three years of probation and 200 hours of community service. Uber has had to pay $148 million to settle the case and has also been fined $1.2 million in the UK and Netherlands as the data breach affected 82,000 UK drivers and close to 175,000 Dutch citizens. "The message in today's guilty verdict is clear: companies storing their customers' data have a responsibility to protect that data and do the right thing when breaches occur," said FBI Special Agent-in-Charge Tripp (USAO, 2022).
- Balenciaga, a fashion house founded in 1917, faced public outrage for its ad campaign released in November 2022 showing children holding teddy bears in bondage harnesses and costumes, by Gabriele Galimberti, an award-winning National Geographic photographer. The Bondage, Dominance, Sadism, and Masochism (BDSM) accessories were also on display at the brand's show at Paris Fashion Week. Balenciaga and its creative director Demna, were widely "panned with

https://doi.org/10.1515/9781501517334-010

the" hashtag #cancelBalenciaga on Twitter (now X) and TikTok, and accused of ignoring the pedophilia and child exploitation implications contained in the ad. Ultimately, the company assumed responsibility for its poor judgment and the ad campaign was withdrawn (Issawi, 2023).

–   On January 24, 2023, a small US firm Hindenburg Research, accused Gautam Adani, one of Asia's wealthiest and most successful businesspeople of accounting fraud, leading to Adani's net worth falling by more than US$50 billion in a matter of days. He strongly denied wrong-doing, and the case continues to unravel (McNamee et al., 2023).

–   On April 28, 2023, Shi Hang (52) a well-known screenwriter and producer in China, was accused by twelve women for sexual harassment. The accusation has generated a tsunami of anger on Chinese social media, as the world waits for the outcome with bated breath (Yuanyuan, 2023).

There are more, many more. All in the last one year. Our research is clear in its outlook: eventually, a brand will face a situation like the cases documented in this book. Unprecedented environmental turbulence notwithstanding, if and when a brand transgresses, an expectation of forgiveness is naïve. Brands will need to regroup and make some tough choices. Many or most will gravitate towards one or more of the first three that come to mind – fight, flight, or freeze. Depending on how the brand and its protagonists view the word "fight," the best response might well be to do so. When a brand transgresses, our invocation of fight involves the eight principles laid out in this book, which we list below:

1. Do The Right Thing
2. Take Accountability
3. Act With Lightning Speed
4. Communicate Transparently
5. Place Principle Above Profit
6. Treat Each Life With Dignity
7. Leadership Sets The Tone
8. Build Brand Authenticity

All bets are off if a brand chooses to ignore any one of these in addressing its perceived bad behavior. In closing, there are a few other considerations that managers should keep in mind when in a bind. These may overlap with some of the principles above but are worth regurgitating.

Transparency Above Opacity. We have covered this adequately in the fourth principle above, but it needs reiteration. Businesses must reorient themselves towards greater transparency. As trivial as this may sound, an ordinary person on the street has access to virtually unlimited information on almost any subject of interest. In such a setting, the belief that obfuscation and camouflage will help a transgressing brand avoid damage mirrors the behavior of an ostrich. Uncomfortably for many, this individual can also communicate with many others in real time. What we called word-of-mouth some years back is now termed viral. And the "information virus" is traveling faster and faster. Dalkon Shield, despite all its deadly effects and the disingenuous company explanations for the harm it caused, survived for almost ten years. Today, it will be lucky to survive more than a few months or weeks.

Equity Above Inequity. There is a tectonic shift on the human brand front as well. The planet struggled with enhancing equity across dimensions of our existence gender, religion, sexual orientation, ethnicity . . . Today, equity enhancing movements are firmly established frameworks, not just for managing businesses but for living life. This flattening of social structures is requiring corporations to reassess how they do their thing. Some have introduced re-crafted mission statements while others have appointed individuals with diverse backgrounds in important positions. Useful as these steps may be, they are short-term "check mark" solutions—some call these tokenism. To reiterate Peter Drucker's words: "Culture eats strategy for breakfast." In other words, how well your strategy performs depends on your culture. Volumes have been written about corporate culture, yet its nebulousness scares many corporations away from owning and committing to it. Ask yourself: What does culture mean to my company? How important is it in our day-to-day decision making? Does my company have a clearly defined set of values it swears and lives by? When was the last time I was part of a Cultural Onboarding training? If the answer to even one of these queries is, "I don't know" or worse "No," it might be time for taking stock. Culture at its core depends on the leadership's core beliefs and values. And a well-defined culture, which places human equity and diversity first—in thought, word, and deed—will trump a lesser one any day in delivering greater happiness to all its stakeholders. It will protect your brand and your firm as we saw in the case of Tylenol and Starbucks and will hurt you as with Dolce & Gabbana and Snow Brand Milk.

Principle Above Profit. The Eight-Principle rubric (and principle # 5 specifically) above argues for a "Principle Over Profit" approach to dealing with brand transgressions. For sure, this lens will invite skepticism with managers schooled in the shareholder value maximization rule as the Miltonian "be all and end all" of all for-profit corporate activity. Their skepticism is understandable. After all, such corporations run the very real risk of ceasing to exist if they keep creating negative financial value consistently. However, note we do not advocate that profit be damned. What we do advocate for is that these companies should not pursue profit relentlessly without regard to other dimensions of running a successful business. Based on innumerable experiences of brands having transgressed, some of which are captured in this book, we believe that the right response to a brand transgression is firmly based on the principles listed above.

Heart Above Intellect. Academic research has shown that a transgression low in severity (for example, a brand's package coming apart) is not viewed as critically by consumers as one high in severity (for example, a smart phone exploding). Speculative case in point: VW's emissions breach barely affected the company's sales, possibly because many consumers did not see this personally affecting them and, therefore, not as a big deal. Further, if consumers are strongly loyal to a brand and have a deep and abiding relationship with it, they may be more forgiving than if they do not hold such a relation or a sense of loyalty. It is also likely that if a brand operates in an environment where consumers do not have much choice and the category is critical (for example, the airline industry, which is largely a duopoly of Boeing and Airbus), a transgression may not receive the same level of pushback. Indeed, all these factors—transgression severity, strength of consumer–brand relationship, brand's market dominance—and others can help managers create a cracker–jack intellectual model of conditions when a transgression will hurt the brand. While pursuing the creation of such a model is valuable in helping understand the moving parts to a transgression and how to deal with it, such pursuit may be misaligned with where the company's heart (or DNA, take your pick) is in its response. It is the heart that matters. And a company's heart is revealed in its approach to its brand's transgression. Is it denial? Is it blame deflection? Is it distraction? Is it deception? Or is it an authentic and relentless pursuit of addressing the needs of the victims first . . . regardless of the factors at play and whether the brand was responsible for the perceived transgression?

Indeed, to err is human, to transgress is brand.

Bibliography

Introduction

Avila, M., Parkin, H., & Galoostian, S. (2019). $16.7 Million To Save One Reputation: How Starbucks Responded Amidst a Racial Sensitivity Crisis. *Pepperdine Journal of Communication Research*, 7(1). https://digitalcommons.pepperdine.edu/pjcr/vol7/iss1/4

Francis, A. (2010, September 3). Case Study: Cadbury Crisis Management (Worm Controversy). *MBA Knowledge Base*. Accessed on October 26, 2023, from https://www.mbaknol.com/management-case-studies/case-study-cadbury-crisis-management-worm-controversy/

Isidore, C. (2020, March 10). The Cost of the Boeing 737 Max Crisis: $18.7 Billion and Counting. CNN. https://www.cnn.com/2020/03/10/business/boeing-737-max-cost/index.html

Koulopoulos, T. (2018, September 28). According to Ray Dalio, Jeff Bezos, and the Dalai Lama, This One Thing Is the Foundation of Trust. *Inc.Com*. Accessed on October 26, 2023, from https://www.inc.com/thomas-koulopoulos/according-to-ray-dalio-jeff-bezos-dalai-lama-this-one-thing-is-foundation-of-trust.html

Leadr Team. (2019, May 10). 5 Leadership Thoughts from John C. Maxwell. *Leadr.Com*. Accessed on October 26, 2023, from https://blog.leadr.com/5-leadership-thoughts-from-john-c-maxwell

Maxwell, J. (2019, April 17). Your Influence Inventory. *John Maxwell Leadership Podcast*. Accessed on October 26, 2023, from https://johnmaxwellleadershippodcast.com/episodes/john-maxwell-your-influence-inventory

Morain, C. (2009, December 28). Tiger Woods Scandal Cost Shareholders up to $12 Billion. *University of California, Davis*. Accessed on October 26, 2023, from https://www.ucdavis.edu/news/tiger-woods-scandal-cost-shareholders-12-billion

NCC Staff. (2022, November 13). Benjamin Franklin's Last Great Quote and the Constitution. *National Constitution Center*. Accessed October 26, 2023, from https://constitutioncenter.org/blog/benjamin-franklins-last-great-quote-and-the-constitution

NDTV. (2021, June 9). France Charges Volkswagen, Former CEO Over "Dieselgate" Scandal. *NDTV.Com*. Accessed on October 26, 2023, from https://www.ndtv.com/world-news/france-charges-volkswagen-former-ceo-martin-winterkorn-over-dieselgate-scandal-2459995

Shah, S. (2020, August 3). When Crisis Led to Consumer Safety the Story of Cadbury. *BusinessWorld*. Accessed on October 26, 2023, from https://www.businessworld.in/article/When-Crisis-led-to-Consumer-Safety-The-Story-of-Cadbury/03-08-2020-304560/

Tsukayama, H. (2018, February 24). How Samsung Moved Beyond its Exploding Phones. *The Washington Post*. https://www.washingtonpost.com/business/how-samsung-moved-beyond-its-exploding-phones/2018/02/23/5675632c-182f-11e8-b681-2d4d462a1921_story.html

Vaid, M. (2006, December 24). How Cadbury's Won the Battle of Worms. *Rediff News*. Accessed on October 26, 2023, from https://www.rediff.com/money/2006/dec/24cad.htm

Chapter 1

ABC News. (2016, November 3). Timeline of the Wells Fargo Accounts Scandal. *ABC News*. https://abcnews.go.com/Business/timeline-wells-fargo-accounts-scandal/story?id=42231128

Baker, M. (2005, May 15). Snow Brand: What Not to Do When It All Goes Wrong. *Bernstein Crisis Management Newsletter*. Accessed on October 26, 2023, from https://www.bernsteincrisismanagement.com/newsletter/crisismgr050515.html#cmu.

BBC News, (2017, 11 April). United Airlines: Shares Drop After Passenger Dragging Video. BBC News, https://www.bbc.com/news/world-us-canada-39563570

Berge, D. (1990). *The First 24 Hours: A Comprehensive Guide to Successful Crisis Communications*. Cambridge, MA: Basil Blackwell.

Broom, G. M. (1994). *Effective Public Relations*. Eds Cutlip, S.M., Center, A.H., & Broom, G.M. Englewood Cliffs, NJ: Prentice-Hall

Caesar-Gordon, A. (2015, October 28). The Perfect Crisis Response? *PRWeek*. https://www.prweek.com/article/1357203?utm_source=website&utm_medium=social

Cohan, W. D. (2016, September 16). Wells Fargo Scandal May Be Sign of a Poisonous Culture. *The New York Times*. https://www.nytimes.com/2016/09/17/business/dealbook/wells-fargo-scandal-may-be-sign-of-a-poisonous-culture.html

Comcowich, W. (2020, February 25). 7 PR Crisis Management Lessons from the Wells Fargo Scandal. *Glean. info*. Accessed on October 26, 2023, from https://glean.info/7-pr-crisis-management-lessons-from-the-wells-fargo-scandal/?doing_wp_cron=1630230539.6082429885864257812500.

Communiqué PR Staff. (2017, July 31). The Tylenol Murders: A Case Study. *Communiqué PR*. Accessed on October 26, 2023, from https://www.communiquepr.com/the-tylenol-murders-a-case-study/9950/

CUB. (2018, March 13). Starbucks Founder Howard Schultz's Shared Values (And Nine Other Tips for Retaining Customers). *CUB Club of United Business*. Accessed on October 26, 2023, from https://cub.club/blog/starbucks-founder-howard-schultzs-shared-values-and-nine-other-tips-for-retaining-customers/

Dept. of Defense. (n.d.). Crises Communication Strategies. Case Study: The Johnson & Johnson Tylenol Crisis. DoD Joint Course in Communication, University of Oklahoma. *Department of Defense, USA*. Accessed on April 4, 2023, from https://www.ou.edu/deptcomm/dodjcc/groups/02C2/Johnson%20&%20Johnson.htm

DiversityInc. (2012). The DiversityInc Top 50 Companies (2012). *Ranking the Brands*. Accessed on October 26, 2023, from https://www.rankingthebrands.com/The-Brand-Rankings.aspx?rankingID=365&year=850

Food Navigator. (n.d.). Snow Brand Milk Scandal Spirals Downwards. *Food Navigator Europe*. Accessed on October 26, 2023, from https://www.foodnavigator.com/Article/2002/02/25/Snow-Brand-Milk-scandal-spirals-downwards#

Friedman, M. (1970, September 13). A Friedman Doctrine-- The Social Responsibility of Business Is to Increase Its Profits. *The New York Times*. https://www.nytimes.com/1970/09/13/archives/a-friedman-doctrine-the-social-responsibility-of-business-is-to.html

Ganger, B. (2021, September 29). Remembering the Victims of the Chicago Tylenol Murders. *Beyond the Dash*. Accessed on October 26, 2023, from https://beyondthedash.com/blog/remembering/remembering-the-victims-chicago-tylenol-murders/7360

Glazer, E., & Rexrode, C. (2016, September 13). Wells Fargo CEO Defends Bank Culture, Lays Blame with Bad Employees. *The Wall Street Journal*. https://www.wsj.com/articles/wells-fargo-ceo-defends-bank-culture-lays-blame-with-bad-employees-1473784452

Greyser, S. A. (1982). Johnson & Johnson: The Tylenol Tragedy. *Harvard Business School*, 9–583–043, 1–3.

Hiltzik, M. (2020, January 27). That Wells Fargo Accounts Scandal was Even Worse than You can Imagine. *Los Angeles Times*. https://www.latimes.com/business/story/2020-01-27/wells-fargo-scandal

Hogg, A. (2013, November 15). Why Values Matter in Business: Five key Lessons from Tylenol Crisis from the "Tylenol Man" Himself. *BizNews*. Accessed on October 26, 2023, from https://www.biznews.com/thought-leaders/2013/11/15/five-key-lessons-from-tylenol-crisis

Japan Times. (2000a, July 9). Snow Brand Scandal Grows. *The Japan Times*. Accessed on October 26, 2023, from https://www.japantimes.co.jp/news/2000/07/09/national/snow-brand-scandal-grows/#.X0V2eshKguU

Japan Times. (2000b, July 26). The Latest Summer Hazard. *The Japan Times*. Accessed on October 26, 2023, from https://www.japantimes.co.jp/opinion/2000/07/26/editorials/the-latest-summer-hazard/

Kast. (2016, November 16). Why Business Ethics is Essential. *KastStories*. Accessed on October 26, 2023, from https://medium.com/kaststories/why-business-ethics-is-essential-dfed29eaf170

Kelly, J. (2020, February 24). Wells Fargo Forced to Pay $3 Billion For the Bank's Fake Account Scandal. *Forbes*. https://www.forbes.com/sites/jackkelly/2020/02/24/wells-fargo-forced-to-pay-3-billion-for-the-banks-fake-account-scandal/?sh=2416d07142d2

Knight, J. (1982, October 11). Tylenol's Maker Shows How to Respond to Crisis. *Washington Post*. https://www.washingtonpost.com/archive/business/1982/10/11/tylenols-maker-shows-how-to-respond-to-crisis/bc8df898-3fcf-443f-bc2f-e6fbd639a5a3/

Knowledge@Wharton. (2012, October 5). Tylenol and the Legacy of J&J's James Burke. *Time*. Accessed on October 26, 2023, from https://business.time.com/2012/10/05/tylenol-and-the-legacy-of-jjs-james-burke/

Larsen, N. (2021, April 6). Do Better Days Lie Ahead for Wells Fargo? *International Banker*. Accessed on October 26, 2023, from https://internationalbanker.com/banking/do-better-days-lie-ahead-for-wells-fargo/

Latson, J. (2014, September 29). How Poisoned Tylenol Became a Crisis-Management Teaching Model. *Time*. https://time.com/3423136/tylenol-deaths-1982/

Lynch, L. J., & Cutro, C. (2017). The Wells Fargo Banking Scandal. *Darden Business Publishing*, UV7267, 1–12.

Markel, H. (2014, September 29). How the Tylenol Murders of 1982 Changed the Way we Consume Medication. *PBS NewsHour*. https://www.pbs.org/newshour/health/tylenol-murders-1982

Rehak, J. (2002, March 23). Tylenol Made a Hero of Johnson & Johnson: The Recall that Started Them All. *The New York Times*. https://www.nytimes.com/2002/03/23/your-money/IHT-tylenol-made-a-hero-of-johnson-johnson-the-recall-that-started.html

Reuters. (2009, January 27). Japan's Snow Brand to Merge with Nippon Milk. *Reuters*. https://www.reuters.com/article/us-japan-milk/japans-snow-brand-to-merge-with-nippon-milk-idINTRE50Q28I20090127

Russell, C. (1982, October 16). Tamper-Resistant Drug Packages Pledged. *Washington Post*. https://www.washingtonpost.com/archive/politics/1982/10/16/tamper-resistant-drug-packages-pledged/1709baa8-9562-48fc-a3e7-6016f6f12f0f/

Tayan, B. (2019). The Wells Fargo Cross-Selling Scandal. *Stanford University Graduate School of Business Research Paper No. 17-1*. Accessed on October 26, 2023, from https://papers.ssrn.com/sol3/papers.cfm?abstract_id=2879102

Taylor, K. & Goggin, B. (2019, May 10). 49 of the Biggest Scandals in Uber's History. *Business Insider*, https://www.businessinsider.com/uber-company-scandals-and-controversies-2017-11

Tedlow, R. S. (2006). James Burke: A Career in American Business (A) & (B). Teaching Note. *Harvard Business School*, 5-309–015, 1–16.

Tedlow, R. S., & Smith, W. (2005b). James Burke: A Career in American Business (B). *Harvard Business School*, 9-390–030, 1–18.

Tedlow, R. S., & Smith, W. K. (2005a). James Burke: A Career in American Business (A). *Harvard Business School*, 9-389–177, 1–25.

UPI Archives. (1982, October 7). Multi-Million Dollar Tylenol Suits Filed. *UPI*. Accessed on October 26, 2023, from https://www.upi.com/Archives/1982/10/07/Multi-million-dollar-Tylenol-suits-filed/6552402811200/

Werhane, P. H., Mead, J., Koehn, D., Saito, A., & Wolfe, R. (2010b). Snow Brand Milk Products (B): Assessing the Possibility for Revitalization. *Darden Business Publishing*, Case E-0348, 7.

Werhane, P. H., Mead, J., Saito, A., Koehn, D., & Wolfe, R. (2010a). Snow Brand Milk Products (A): Assessing the Possibility for Revitalization. *Darden Business Publishing*, Case E-0347, 11.

Chapter 2

Anna, C. (2016, March 28). "Instrument of Torture": The Dalkon Shield Disaster. *Planned Parenthood*. Accessed on October 27, 2023, from http://advocatesaz.org/2016/03/28/instrument-of-torture-the-dalkon-shield-disaster/

Bahr, A. (2012, August 29). As Memories of Dalkon Shield Fade, Women Embrace IUDs Again. *Ms. Magazine*. Accessed on October 27, 2023, from https://msmagazine.com/2012/08/29/as-memories-of-dalkon-shield-fade-women-embrace-iuds-again/

Burke, K. (2014, May 14). Truth, Transparency & Target: A Lesson in Crisis Communications. *HubSpot*. Accessed on October 27, 2023, from https://blog.hubspot.com/marketing/target-corporate-crisis-communications

Byrne, J.-A. (1985, May 19). Chief Minnesota Judge Retires. *UPI*. Accessed on October 27, 2023, from https://www.upi.com/Archives/1985/05/19/Chief-Minnesota-judge-retires/7227485323200/

Cassidy-Brinn, G. (2011, January 1). Not Your Mother's IUD: Risks and Benefit's of Modern IUDs. *National Women's Health Network*. Accessed on October 27, 2023, from https://nwhn.org/not-your-mothers-iud-risks-and-benefits-of-modern-iuds/

Connolly, K. (2013, June 28). Lawsuits Over Mirena IUD Bring Back Memories of Dalkon Shield. *Drugwatch. Com*. Accessed on October 27, 2023, from https://www.drugwatch.com/news/2013/06/28/mirena-litigation-dalkon-shield-injuries/

Covey, S. R. (2004). *The 7 Habits of Highly Effective People: Powerful Lessons in Personal Change* (Revised edition). New York, NY: Free Press.

Deloitte. (2016). *Reputation Matters. Developing Reputational Resilience Ahead of Your Crisis. Deloitte Risk Advisory*. Deloitte. Accessed on October 27, 2023, from https://www2.deloitte.com/content/dam/Deloitte/uk/Documents/risk/deloitte-uk-reputation-matters-june-2016.pdf

Dhanaraj, C., Mukherjee, M., & Bindu, H. (2011). A Bomb in Your Pocket? Crisis Leadership at Nokia India (A). *IVEY Publishing*, 910M64, 1–11.

Dhanaraj, C., Sumukadas, N., Johnson, P. F., & Malvankar, M. (2011). Nokia India: Battery Recall Logistics. *IVEY Publishing*, W11082, 1–13.

Dowie, M., Ehrenreich, B., & Minkin, S. (1979, December). The Charge: Gynocide. *Mother Jones*. Accessed on October 27, 2023, from https://www.motherjones.com/politics/1979/11/charge-gynocide/

ET Bureau. (2008, June 10). BE Survey: Nokia is India's Most Trusted BranD. *The Economic Times*. Accessed on October 27, 2023, from https://economictimes.indiatimes.com/be-survey-nokia-is-indias-most-trusted-brand/articleshow/3115558.cms

Goldstein, S. (2007, August 24). Matsushita to Bear Costs of Nokia Battery Recall. *MarketWatch*. Accessed on October 27, 2023, from https://www.marketwatch.com/story/matsushita-to-pay-the-174-mln-tab-for-nokia-battery-recall

Horwitz, R. (2018, January 10). The Dalkon Shield. *Arizona State University Embryo Project Encyclopedia*. Accessed on October 27, 2023, from https://embryo.asu.edu/pages/dalkon-shield

Kenney, K. (1985, April 30). Dalkon Shield Gives Birth to a Generation of Lawsuits. *Chicago Tribune*. https://www.chicagotribune.com/news/ct-xpm-1985-04-30-8501260779-story.html

Krismann, C. H. (2015, December 17). Dalkon Shield | Contraceptive Device & Health Risks. *Britannica*. Accessed on October 27, 2023, from https://www.britannica.com/science/Dalkon-Shield

Lindenfeld, E. (2016). The Unintended Pregnancy Crisis: A No-Fault Fix. *Marquette Benefits and Social Welfare Law Review*, *17*(2). https://scholarship.law.marquette.edu/benefits/vol17/iss2/5

McDowell, A. (2017, May 2). 15 Quotes from the Last Lecture Everyone Needs to Hear. *Odyssey*. Accessed on October 27, 2023, from https://www.theodysseyonline.com/15-quotes-from-the-last-lecture-everyone-needs-hear

Merriam-Webster. (2023a). Accountability. *Merriam-Webster.Com Dictionary*. Accessed on November 9, 2023, from https://www.merriam-webster.com/dictionary/accountability

Merriam-Webster. (2023b). Head-in-the-sand. *Merriam-Webster.Com Dictionary*. Accessed on November 9, 2023, from https://www.merriam-webster.com/dictionary/head-in-the-sand

Miller, J. A. (1996, September 1). Money for Mischief: USAID and Pathfinder Tag-Team Women in the Developing World. *Population Research Institute*. Accessed on October 27, 2023, from https://www.pop.org/money-for-mischief-usaid-and-pathfinder-tag-team-women-in-the-developing-world/

MMWR. (1974, June 29). IUD Safety: Report of a Nationwide Physician Survey. *U.S. Centers for Disease Control and Prevention*. Accessed on October 27, 2023, from https://www.cdc.gov/mmwr/preview/mmwrhtml/lmrk107.htm

NYT. (1984, March 2). Judge Lambastes Company in Suit on Intrauterine Device. *The New York Times*. Section B, p. 16. Accessed on November 9, 2023, from https://www.nytimes.com/1984/03/02/us/judge-lambastes-company-in-suit-on-intrauterine-device.html

Rediff News. (2007, September 3). Nokia Blames Fake Batteries; Gets Support. *Rediff News*. Accessed on October 27, 2023, from https://www.rediff.com/money/2007/sep/03nokia.htm

Roepke, C. L., & Schaff, E. A. (2014). Long Tail Strings: Impact of the Dalkon Shield 40 Years Later. *Open Journal of Obstetrics and Gynecology, 04*(16), 996–1005. https://doi.org/10.4236/ojog.2014.416140

Rutchick, J. (1984, November 15). Attorney Says Dalkon Money Won't Offset Losses. *UPI*. Accessed on October 27, 2023, from https://www.upi.com/Archives/1984/11/15/Attorney-says-Dalkon-money-wont-offset-losses/6316469342800/

Shepard, J. (2009, November 15). Nokia Announces Charger Recall Program. EE Power. Accessed on October 27, 2023, from https://eepower.com/news/nokia-announces-charger-recall-program/

Stanley, J. (2017, June 7). Choice/Less: The Backstory, Episode 2: Loretta Ross on the Dalkon Shield Disaster. *Rewire News Group*. Accessed on October 27, 2023, from https://rewirenewsgroup.com/2017/06/07/choiceless-backstory-episode-2-loretta-ross-dalkon-shield-disaster/

Taylor, J. (1990, March 31). Family's Only Link to A.H. Robins is the Name Now. *Greensboro News & Record*. https://greensboro.com/familys-only-link-to-a-h-robins-is-the-name-now/article_b6cdc5f1-e8b8-5376-8d7a-0ad74024baae.html

Teach Different. (2023). "It's not what happens to you, but how you react to it that matters." *Epictetus. Teach Different*. Accessed on October 27, 2023, from https://teachdifferent.com/podcast/its-not-what-happens-to-you-but-how-you-react-to-it-that-matters-teach-different-with-epictetus/

Yakola, D. (2014, March 1). Ten Tips for Leading Companies Out of Crisis. *McKinsey & Company*. Accessed on October 27, 2023, from https://www.mckinsey.com/capabilities/strategy-and-corporate-finance/our-insights/ten-tips-for-leading-companies-out-of-crisis

Chapter 3

ABC News (2018, April 19). Men Arrested at Starbucks Speak Out. *ABC News*. Accessed on October 31, 2023, from https://www.youtube.com/watch?v=NWOz3OZ6J9M

Adilabadkar, S. (2020, April 22). Post Maggi Crisis, Nestle Looks for More Winners. *Trendlyne.Com*. Accessed on October 31, 2023, from https://trendlyne.com/posts/2321300/post-maggi-crisis-nestle-looks-for-more-winners

Associated Press. (2018a). Philadelphia Starbucks: Protests Happening After Black Men Arrested. *USA Today*. https://www.usatoday.com/story/money/2018/04/16/starbucks-protests-philadelphia-black-men-arrests-racial-profiling/519706002/

Associated Press. (2018b, April 14). Police Chief: Officers Did Nothing Wrong in Arrest of Black Men at Starbucks. *NBC News*. https://www.nbcnews.com/news/us-news/police-chief-officers-did-nothing-wrong-arrest-black-men-starbucks-n866061

Associated Press. (2018c, April 16). "Starbucks Coffee is Anti-Black" Say Chanting Protesters at Philadelphia Starbucks Where 2 Black Men were Arrested. *USA TODAY*. https://www.usatoday.com/story/money/2018/04/16/starbucks-protests-philadelphia-black-men-arrests-racial-profiling/519706002/

Associated Press. (2018, April 16). Philadelphia: Protesters at Starbucks Chant Company is "Anti-Black." *The New Indian Express*. Accessed on October 30, 2023, from https://www.newindianexpress.com/world/2018/apr/16/philadelphia-protesters-at-starbucks-chant-company-is-anti-black-1802317.html

Avila, M., Parkin, H., & Galoostian, S. (2019). $16.7 Million To Save One Reputation: How Starbucks Responded Amidst a Racial Sensitivity Crisis. *Pepperdine Journal of Communication Research*, 7(1). https://digitalcommons.pepperdine.edu/pjcr/vol7/iss1/4

Balakrishnan, R., & Bapna, A. (2015, June 10). Maggi Row: How Not to Handle a Major Crisis. *ETBrandEquity.Com*. Accessed on October 30, 2023, from http://brandequity.economictimes.indiatimes.com/news/marketing/maggi-row-how-not-to-handle-a-major-crisis/47610304

Ben-Yaacov, S. (2018, April 15). Protesters Demand Firing of Philly Starbucks Manager Following Arrests of Two Black Men. *WHYY*. Accessed on October 30, 2023, from https://whyy.org/articles/starbucks-ceo-en-route-to-philly-protests-underway-following-arrests-of-two-black-men/

Bhushan, R. (2015, June 9). Maggi Row: A Timeline of Key Events and What Went Wrong. *ETBrandEquity.Com*. Accessed on October 30, 2023, from http://brandequity.economictimes.indiatimes.com/news/marketing/maggi-row-a-timeline-of-key-events-and-what-went-wrong/47596934

Bown, J. (2019, July 8). How Social Media Could Ruin your Business. *BBC News*. https://www.bbc.com/news/business-48871456

Business Insider. (2015, June 9). All Work and No Play – That's How Maggi Employees are Living their Life These Days. *Business Insider India*. Accessed on October 31, 2023, from https://www.businessinsider.in/all-work-and-no-play-thats-how-maggi-employees-are-living-their-life-these-days/articleshow/47600753.cms

CBS News. (2018, May 2). Black Men Arrested at Starbucks Settle for $1 Each, Promise of $200K Program. *CBS News*. https://www.cbsnews.com/news/black-men-arrested-starbucks-settle-for-1-each-promise-of-200k-program-philadelphia/

Domonoske, C. (2017, April 11). After Unsatisfying Answers, United Offers 'Deepest Apology' For Violent Confrontation. NPR, https://www.npr.org/sections/thetwo-way/2017/04/11/523451560/after-unsatisfying-answers-united-offers-deepest-apology-for-violent-video

Datta, A. (2018, January 17). When It Comes to Putting Out Fires, Nestlé India's Suresh Narayanan Is No Novice. *Forbes*. https://www.forbes.com/sites/forbesasia/2018/01/17/when-it-comes-to-putting-out-fires-nestle-indias-suresh-narayanan-is-no-novice/

Davis, S. (2018, April 25). When Starbucks Looked Its Brand Purpose in the Eyes. *Forbes*. https://www.forbes.com/sites/scottdavis/2018/04/25/when-starbucks-looked-its-brand-purpose-in-the-eyes/

DePino, M. (2018). Social Media Video Shows Arrests of Black Men at Philadelphia Starbucks. YouTube. *Guardian News*. Accessed on October 30, 2023, from https://www.youtube.com/watch?v=xWBVxTEgoYk

Durbin, D.-A. (2022, July 12). Starbucks Closing 16 US Stores for Safety Issues. *Associated Press*. Accessed on October 30, 2023, from https://apnews.com/article/oregon-portland-seattle-183c298121860422c7b93b7b5a13c088

Dutta, A. (2020, June 4). Return of Maggi: Volume and Value Surpasses Pre-Ban Level of 2014. *Business Standard*. Accessed on October 31, 2023, from https://www.business-standard.com/article/companies/return-of-maggi-volume-and-value-surpasses-pre-ban-level-of-2014-120060401532_1.html

Filloon, W. (2018, April 16). Arrest of Black Men at Starbucks Spurs Outrage on Social Media. *Eater*. Accessed on October 30, 2023, from https://www.eater.com/2018/4/16/17242350/starbucks-arrest-black-men-racist-twitter-reactions

Fry, E. (2016, April 26). Nestle's Half Billion Dollar Noodle Debacle in India. *Forbes*. https://fortune.com/longform/nestle-maggi-noodle-crisis/

Giammona, C. (2018, May 29). Starbucks Investors Question Cost of Bias Training, Schultz Says. *BNN Bloomberg*. Accessed on October 30, 2023, from https://www.bnnbloomberg.ca/starbucks-investors-question-cost-of-bias-training-schultz-says-1.1084396

Gino, F., Coffman, K., & Huizinga, J. (2020). Starbucks: Reaffirming Commitment to the Third Place Ideal. *Harvard Business School*, 920016, 1–30.

Griffin, A. (2008). *New Strategies for Reputation Management: Gaining Control of Issues, Crises & Corporate Social Responsibility*. London, UK: Kogan Page.

Herrero, A. G., & Pratt, C. B. (1996). An Integrated Symmetrical Model for Crisis-Communications Management. *Journal of Public Relations Research*, 8(2), 79–105. https://doi.org/10.1207/s1532754xjprr0802_01

Horton, A. (2018, April 16). "Absolute Discrimination": Public Relations Disaster for Starbucks as Company Hit by Race Scandal. *The Sydney Morning Herald*. https://www.smh.com.au/business/companies/absolute-discrimination-public-relations-disaster-for-starbucks-as-company-hit-by-race-scandal-20180416-p4z9sw.html

Hyken, S. (2018, May 10). Starbucks Gets an A in Crisis Management. *Forbes*. https://www.forbes.com/sites/shephyken/2018/05/10/starbucks-gets-an-a-in-crisis-management/?sh=7689dfc97998

Iyer, L. (2015, June 5). The Man who Called Nestle's MSG Bluff. *Bangalore Mirror*. Accessed on October 31, 2023, from https://bangaloremirror.indiatimes.com/news/india/msg-nestle-maggie/articleshow/47559532.cms

Kamnetz, T. (2018, July 24). What You Can Learn from How Starbucks Handled PR Crisis. *www.Fastcasual.Com*. Accessed on October 30, 2023, from https://www.fastcasual.com/blogs/starbucks-foundation-shakes-as-crisis-lingers/

Kang, C & Frenkel, S. (2018, April 4). Facebook Says Cambridge Analytica Harvested Data of Up to 87 Million Users. The New York Times, https://www.nytimes.com/2018/04/04/technology/mark-zuckerberg-testify-congress.html

Kellerman, B. (2006, April 1). When Should a Leader Apologize – And When Not? *Harvard Business Review*. https://hbr.org/2006/04/when-should-a-leader-apologize-and-when-not

Knowledge@Wharton. (2018, April 20). What Brands Can Learn from Starbucks' Crisis Response. *Knowledge at Wharton*. Accessed on October 30, 2023, from https://knowledge.wharton.upenn.edu/podcast/knowledge-at-wharton-podcast/starbucks-arrest-response/

Madej, P. (2018a, April 17). Inquirer Photographer Describes Image Behind Viral Starbucks Meme. *Philadelphia Inquirer*. Accessed on October 30, 2023, from https://www.inquirer.com/philly/news/philadelphia-starbucks-protest-photo-meme-twitter-black-men-arrest-20180417.html

Madej, P. (2018b, April 19). Philadelphia Starbucks Case: What we've Learned Since the Arrests. *Philadelphia Inquirer*. Accessed on October 30, 2023, from https://www.inquirer.com/philly/news/starbucks-philadelphia-arrests-black-controversy-boycott-timeline-20180419.html

Madej, P., DiStefano, J. N., & Adelman, J. (2018, April 14). Black Men's Arrests at Philadelphia Starbucks Prompt City Probes Amid National Outcry. *Philadelphia Inquirer*. Accessed on October 30, 2023, from https://www.inquirer.com/philly/news/starbucks-philadelphia-police-viral-video-investigation-race-20180414.html

McGregor, J. (2018, April 19). Anatomy of a PR Response: How Starbucks is handling its Philadelphia Crisis. *The Washington Post*. https://www.washingtonpost.com/news/on-leadership/wp/2018/04/19/anatomy-of-a-pr-response-how-starbucks-is-handling-its-philadelphia-crisis/

McLaughlin, E. C. (2018, April 16). Starbucks Arrests: Cafe Shut Down After Protesters Enter, Chanting "Starbucks Coffee is Anti-Black!" *CNN*. https://edition.cnn.com/2018/04/16/us/philadelphia-police-starbucks-arrest-protests/index.html

Mitra, S. (2017, February 15). The Maggi Ban: How India's Favourite Two-Minute Noodles Lost 80% Market Share. *Mint*. Accessed on October 31, 2023, from https://www.livemint.com/Companies/1JKHsutTXLWtTcVwdIDg0H/The-Maggi-ban-How-Indias-favourite-twominute-noodles-lost.html

Nair, H. V. (2016, September 23). Nestle to Destroy 54 Crore Maggi Packets. *India Today*. Accessed on October 30, 2023, from https://www.indiatoday.in/mail-today/story/nestle-maggi-lead-msg-presence-342693-2016-09-23

Newman, D. (2015, October 13). Customer Experience is the Future of Marketing. *Forbes*. Accessed on October 30, 2023, from https://www.forbes.com/sites/danielnewman/2015/10/13/customer-experience-is-the-future-of-marketing/

Ramanna, K., & Kak, R. (2016a). The Maggi Noodle Safety Crisis in India (A). *Harvard Business School*, 9-116–013, 1–23.

Ramanna, K., & Kak, R. (2016b). The Maggi Noodle Safety Crisis in India (B). *Harvard Business School*, 9-116–014, 1–3.

Ramanna, K., & Markovich, Z. (2016). The Maggi Noodle Safety Crisis in India (A), (B), and (C). *Harvard Business School*, 5-116–049, 1–23.

Rock, A. (2022, August 2). Here's Why Martha Stewart Went to Jail, & What She's Said About It. *Hollywood Life*. Accessed on November 9, 2023, from https://hollywoodlife.com/feature/martha-stewart-jail-4808313/

Rowe, W. G., & Mark, K. (2019). Starbucks, Howard Schultz, and the Trump Effect. *IVEY Publishing*, W19512, 1–12.

Shah, R. (2018, March 20). How Much did Maggi Ban Cost Nestle India? *DNA*. Accessed on October 31, 2023, from https://www.dnaindia.com/business/report-how-much-did-maggi-ban-cost-nestle-india-2140196

Shane, D., & Horowitz, J. (2018, May 21). Starbucks: You Don't Need to Buy Anything to Hang Out in Our Stores. *CNN Business*. https://money.cnn.com/2018/05/20/news/companies/starbucks-bathroom-policy/index.html

Sinha, A. (2016, December 8). Corporate Resurrecting Brand Maggi. *Business World*. Accessed on October 31, 2023, from https://www.businessworld.in/article/Corporate-Resurrecting-Brand-Maggi/08-12-2016-109396/

Starbucks (2018, May 2). Starbucks Reaches Agreement with Donte Robinson and Rashon Nelson. Accessed April 6, 2024. https://stories.starbucks.com/press/2018/starbucks-reaches-agreement-with-donte-robinson-and-rashon-nelson/

Starbucks. (2020, February 24). An update on Starbucks Civil Rights Assessment. *Starbucks Stories*. Accessed on October 30, 2023, from https://stories.starbucks.com/press/2020/an-update-on-starbucks-civil-rights-assessment/

Statista. (2023). Number of Starbucks Stores Worldwide 2022. *Statista*. Accessed on October 30, 2023, from https://www.statista.com/statistics/266465/number-of-starbucks-stores-worldwide/

Stevens, M., & Haag, M. (2019, February 22). Jeffrey Skilling, Former Enron Chief, Released After 12 Years in Prison. *The New York Times*. https://www.nytimes.com/2019/02/22/business/enron-ceo-skilling-scandal.html

Synder, M. (2015, February 2). How Maggi Noodles Became India's Favourite Comfort Food. *Quartz*. Accessed on October 31, 2023, from https://qz.com/india/337224/how-maggi-noodles-became-indias-favourite-comfort-food

Tavuchis, N. (1991). *Mea Culpa: A Sociology of Apology and Reconciliation*. Stanford, CA: Stanford University Press.

Varma, V., & Yamashita, K. (2020, January 9). Case Study of Crisis and an Affirmation of Character. *SHRM*. Accessed on October 30, 2023, from https://www.shrm.org/executive/resources/people-strategy-journal/winter2020/pages/starbucks-feature.aspx

Zara, C. (2018, April 18). Here's How Quickly "Boycott Starbucks" Spread Across the Internet. *Fast Company*. Accessed on October 30, 2023, from https://www.fastcompany.com/40560741/heres-how-quickly-boycott-starbucks-spread-across-the-internet

Chapter 4

Alter, C. (2015, November 19). Meet the Man Who Brought Down Volkswagen. *Time*. https://time.com/4119981/the-man-who-brought-down-volkswagen/

Amelang, S., & Wehrmann, B. (2020, May 25). "Dieselgate" – A Timeline of the Car Emissions Fraud Scandal in Germany. *Clean Energy Wire*. Accessed on November 1, 2023, from https://www.cleanenergywire.org/factsheets/dieselgate-timeline-car-emissions-fraud-scandal-germany

ATE. (2015, September 18). VW Faced Ultimatum from U.S. Environmental Regulators Over Diesel Emissions. *Automotive News Europe*. Accessed on November 1, 2023, from https://europe.autonews.com/article/20150921/COPY/309219920/vw-faced-ultimatum-from-u-s-environmental-regulators-over-diesel-emissions

Bell, E. (2020, May 8). 14 Things You Should Know About Stolichnaya Vodka. *VinePair*. Accessed on November 1, 2023, from https://vinepair.com/articles/stolichnaya-vodka-elit-stoli-guide/

Bomey, N. (2018, April 12). New Volkswagen CEO: Herbert Diess replaces Matthias Mueller. *USA Today*. https://www.usatoday.com/story/money/cars/2018/04/12/volkswagen-ceo-herbert-diess-matthias-mueller/511663002/

Boston, W. (2015, October 5). Volkswagen Emissions Investigation Zeroes in on Two Engineers. *The Wall Street Journal*. https://www.wsj.com/articles/vw-emissions-probe-zeroes-in-on-two-engineers-1444011602

Bowler, T. (2015, September 25). Volkswagen: From the Third Reich to Emissions Scandal. *BBC News*. https://www.bbc.com/news/business-34358783

Bruce, C. (2016, April 25). VW Won't Release Diesel Scandal Investigation Report. *Autoblog*. Accessed on November 1, 2023, from https://www.autoblog.com/2016/04/25/vw-diesel-scandal-investigation-report/

Burger, L., & Martin, M. (2019, April 15). Former Volkswagen CEO Winterkorn Charged with Fraud by German Prosecutors. *Reuters*. https://www.reuters.com/article/us-volkswagen-emissions-winterkorn/former-volkswagen-ceo-winterkorn-charged-with-fraud-by-german-prosecutors-idUSKCN1RR11O

Carbonnel, A. de. (2016, December 8). EU Takes Legal Action Against Germany, UK Over VW Scandal. *Reuters*. https://www.reuters.com/article/us-volkswagen-emissions-eu/eu-takes-legal-action-against-germany-uk-over-vw-scandal-idUSKBN13X14N

Cheng, Y., Funkhouser, C., Raabe, T., & Cross, R. (2022). Examining Organization–Public Relationships in Crises: A Thematic Meta-Analysis of Updated Literature From 1997 to 2019. *Journal of Contingencies and Crisis Management, 30*(2), 148–160. https://doi.org/10.1111/1468-5973.12370

Cremer, A. (2017, January 19). Ex-Volkswagen CEO Denies Early Knowledge of Diesel Emissions Cheating. *Reuters*. https://www.reuters.com/article/cbusiness-us-volkswagen-emissions-winter-idCAKBN15318J

Davis, B. (2015, September 28). Social Media and Crisis Management: A Volkswagen Case Study. *Econsultancy*. Accessed on November 1, 2023, from https://econsultancy.com/social-media-and-crisis-management-a-volkswagen-case-study/

Dodds, E. (2013, August 5). In Gay-Rights Activists' Boycott of Russian Vodka, Faulty Logic. *Time*. https://nation.time.com/2013/08/05/the-faulty-logic-of-the-russian-vodka-boycott/

Eddy, M. (2019, July 31). Rupert Stadler, Ex-Audi Chief, is Charged with Fraud in Diesel Scandal. *The New York Times*. https://www.nytimes.com/2019/07/31/business/audi-diesel-emissions-rupert-stadler.html

Erickson, S. (2021). Communication in a Crisis and the Importance of Authenticity and Transparency. *Journal of Library Administration, 61*(4), 476–483. https://doi.org/10.1080/01930826.2021.1906556

Ewing, J. (2015, October 29). Volkswagen, Hit by Emissions Scandal, Posts Its First Loss in Years. *The New York Times*. https://www.nytimes.com/2015/10/29/business/international/volkswagen-earnings-q3.html

Ewing, J. (2016, February 19). Volkswagen Memos Suggest Company Misled U.S. Regulators. *The New York Times*. https://www.nytimes.com/2016/02/19/business/volkswagen-memos-suggest-emissions-problem-was-known-earlier.html?_r=0

Ewing, J. (2017, May 17). VW Engineers Wanted O.K. From the Top for Emissions Fraud, Documents Show. *The New York Times*. https://www.nytimes.com/2017/05/17/business/volkswagen-muller-diesel-emissions.html

Ewing, J. (2018a, January 28). German Carmakers Criticized for Emissions Research on Monkeys. *The New York Times*. https://www.nytimes.com/2018/01/28/business/german-carmakers-diesel-monkeys.html

Ewing, J. (2018b, June 13). Volkswagen Agrees to $1.2 Billion German Fine in Emissions-Cheating Scheme. *The New York Times*. https://www.nytimes.com/2018/06/13/business/volkswagen-emissions-germany-fine.html

Forbes. (2015, May 6). Forbes' 13th Annual Global 2000: The World's Biggest Public Companies. *Forbes*. https://www.forbes.com/sites/forbespr/2015/05/06/forbes-13th-annual-global-2000-the-worlds-biggest-public-companies/

Gallagher, J. (2012, June 12). Diesel Exhausts Do Cause Cancer, Says WHO. *BBC News*. https://www.bbc.com/news/health-18415532

GayCities. (2014, February 7). Gay Bar Lifts Ban on Stoli Vodka, Boycott Ends. *GayCities Wanderlust*. Accessed on November 1, 2023, from https://www.gaycities.com/articles/31518/chicagos-bar-sidetrack-lifts-boycott-of-stoli-vodka/

Hakim, D. (2016, February 26). VW's Crisis Strategy: Forward, Reverse, U-Turn. *The New York Times*. https://www.nytimes.com/2016/02/28/business/international/vws-crisis-strategy-forward-reverse-u-turn.html

Halperin, B., Ho, B., List, J. A., & Muir, I. (2019). Toward an Understanding of the Economics of Apologies: Evidence from a Large-Scale Natural Field Experiment. *National Bureau of Economic Research*, NBER Working Papers 25676. Accessed on November 1, 2023, from https://ideas.repec.org//p/nbr/nberwo/25676.html

Higgins, A. (2013, September 8). Facing Fury Over Antigay Law, Stoli Says 'Russian? Not Really.' *The New York Times*. https://www.nytimes.com/2013/09/08/world/europe/facing-fury-over-antigay-law-stoli-says-russian-not-really.html

Holland, D., Krause, A., Provencher, J., & Seltzer, T. (2018). Transparency Tested: The Influence of Message Features on Public Perceptions of Organizational Transparency. *Public Relations Review, 44*(2), 256–264. https://doi.org/10.1016/j.pubrev.2017.12.002

Holland, D., Seltzer, T., & Kochigina, A. (2021). Practicing Transparency in a Crisis: Examining the Combined Effects of Crisis Type, Response, and Message Transparency on Organizational Perceptions. *Public Relations Review, 47*(2), 102017. https://doi.org/10.1016/j.pubrev.2021.102017

HRW. (2018, December 11). No Support: Russia's "Gay Propaganda" Law Imperils LGBT Youth. *Human Rights Watch*. Accessed on November 1, 2023, from https://www.hrw.org/report/2018/12/12/no-support/russias-gay-propaganda-law-imperils-lgbt-youth

Jaffe, E. (2015, September 24). The Study That Brought Down Volkswagen. *Bloomberg*. https://www.bloomberg.com/news/articles/2015-09-24/the-west-virginia-study-that-started-the-volkswagen-scandal

Jolly, J. (2022, May 25). Volkswagen Settles Initial 'Dieselgate' Claims with £193m Payout. *The Guardian*. https://www.theguardian.com/business/2022/may/25/volkswagen-settles-uk-dieselgate-claims-with-193m-payout

Jung, J. C., & Sharon, E. (2019). The Volkswagen Emissions Scandal and its Aftermath. *Global Business and Organizational Excellence, 38*(4), 6–15. https://doi.org/10.1002/joe.21930

Kiley, D. (2017, December 6). VW Executive Oliver Schmidt Sentenced to 7 Years for Dieselgate. *Forbes*. https://www.forbes.com/sites/davidkiley5/2017/12/06/vw-exec-oliver-schmidt-gets-seven-years-in-jail-for-dieselgate/?sh=12fc429e5cc4

Kitman, J. L. (2015, October 1). Volkswagen Lied and Cheated 11 Million Times. Will Anyone Go to Jail for That? *The Nation*. Accessed on November 1, 2023, from https://www.thenation.com/article/archive/what-will-vw-pay/

Kottasova, I. (2015, December 4). Volkswagen's Sales are Collapsing. *CNN Business*. https://money.cnn.com/2015/12/04/news/companies/volkswagen-sales-down/

Leong, L. (2016, April 26). Presentation Shows VW Execs Cheated Because Fix was Too Costly. *TechRadar*. Accessed on November 1, 2023, from https://www.techradar.com/news/car-tech/presentation-shows-vw-execs-cheated-because-fix-was-too-costly-1319856

Liptak, A. (2018, September 23). Porsche Says That It Will no Longer Make Diesel Vehicles. The Verge. Accessed on November 1, 2023, from https://www.theverge.com/2018/9/23/17892768/porsche-discontinuing-diesel-vehicles-electric-hybrids-dieselgate

Lynch, L. J., Cutro, C., & Bird, E. (2018). The Volkswagen Emissions Scandal. *Darden Business Publishing*, *UV7245*, 1–17.

McGee, P. (2018, January 18). What Went so Right with Volkswagen's Restructuring? *Financial Times*. https://www.ft.com/content/a12ec7e2-fa01-11e7-9b32-d7d59aace167

Miller, E. (2015, September 22). VW Could Fool the EPA, But It Couldn't Trick Chemistry. *Wired*. Accessed on November 1, 2023, from https://www.wired.com/2015/09/vw-fool-epa-couldnt-trick-chemistry/

Noack, R. (2015, September 23). For Germans, the Volkswagen Scandal is a National Embarrassment. *The Washington Post*. https://www.washingtonpost.com/news/worldviews/wp/2015/09/23/for-germans-the-volkswagen-scandal-is-a-national-embarrassment/

NYT. (2015, September 23). What Was Volkswagen Thinking? *The New York Times*. https://www.nytimes.com/2015/09/23/opinion/what-was-volkswagen-thinking.html

Odell, P. (2015, November 9). How Stoli Survived the "Dump Stoli" Crisis. Chief Marketer. Accessed on November 1, 2023, from https://www.chiefmarketer.com/stoli-survived-dump-stoli-crisis/

OPA. (2017, January 11). Volkswagen AG Agrees to Plead Guilty and Pay $4.3 Billion in Criminal and Civil Penalties; Six Volkswagen Executives and Employees are Indicted in Connection with Conspiracy to Cheat U.S. Emissions Tests. *Office of Public Affairs, U.S. Department of Justice*. Accessed on November 1, 2023, from https://www.justice.gov/opa/pr/volkswagen-ag-agrees-plead-guilty-and-pay-43-billion-criminal-and-civil-penalties-six

Quittner, J. (2013, July 13). The Latest Twist in the Long, Sordid Tale of Stolichnaya Vodka. *Inc.Com*. Accessed on November 1, 2023, from https://www.inc.com/jeremy-quittner/stolichnaya-vodka-spi-group-gay-boycott.html

Reuters. (2018a, June 12). Daimler Recalls 774,000 Diesel Mercedes Cars After CEO Meets with Minister. *Clean Energy Wire*. Accessed on November 1, 2023, from https://www.cleanenergywire.org/news/dieselgate-ensnares-daimler-germany-rejects-eu-renewable-ambitions/daimler-recalls-774000-diesel-mercedes-cars-after-ceo-meets-minister

Reuters. (2018b, September 10). VW Investors Seek $11B in Damages Over Dieselgate Scandal. *Reuters*. https://www.reuters.com/article/volkswagen-emissions-trial-idINL5N1VW1KT

Reuters. (2018c, October 16). German Prosecutors Fine Audi 800 Million Euros for Diesel Violations. *Reuters*. https://www.reuters.com/article/us-volkswagen-emissions-audi/german-prosecutors-fine-audi-800-million-euros-for-diesel-violations-idUSKCN1MQ12Z

Reuters. (2019, May 23). Prosecutors Fine Bosch 90 Million Euros for Emissions Cheating Role. *Reuters*. https://www.reuters.com/article/us-bosch-emissions-fine/prosecutors-fine-bosch-90-million-euros-for-emissions-cheating-role-idUSKCN1ST10C

Reuters. (2020a, April 20). Volkswagen Settles Emissions Class Action with Three-Quarters of Claimants. *Reuters*. https://www.reuters.com/article/us-volkswagen-emissions/volkswagen-settles-emissions-class-action-with-three-quarters-of-claimants-idUSKBN2220U7

Reuters. (2020b, September 16). Ex-VW CEO to Face Charges of Organised Commercial Fraud. *Reuters*. https://www.reuters.com/article/volkswagen-emissions-int/ex-vw-ceo-to-face-charges-of-organised-commercial-fraud-idUSKBN260243

Reuters. (2023, March 28). German Court Expects Conviction for Former Audi Boss in Diesel Scandal. *Reuters*. https://www.reuters.com/business/autos-transportation/german-court-expects-conviction-former-audi-boss-diesel-scandal-2023-03-28/

Ruddick, G. (2015a, September 22). Volkswagen Scandal: US Chief Says Carmaker "Totally Screwed Up." *The Guardian*. https://www.theguardian.com/business/2015/sep/22/volkswagen-scandal-us-chief-carmaker-totally-screwed-up-michael-horn

Ruddick, G. (2015b, December 10). VW Admits Emissions Scandal was Caused by "Whole Chain" of Failures. *The Guardian*. https://www.theguardian.com/business/2015/dec/10/volkswagen-emissions-scandal-systematic-failures-hans-dieter-potsch

Savage, D. (2013, July 24). Why I'm Boycotting Russian Vodka. *The Stranger*. Accessed on November 1, 2023, from https://www.thestranger.com/blogs/2013/07/24/17333522/why-im-boycotting-russian-vodka

Schmitt, B. (2016, August 31). How Different Countries Are Playing Dieselgate – And VW – To Their Advantage. *Forbes*. https://www.forbes.com/sites/bertelschmitt/2016/08/31/triple-standards-dieselgate-the-continuation-of-industrial-policy-by-other-means/

Schuetz, M., & Woo, C. H. L. (2016). Dieselgate – Heavy Fumes Exhausting the Volkswagen Group. *ACRC The University of Hongkong Asia Case Research Centre*, HK1089, 1–27.

Schwartz, J. (2018, September 10). VW Investors Sue for Billions of Dollars Over Diesel Scandal. *Reuters*. https://www.reuters.com/article/uk-volkswagen-emissions-trial-idUKKCN1LQ0WD

Shah, G., Rovenpor, J., & Jafar, M. (2016). A Brand Under Attack: The Boycott of Stoli Vodka and the Power of Social Media NA0403. *Case Research Journal*, *36*(2), 1–20. https://hbsp.harvard.edu/product/NA0403-PDF-ENG

Shepardson, D. (2017, January 31). VW, Robert Bosch Agree to Pay $1.55 Billion to Settle U.S. Diesel Claims. *Reuters*. https://www.reuters.com/article/us-volkswagen-emissions/vw-robert-bosch-agree-to-pay-1-55-billion-to-settle-u-s-diesel-claims-idUSKBN15G3NX

Shepardson, D., & Taylor, E. (2018, May 3). Ex-Volkswagen CEO Winterkorn Charged in U.S. Over Diesel Scandal. *Reuters*. https://www.reuters.com/article/us-volkswagen-emissions/ex-volkswagen-ceo-winterkorn-charged-in-u-s-over-diesel-scandal-idUSKBN1I42I3

Shepardson, D., & White, J. (2017, August 25). VW Engineer Sentenced to 40-Month Prison Term in Diesel Case. *Reuters*. https://www.reuters.com/article/volkswagen-emissions-sentencing/vw-engineer-sentenced-to-40-month-prison-term-in-diesel-case-idUSL2N1LA1OU

Sherter, A. (2015, October 6). Emissions Scandal Could Cost Volkswagen More Than $35 billion. *CBS News*. https://www.cbsnews.com/news/emissions-scandal-could-cost-volkswagen-more-than-35-billion/

Smith, N. C., & McCormick, E. (2018). Volkswagen's Emissions Scandal: How Could It Happen? *INSEAD*, IN1465, 1–23.

Steitz, C., Cremer, A., & Shepardson, D. (2016, March 2). VW Says 2014 Diesel Warnings did Not Get CEO's Attention. *Reuters*. https://www.reuters.com/article/volkswagen-emissions/vw-says-2014-diesel-warnings-did-not-get-ceos-attention-idINKCN0W50DQ

Sun, M. (2020, September 15). Volkswagen Completes Compliance Monitoring After Emissions Scandal. *Wall Street Journal*. https://www.wsj.com/articles/volkswagen-completes-compliance-monitoring-after-emissions-scandal-11600191807

Tabuchi, H., & Ewing, J. (2016, June 27). Volkswagen to Pay $14.7 Billion to Settle Diesel Claims in U.S. *The New York Times*. https://www.nytimes.com/2016/06/28/business/volkswagen-settlement-diesel-scandal.html

Telford, T. (2019, September 24). Top Volkswagen Executives Charged with Market Manipulation in Emissions Scandal. *Washington Post*. https://www.washingtonpost.com/business/2019/09/24/top-volkswagen-executives-charged-with-market-manipulation-emissions-scandal/

Vellequette, L. P. (2017, January 16). VW's Plot to Fool the Feds: How High Up Did It Go? Automotive News. Accessed on November 1, 2023, from https://www.autonews.com/article/20170116/OEM11/301169949/vw-s-plot-to-fool-the-feds-how-high-up-did-it-go

VW. (2014). Volkswagen Konzern – AR 2014 – Moving Progress. *Volkswagen Group*. Accessed on November 1, 2023, from https://annualreport2014.volkswagenag.com/

Welch, J. (2019). The Volkswagen Recovery: Leaving Scandal in the Dust. *Journal of Business Strategy*, *40*(2), 3–13. https://doi.org/10.1108/JBS-04-2018-0068

Winterkorn, M. (2014). Volkswagen Konzern – AR 2014 – Letter to Our Shareholders. *Volkswagen Group*. Accessed on November 1, 2023, from https://annualreport2014.volkswagenag.com/strategy/letter-to-our-shareholders.html

Zacks. (2016, September 21). 1400 Investors File Claims Against Volkswagen for Over $9 Billion. *Yahoo News*. https://www.yahoo.com/news/1400-investors-file-claims-against-223610984.html

Zax, D. (2012, December 3). Many Cars Have a Hundred Million Lines of Code. *MIT Technology Review*. Accessed on November 1, 2023, from https://www.technologyreview.com/2012/12/03/181350/many-cars-have-a-hundred-million-lines-of-code/

Chapter 5

Baker, S. (2019, May 19). Boeing's Response to the 737 Max Crisis Confused and Frightened People, Making it Hard to Believe its Apologies, Experts Say. *Business Insider*. https://www.businessinsider.com/boeing-737-max-crisis-response-confusing-hard-to-trust-experts-2019-5

BBC. (2020, October 28). Boeing to Cut 20% of Workforce by End of 2021. *BBC News*. https://www.bbc.com/news/business-54716296

Beene, R., Suhartono, H., & Bloomberg. (2020, January 14). Boeing Mocked Lion Air for Requesting Extra 737 Max Pilot Training Year Before Crash. *Fortune*. https://fortune.com/2020/01/14/boeing-lion-air-extra-737-max-pilot-training-simulator-crash/

Beresnevicius, R. (2020a, October 22). Boeing 737 MAX Crisis: A Timeline (Part I). *Aerotime Hub*. Accessed on November 4, 2023, from https://www.aerotime.aero/articles/23728-boeing-737-max-crisis

Beresnevicius, R. (2020b, October 22). Boeing 737 MAX Crisis: Burned Bridges (Part III). *Aerotime Hub*. Accessed on November 4, 2023, from https://www.aerotime.aero/articles/23758-boeing-737-max-crisis-burned-bridges

Betz, U., & De Paoli, I. (n.d.). Merck – Curious Minds Dedicated to Human Progress. *Nature Portfolio*. Accessed on September 21, 2021, from https://www.nature.com/articles/d42473-021-00195-3

Blackman, J. & Romero, D. (2024, January 5). FAA Orders Temporary Grounding of Boeing 737 Max 9 after Alaska Airlines Plane Panel Detaches Midair. NBC News.https://www.nbcnews.com/news/us-news/alaska-airlines-flight-makes-emergency-landing-part-plane-appears-deta-rcna132618

Boeing. (n.d.). What Defines Us. *Boeing Intelligence & Analytics | Strategic Solutions*. Accessed on November 6, 2023, from https://www.bia-boeing.com/what-defines-us

Boeing. (2011, December 11). Boeing 737 MAX Logs First Firm Order from Launch Customer Southwest Airlines. *Boeing MediaRoom*. Accessed on November 4, 2023, from https://boeing.mediaroom.com/2011-12-13-Boeing-737-MAX-Logs-First-Firm-Order-from-Launch-Customer-Southwest-Airlines

Boeing. (2018a). 2017 Top DOW Performer. *Boeing Company Annual Report*. Accessed on November 6, 2023, from https://investors.boeing.com/investors/reports/

Boeing. (2018b, October 29). Boeing Statement on Lion Air Flight 610 Preliminary Report. *Boeing MediaRoom*. Accessed on November 6, 2023, from https://boeing.mediaroom.com/news-releases-statements?item=130336

Boeing. (2018c, November 6). Boeing Statement on AOA Disagree Alert. *Boeing MediaRoom*. Accessed on November 6, 2023, from https://boeing.mediaroom.com/news-releases-statements?item=130431

Boeing. (2019, March 13). In Consultation with the FAA, NTSB and its Customers, Boeing Supports Action to Temporarily Ground 737 MAX Operations. *Boeing MediaRoom*. Accessed on November 4, 2023, from https://boeing.mediaroom.com/news-releases-statements?item=130404

Boghani, P. (2021, September 14). *What Has Happened to Boeing Since the 737 Max Crashes. PBS Frontline*. https://www.pbs.org/wgbh/frontline/article/what-has-happened-to-boeing-since-the-737-max-crashes/

Bushey, C., & Meyer, G. (2020, January 29). Boeing Expects 737 Max Crisis Costs to Reach $18.6bn. *Financial Times*. https://www.ft.com/content/0e9a99de-428d-11ea-a43a-c4b328d9061c

Callahan, P. (2004, February 29). Airbus is Taking its Passenger Plane Business . . . An Ethics Scandal is Sapping Defense Orders . . . Many Employees Pine for the Days Before he Arrived . . . *Chicago Tribune*. https://www.chicagotribune.com/news/ct-xpm-2004-02-29-0402290256-story.html

Casadesus-Masanell, R., & Elterman, K. (2019a). Airbus vs. Boeing (G): New Planes and Upgrades (2011). *Harvard Business School, 9-720–382*, 1–7.

Casadesus-Masanell, R., & Elterman, K. (2019b). Airbus vs. Boeing (M): MAX 8 Disasters (July 2019). *Harvard Business School, 9-720–388, 1–2*.

Cava, M. della. (2019, June 16). Boeing CEO Calls Handling of 737 Max Crashes a "Mistake," Vows Improvements. *USA Today*. https://www.usatoday.com/story/news/nation/2019/06/16/boeing-ceo-called-its-handling-two-737-crashes-mistake/1472252001/

CNN. (2019, April 5). Boeing Acknowledges its Software's Role in Plane Crashes that Killed Hundreds. *CNN*. https://www.wrdw.com/content/news/Boeing-acknowledges-its-softwares-role-in-plane-crashes-that-killed-hundreds-508163721.html?ref=721

Corliss, B. (2023, April 26). Boeing Says it Still Will Deliver up to 450 737s This Year. *Leeham News*. Accessed on November 6, 2023, from https://leehamnews.com/2023/04/26/boeing-says-it-still-will-deliver-up-to-450-737s-this-year/

Czarnecki, S. (2019, March 13). Timeline of a Crisis: Boeing Under the Microscope. *PR Week*. https://www.prweek.com/article/1579055/timeline-crisis-boeing-microscope

Driscoll, D.-M. (2017, May 4). Why Ethics Matter: A Business Without Values Is a Business at Risk. *Corporate Compliance Insights*. Accessed on November 6, 2023, from https://www.corporatecomplianceinsights.com/why-ethics-matter-a-business-without-values-is-a-business-at-risk/

Duguid, K., Franklin, J., & Shepardson, D. (2020, May 1). How Boeing Went from Appealing for Government Aid to Snubbing it. *Reuters*. https://www.reuters.com/article/us-boeing-debt-investors-analysis-idUSKBN22E025

Ebbs, W. (2020, September 25). Boeing's Shocking Debris Problem Exposes the Company's Dangerous Monopoly. *CCN*. https://www.ccn.com/boeing-debris-problem-exposes-the-companys-dangerous-monopoly/

FAA Report. (2020, December 18). Wicker Releases Committee's FAA Investigation Report. *U.S. Senate Committee on Commerce, Science, and Transportation*. Accessed on November 6, 2023, from https://www.commerce.senate.gov/2020/12/wicker-releases-committee-s-faa-investigation-report

Feeley, J. (2021, February 9). Boeing Board Let CEO Mislead on 737 Max Crashes, Suit Says. *Bloomberg*. https://www.bloomberg.com/news/articles/2021-02-09/boeing-board-let-ceo-mislead-on-737-max-crash-causes-suit-says

FOX (2019, June 18). Boeing 737 Max Jet: A Timeline of the Crisis and Where the Plane Maker Stands Now. *FOX Business*. https://www.foxbusiness.com/features/timeline-a-brief-history-of-the-737-max-plane-and-how-boeing-reacted-to-fatal-crashes

Frost, N. (2020, January 3). How the McDonnell Douglas-Boeing Merger Led to the 737 Max Crisis. *Quartz*. Accessed on November 6, 2023, from https://qz.com/1776080/how-the-mcdonnell-douglas-boeing-merger-led-to-the-737-max-crisis

Gates, B. (2014, May 16). A Story from One of my Heroes. *GatesNotes*. Accessed on November 6, 2023, from https://www.gatesnotes.com/Story-of-A-Hero-Bill-Foege

Gates, D. (2018, October 29). Search for Cause of Deadly Boeing 737 MAX Lion Air Crash Begins. *The Seattle Times*. https://www.seattletimes.com/business/boeing-aerospace/search-for-cause-of-deadly-737-lion-air-crash-begins/

Gates, D., & Miletich, S. (2019, July 3). Boeing's $100 Million Pledge for 737 MAX Crash Victims Sparks Criticism and Questions. *The Seattle Times*. https://www.seattletimes.com/business/boeing-aerospace/boeing-will-give-100-million-to-max-crash-victims-families-and-communities/

Gelles, D., Kitroeff, N., Nicas, J., & Ruiz, R. (2019, March 23). Boeing Was 'Go, Go, Go' to Beat Airbus With the 737 Max. *The New York Times*. https://www.nytimes.com/2019/03/23/business/boeing-737-max-crash.html

German, K. (2021, June 19). 2 Years after Being Grounded, the Boeing 737 Max is Flying Again. *CNET*. Accessed on November 6, 2023, from https://www.cnet.com/tech/tech-industry/boeing-737-max-8-all-about-the-aircraft-flight-ban-and-investigations/

Gunerigok, S. (2019, October 29). Boeing CEO Says "Deeply Sorry" for 737 Airplane Crashes. *AA Americas*. Accessed on November 6, 2023, from https://www.aa.com.tr/en/americas/boeing-ceo-says-deeply-sorry-for-737-airplane-crashes/1629995

Hayward, J. (2020, August 3). The History of the Boeing 737. *Simple Flying*. Accessed on November 6, 2023, from https://simpleflying.com/boeing-737/

Hickman, A. (2019, April 1). Flop of the Month: Boeing Delay Allows Others to Take Control of Narrative. *PR Week*. Accessed on November 6, 2023, from https://www.prweek.com/article/1580584/flop-month-boeing-delay-allows-others-control-narrative

IEP. (n.d.). *Kant, Immanuel | Internet Encyclopedia of Philosophy*. Accessed on November 6, 2023, from https://iep.utm.edu/kantview/

Johnson, E. M. (2020, November 18). TIMELINE-Boeing's 737 MAX Crisis. *Reuters*. https://www.reuters.com/article/boeing-737max-timeline-idUSL1N2I417A

Johnsson, J. (2020, September 26). Boeing Job Cuts: Executive Roles at Risk and Real Estate to Be Sold in New Plan. *Bloomberg*. https://www.bloomberg.com/news/articles/2020-09-26/boeing-prepares-deeper-cuts-from-executive-ranks-to-real-estate

Josephs, L. (2019, March 28). Warren Buffett: Boeing 737 Max Problems "Aren't Going to Change the Industry." *CNBC*. https://www.cnbc.com/2019/03/28/buffett-boeing-737-max-problems-arent-going-to-change-the-industry.html

Josephs, L. (2021a, January 12). Boeing's 2020 Aircraft Cancellations Worst on Record, Despite December Max Orders. *CNBC*. https://www.cnbc.com/2021/01/12/boeings-2020-aircraft-cancellations-worst-on-record-despite-december-max-orders.html

Josephs, L. (2021b, April 28). Boeing Post Sixth Consecutive Quarterly Loss, Expects Turning Point in 2021. *CNBC*. https://www.cnbc.com/2021/04/28/boeing-ba-q1-2021-earnings.html

Kelly, J. (2019, October 30). When A Company Prioritizes Profit Over People: Boeing CEO Tells Congress That Safety Is 'Not Our Business Model.' *Forbes*. https://www.forbes.com/sites/jackkelly/2019/10/30/when-companies-prioritize-profits-over-employee-and-consumer-safety-after-fatal-boeing-737-max-crashes-ceo-tells-congress-that-safety-is-not-our-business-model/?sh=286af7c4151a

Kitroeff, N., Gelles, D., & Nicas, J. (2019, July 27). The Roots of Boeing's 737 Max Crisis: A Regulator Relaxes Its Oversight. *The New York Times*. https://www.nytimes.com/2019/07/27/business/boeing-737-max-faa.html

Langewiesche, W. (2019, September 18). What Really Brought Down the Boeing 737 Max? *New York Times Magazine*. https://www.nytimes.com/2019/09/18/magazine/boeing-737-max-crashes.html

Leggett, T. (2020, January 10). Boeing Faces Fine for 737 Max Plane "Designed by Clowns." *BBC News*. https://www.bbc.com/news/business-51058929

Levin, A. (2020, September 16). Failures, Deception, Errors – What Led to Boeing 737 Max Crashes, According to US Probe. *The Print*. Accessed on November 6, 2023, from https://theprint.in/world/failures-deception-errors-what-led-to-boeing-737-max-crashes-according-to-us-probe/504266/

MacGillis, A. (2019, November 11). The Case Against Boeing. *The New Yorker*. https://www.newyorker.com/magazine/2019/11/18/the-case-against-boeing

Martin, W., & Slotnik, D. (2020, January 29). Boeing Reports Worst Full-Year Loss in its History, but CEO Calhoun Vows "we'll' Get Through it. *The Seattle Times*. https://www.seattletimes.com/subscribe/signup-offers/

Matthews, K. (2019, March 25). Boeing is Doing Crisis Management all Wrong – Here's What a Company Needs to do to Restore the Public's Trust. *The Conversation*. Accessed on November 6, 2023, from http://theconversation.com/boeing-is-doing-crisis-management-all-wrong-heres-what-a-company-needs-to-do-to-restore-the-publics-trust-114051

McCarthy, N. (2019, December 17). 737 Max Crisis Sees Airbus Overtake Boeing in Deliveries. *Forbes*. https://www.forbes.com/sites/niallmccarthy/2019/12/17/737-max-crisis-sees-airbus-overtake-boeing-in-deliveries-infographic/

McFadden, C., Schecter, A., Monahan, K., & Schapiro, R. (2019, December 9). Former Boeing Manager Says He Warned Company of Problems Prior to 737 Crashes. *NBC News*. https://www.nbcnews.com/news/us-news/former-boeing-manager-says-he-warned-company-problems-prior-737-n1098536

Merck. (2022, May 25). 35 Years: The Mectizan® Donation Program. *Merck.Com*. Accessed on November 6, 2023, from https://www.merck.com/stories/mectizan/

Nicas, J., Kitroeff, N., Gelles, D., & Glanz, J. (2019, June 1). Boeing Built Deadly Assumptions Into 737 Max, Blind to a Late Design Change. *The New York Times*. https://www.nytimes.com/2019/06/01/business/boeing-737-max-crash.html

Onyanga-Omara, J., Bacon, J., & Stanglin, D. (2019, April 4). Boeing CEO Accepts Blame for Two Plane Crashes, Apologizes to Families of Victims: "We Own It." *USA Today*. https://www.usatoday.com/story/news/world/2019/04/04/ethiopia-plane-crash-boeing/3361880002/

Pandey, B. K. (2020). The Boeing 737 Max Roars Back into the Skies. *Issue 6. SP's Airbuz*. Accessed on November 6, 2023, from https://www.spsairbuz.com/story/?id=1110

Paur, J. (2011, August 31). Boeing Opts to Upgrade 737. *WIRED*. Accessed on November 6, 2023, from https://www.wired.com/2011/08/boeing-opts-to-upgrade-737/

Peterson, M. (2019, April 8). The Ethical Failures Behind the Boeing Disasters. *Blog of the APA*. Accessed on November 6, 2023, from https://blog.apaonline.org/2019/04/08/the-ethical-failures-behind-the-boeing-disasters/

PRNewswire. (2019, March 17). Boeing CEO Muilenburg Issues Statement on Ethiopian Airlines Flight 302 Accident Investigation. *Boeing MediaRoom*. Accessed on November 6, 2023, from https://boeing.mediaroom.com/2019-03-17-Boeing-CEO-Muilenburg-Issues-Statement-on-Ethiopian-Airlines-Flight-302-Accident-Investigation

Reinicke, C. (2019, December 17). Boeing Sees $11 Billion of Market Value Erased in Just 2 Days as its 737 Max Disaster Worsens. *Business Insider*. https://markets.businessinsider.com/news/stocks/boeing-stock-price-falls-erases-billions-2-days-737-max-halt-2019-12-1028769301

Reuters. (2011, November 12). AIRSHOW-Boeing 737 Draft Orders Reach 700. *Reuters*. https://www.reuters.com/article/us-dubai-airshow-boeing-idUSTRE7AB0JF20111112

Sharma, A. (2020, April 18). Boeing Prepares for a Second Round of Layoffs. *People Matters*. Accessed on November 6, 2023, from https://www.peoplemattersglobal.com/site/interstitial?return_to=%2Fnews%2Femployee-relations%2Fboeing-prepares-for-second-round-of-layoffs-26695

Sheetz, M., & Macias, A. (2019, January 30). Boeing Shares Surge After Monster Earnings Beat and a Record $101 Billion in Annual Revenue. *CNBC*. https://www.cnbc.com/2019/01/30/boeing-earnings-q4-2018.html

Singh, C. (2019, September 27). Boeing Settles First 737 MAX Lion Air Crash Case for $1.2 Million. *News 18*. Accessed on November 6, 2023, from https://www.news18.com/news/auto/boeing-settles-first-737-max-lion-air-crash-case-for-1-2-million-2323141.html

Slotnick, D. (2019, September 20). The Boeing 737 Max Has Had a Troubled Existence that Culminated in 2 Fatal Crashes Just 5 Months Apart. Here is the Complete Timeline of the Besieged Jetliner, from its Birth to the Present Day. *Business Insider Africa*. https://africa.businessinsider.com/lifestyle/the-boeing-737-max-has-had-a-troubled-existence-that-culminated-in-2-fatal-crashes/ldbmtgw

Slotnick, D. (2020, October 29). The First Boeing 737 Max Crash was 2 Years Ago Today. Here's the Complete History of the Plane that's Been Grounded Since 2 Crashes Killed 346 People 5 Months Apart. *Business Insider*. https://www.businessinsider.com/boeing-737-max-timeline-history-full-details-2019-9

Steiner, J. F., & Steiner, G. A. (2012). *Business, Government, and Society: A Managerial Perspective -Text and Cases* (13th ed). New York, NY: McGraw-Hill Irwin.

Tangel, A., & Cameron, D. (2020, March 27). Boeing to Emerge as Big Stimulus Winner. *Wall Street Journal*. https://www.wsj.com/articles/boeing-to-emerge-as-big-stimulus-winner-11585331293

Temin, D. (2019, April 7). Great Crisis Management Is Counterintuitive: That's Why Boeing, Wells Fargo Are Getting It So Wrong. *Forbes*. https://www.forbes.com/sites/daviatemin/2019/04/07/great-crisis-management-is-counter-intuitive-thats-why-boeing-wells-fargo-are-getting-it-so-wrong/?sh=432cca786ba7

The Business Enterprise Trust, Hanson, K. O., Bollier, D., & Weiss, S. (1991). Merck & Co., Inc.: Addressing Third-World Needs (C). *The Business Enterprise Trust, 9-991–023*. https://hbsp.harvard.edu/product/991023-PDF-ENG?Ntt=Merck%20The%20enterprise%20trust

Tkacik, M. (2019, September 18). Crash Course: : How Boeing's Managerial Revolution Created the 737 MAX Disaster. *The New Republic*. Accessed on November 6, 2023, from https://newrepublic.com/article/154944/boeing-737-max-investigation-indonesia-lion-air-ethiopian-airlines-managerial-revolution

Useem, J. (2000, October 2). Boeing VS. Boeing America's Export Champion is Going Head-to-Head with a Company Even Tougher than Airbus Itself. In *CNN Money*. https://money.cnn.com/magazines/fortune/fortune_archive/2000/10/02/288426/

Useem, J. (2019, November 20). The Long-Forgotten Flight That Sent Boeing Off Course. *The Atlantic*. Accessed on November 6, 2023, from https://www.theatlantic.com/ideas/archive/2019/11/how-boeing-lost-its-bearings/602188/

Vagelos, P. R., & Galambos, L. (2006). *The Moral Corporation – Merck Experiences*. New York, NY: Cambridge University Press.

Volkov, M. (2020, October 2). Boeing 737 MAX Accountability: Shareholder Litigation Against Boeing Board & House Transportation Committee Issues Scathing Report (Part I of II) | The Volkov Law Group. *JDSupra*. Accessed on November 6, 2023, from https://www.jdsupra.com/legalnews/boeing-737-max-accountability-95384/

Wasson, L. (2019, December 23). Boeing's Turbulent Year: A Timeline of the 737 Max Crisis. *The Globe and Mail*. https://www.theglobeandmail.com/business/international-business/article-boeings-turbulent-year-a-timeline-of-the-737-max-crisis/

Waters, H. R., Rehwinkel, J. A., & Burnham, G. (2004). Economic Evaluation of Mectizan Distribution. *Tropical Medicine & International Health: TM & IH, 9(4)*, A16-25. https://doi.org/10.1111/j.1365-3156.2004.01210.x

Wattles, J. (2020, July 29). Boeing Posts Three-Month Loss of $2.4 Billion. *CNN Business*. https://edition.cnn.com/2020/07/29/tech/boeing-earnings-covid/index.html

Willis, P. (2020, August 27). What Broke the 737 Max? *Aerospace Testing International*. Accessed on November 6, 2023, from https://www.aerospacetestinginternational.com/features/what-broke-the-737-max.html

Wolfe, F. (2020, January 30). Boeing Targets Middle of Year for 737 MAX Return to Service. *Aviation International*. Accessed on November 6, 2023, from https://www.aviationtoday.com/2020/01/30/boeing-targets-middle-of-year-for-737-max-return-to-service/

Zhang, B. (2019, March 13). The US Government Says it has No Reason to Ground the Boeing 737 MAX that has Crashed Twice since October. *Business Insider India*. https://www.businessinsider.in/the-us-government-says-it-has-no-reason-to-ground-the-boeing-737-max-that-has-crashed-twice-since-october/articleshow/68384313.cms

Chapter 6

Adegeest, D.-A. (2018, November 22). Dolce & Gabbana, a History of PR Disasters. *Fashion United*. Accessed on November 7, 2023 from https://fashionunited.uk/news/fashion/dolce-gabbana-a-history-of-pr-disasters/2018112240119

Ap, T. (2023, January 12). Dolce & Gabbana is Trying to Rehab its China Image by Dressing the Wrong Demographic. *Yahoo!Finance*. https://finance.yahoo.com/news/dolce-gabbana-trying-rehab-china-203900698.html

B Corp. (2023, October 6). B Corp Certification Demonstrates a Company's Entire Social and Environmental Impact. *B Corp*. Accessed on November 7, 2023 from https://www.bcorporation.net/en-us/certification

Bahler, K. (2019, July 16). Every Brand Wants to be "Woke." Ben & Jerry's Actually Is. *Money*. Accessed on November 7, 2023 from https://money.com/ben-and-jerrys-woke-marketing/

Bain, M. (2019, July 19). Chinese Web Users have Shunned Dolce & Gabbana Since its Racism Controversy. *Quartz*. Accessed on November 7, 2023 from https://qz.com/1670526/dolce-gabbana-still-shunned-online-in-china-after-racism-controversy

B&J. (2021, July 18). Ben & Jerry's Will End Sales of Our Ice Cream in the Occupied Palestinian Territory. *Ben & Jerry's*. Accessed on November 7, 2023 from https://www.benjerry.com/about-us/media-center/opt-statement

Cristoferi, C. (2019, August 27). Dolce & Gabbana sees Sales Slowdown in China After Ad Backlash. *Reuters*. https://www.reuters.com/article/us-dolce-gabbana-results-idUSKCN1VH1EV

Dalton, M. (2018, November 23). Chinese Online Retailers Stop Selling Dolce & Gabbana After Racism Uproar. *The Wall Street Journal*. https://www.wsj.com/articles/some-chinese-online-retailers-pull-dolce-gabbana-products-from-their-sites-1542993574

Darmstadter, H. (2016). *The Times* and General Motors: What Went Wrong? *Cogent Arts & Humanities*, *3*(1), 1134030. https://doi.org/10.1080/23311983.2015.1134030

EHRC. (2019, August 16). Human Rights and Business. *Equality and Human Rights Commission*. Accessed on November 7, 2023 from https://www.equalityhumanrights.com/human-rights/human-rights-and-business?return-url=https%3A%2F%2Fwww.equalityhumanrights.com%2Fsearch%3Fkeys%3DEquality%2B%2526%2BHuman%2BRights%2BCommission.%2B%25282019%252C%2BAugust%2B16%2529.%2BHuman%2Brights%2Band%2Bbusiness

ERC. (2017, January 18). Respect: The Key to Customer Service Excellence. *ERC*. Accessed on November 7, 2023 from https://yourerc.com/blog/respect-the-key-to-customer-service-excellence/

Hayden, B. (2016, September 11). Why the Golden Rule Must Be Practiced in Business. *Entrepreneur*. Accessed on November 7, 2023 from https://www.entrepreneur.com/business-news/why-the-golden-rule-must-be-practiced-in-business/281387

Hills, M. C. (2021, June 17). Three Years After Ad Controversy, D&G is Still Struggling to Win Back China. *CNN*. https://www.cnn.com/style/article/dolce-gabbana-karen-mok-china/index.html

Josephs, L. (2018, March 6). United Airlines is Sending Employees To Compassion Training. *CNBC*. https://www.cnbc.com/2018/03/06/can-you-teach-compassion-in-four-hours-united-airlines-is-giving-it-a-go.html

Keen, A. (2015, January 27). Are Business Ethics at a Low Ebb? *Entrepreneur*. Accessed on November 7, 2023 from https://www.entrepreneur.com/growing-a-business/are-business-ethics-at-a-low-ebb/242247

Krishna, R. (2018, November 21). Dolce & Gabbana Says Its Accounts Were Hacked After People Criticizing It Received Racist Abuse. *Buzz Feed News*. https://www.buzzfeednews.com/article/krishrach/dolce-gabbana-hacked-racist

Lucas, R. W. (2022). Customer Service Skills for Success (Eighth Edition). McGraw Hill. Accessed on November 7, 2023 from https://www.customerserviceskillsbook.com/wordpress/customer-service-culture-quote-jerry-fritz/

Michalak, R. (2019, May 1). Ben & Jerry's and the "Linked Prosperity" Business Model. *Fast Company*. Accessed on November 7, 2023 from https://www.fastcompany.com/90287777/this-key-metric-is-how-ben-jerrys-measures-success

Northman, T. (2018, November 21). Stefano Gabbana's Latest Problematic Statement Says That Chinese People Eat Dogs. *Hypebae*. Accessed on November 7, 2023 from https://hypebae.com/2018/11/ste fano-gabbana-controversial-comments-china-racist-messages

Quiroz-Gutierrez, M. (2021, July 21). "No-Go Topics" Don't Exist for Ben and Jerry's, Says CEO. *Fortune*. https://fortune.com/2021/07/21/ben-and-jerrys-activism-ceo-matthew-mccarthy-occupied-palestinian-territory/

Reiger, T. (2012, August 9). Why Dignity is the Key to Customer Service. *American Express | Business Class: Trends and Insights*. Accessed on November 7, 2023 from https://www.americanexpress.com/en-us/business/trends-and-insights/articles/why-dignity-is-the-key-to-customer-service/

Romero, A., Rojas, E., & Serrano, L. (2017, June 22). The United Case: How Reputation Crises Have Changed in Today's World. *IDEAS LLYC*. Accessed on November 7, 2023 from https://ideasen.llorenteycuenca.com/2017/06/22/the-united-case-how-reputation-crises-have-changed-in-todays-world/

Solis, M. (2020, August 20). Ben & Jerry's Showed America What Real Corporate Activism Looks Like. *HuffPost*. Accessed on November 7, 2023 from https://www.huffpost.com/entry/ben-jerry-ice-cream-corporate-activism_n_5f1b11dec5b6296fbf423019

Stevenson, T. (2020, August 27). How Dolce & Gabbana Lost 98% of Their Chinese Market with One Video. *Medium*. Accessed on November 7, 2023 from https://bettermarketing.pub/how-dolce-gabbana-lost-98-of-their-chinese-market-with-one-video-cb2baacb4a10

TR Center. (n.d.). Theodore Roosevelt Quotes. *Theordore Roosevelt Center*. Accessed on November 7, 2023, from https://www.theodorerooseveltcenter.org/Learn-About-TR/TR-Quotes?page=112

Watarastaporn, T. (2020, June 9). Ben & Jerry's Releases Series of Politically Charged Ice Cream Flavors. *The Stanford Daily*. Accessed on November 7, 2023 from https://stanforddaily.com/2020/06/09/ben-jerrys-releases-series-of-politically-charged-ice-cream-flavors/

Wunsch, N.-G. (2021, February 11). The Leading Ice Cream Brands of the United States in 2020, Based on Sales. *Statista*. Accessed on November 7, 2023 from https://www.statista.com/statistics/190426/top-ice-cream-brands-in-the-united-states/

Zhou, M. (2018, December 19). China Crisis: What Can we Learn from the D&G Disaster? *Up*. Accessed on November 7, 2023 from https://www.upthereeverywhere.com/blog/how-to-avoid-a-crisis-like-what-happened-to-dg-in-china

Chapter 7

Agnihotri, A., & Bhattacharya, S. (2018). Nike: Ethics Versus Reputation in the #MeToo Era. *IVEY Publishing*, *W18614*, 1–12.

Aurthur, K. (2021, July 6). Gretchen Carlson: Five Years After Her Lawsuit Against Roger Ailes. *Variety*. https://variety.com/2021/tv/news/gretchen-carlson-sexual-harassment-lawsuit-five-year-anniversary-1235010908/

Biswas, S. (2018, November 26). Mumbai 26/11 Attacks: Six Corpses, a Mobile Phone Call and One Survivor. *BBC News*. https://www.bbc.com/news/world-asia-india-46314555

Bowman, E. (2022, February 13). Gretchen Carlson Praises Bill that Ends Forced Arbitration in Sexual Assault Cases. *NPR*. https://www.npr.org/2022/02/12/1080420139/gretchen-carlson-forced-arbitration-bill

Brockes, E. (2018, January 15). #MeToo founder Tarana Burke: 'You have to use your privilege to serve other people.' *The Guardian*. https://www.theguardian.com/world/2018/jan/15/me-too-founder-tarana-burke-women-sexual-assault

Byers, D. (Director). (2021, June 29). Fox News Agrees to $1 Million Fine as Part of Human Rights Investigation Settlement. *NBC News*. https://www.nbcnews.com/media/fox-news-agrees-1-million-fine-part-human-rights-investigation-settlem-rcna1301

Chenoweth, N. (2016, July 23). Behind the Murdochs' Media Play that Sank Roger Ailes. *Financial Review*. https://www.afr.com/companies/media-and-marketing/behind-the-murdochs-media-play-that-sank-roger-ailes-20160722-gqbsck

Cherry, K. (2021, July 28). Gardner's Theory of Multiple Intelligences. *Verywell Mind*. Accessed on November 7, 2023, from https://www.verywellmind.com/gardners-theory-of-multiple-intelligences-2795161

Condé Nast Traveller. (2021, June 25). IHCL's Taj Named the Strongest Hotel Brand in the World. *Condé Nast Traveller*. Accessed on November 7, 2023, from https://www.cntraveller.in/story/ihcls-taj-named-the-strongest-hotel-brand-in-the-world/

Crockett, E. (2016, August 15). Here are the Women who Have Publicly Accused Roger Ailes of Sexual Harassment. *Vox*. https://www.vox.com/2016/8/15/12416662/roger-ailes-fox-sexual-harassment-women-list

Deshpande, R., & Raina, A. (2011). The Ordinary Heros of the Taj. *Harvard Business Review*, *R1112J*, 1–6.

Dickinson, T. (2011, May 25). How Roger Ailes Built the Fox News Fear Factory. *RollingStone*. https://www.rollingstone.com/politics/politics-news/how-roger-ailes-built-the-fox-news-fear-factory-244652/

Dockterman, E. (2019, December 16). The True Story Behind Bombshell and the Fox News Scandal. *Time*. https://time.com/5748267/bombshell-true-story-fox-news/

Ellison, S. (2016, September 22). Inside the Final Days of Roger Ailes's Reign at Fox News. *Vanity Fair*. https://www.vanityfair.com/news/2016/09/roger-ailes-fox-news-final-days

Garrahan, M. (2017, May 1). Shine Follows Ailes and O'Reilly out of Fox News. *Financial Times*. https://www.ft.com/content/15bb0004-2ea5-11e7-9555-23ef563ecf9a

Gross, T. (2016, July 26). The Rise and Fall of FOX News CEO Roger Ailes. *WEKU*. Accessed on November 7, 2023, from https://www.weku.org/2016-07-26/the-rise-and-fall-of-fox-news-ceo-roger-ailes

Harter, J. (2021, July 29). U.S. Employee Engagement Data Hold Steady in First Half of 2021. *Gallup.Com*. Accessed on November 7, 2023, from https://www.gallup.com/workplace/352949/employee-engagement-holds-steady-first-half-2021.aspx

IHCL. (2020, January 14). Mice Times Ahead. *IHCL*. Accessed on November 7, 2023, from https://www.ihcltata.com/ihcl/press-room/mice-times-ahead/

Keltner, D. (2017, October 13). Sex, Power, and the Systems That Enable Men Like Harvey Weinstein. *Harvard Business Review*, *H03YL9*. https://hbsp.harvard.edu/product/H03YL9-PDF-ENG?Ntt=SEX%20AND%20POWER%20SYSTEMS

Kenny, G. (2018, December 7). Divide and Conquer: The Story of Roger Ailes. *RogerEbert.Com*. Accessed on November 7, 2023, from https://www.rogerebert.com/reviews/divide-and-conquer-the-story-of-roger-ailes-2018

Kramer, R. M. (2006, February 1). Great Intimidators. *Harvard Business Review, R0602D*. https://hbsp.harvard.edu/product/R0602D-PDF-ENG?Ntt=the%20great%20itimidators

Luo, H., & Zhang, L. (2021, May 19). Measuring the Impact of #MeToo on Gender Equity in Hollywood. *Harvard Business Review, H06D1Q*. https://hbsp.harvard.edu/product/H06D1Q-PDF-ENG?Ntt=Measuring%20the%20Impact%20of%20%23MeToo%20on%20gender%20equity%20in%20Hollywood.

Nicolaou, E., & Smith, C. E. (2019, October 5). Me Too Movement 2-Year Timeline Most Important Moments. *Refinery29*. Accessed on November 7, 2023, from https://www.refinery29.com/en-us/2018/10/212801/me-too-movement-history-timeline-year-weinstein

Parloff, R. (2016, July 8). Why Gretchen Carlson Sued Only Roger Ailes – Not Fox News. *Fortune*. https://fortune.com/2016/07/08/gretchen-carlson-sued-only-ailes-not-fox/

Rogers, J. (2017, December 1). #MeToo: How an 11-year-old Movement Became a Social Media Phenomenon. *Fox News*. https://www.foxnews.com/tech/metoo-how-an-11-year-old-movement-became-a-social-media-phenomenon

Shugerman, E. (2017, May 11). Sexual Harassment Costs Fox News up to $110 Million in Last Nine Months. *The Independent*. https://www.independent.co.uk/news/world/americas/fox-news-sexual-harassment-cases-payouts-settlements-bill-o-reilly-roger-ailes-a7730556.html

Stanglin, D. (2017, May 18). Fox News Mastermind Roger Ailes Dies at 77, a Year After Being Ousted. *USA Today*. https://www.usatoday.com/story/news/2017/05/18/roger-ailes-former-fox-news-chairman-dead-77/101823530/

Stelter, B. (Director). (2016, September 6). Fox News Settles with Gretchen Carlson and "Handful" of Other Women. *CNN Business*. https://money.cnn.com/2016/09/06/media/gretchen-carlson-fox-news-lawsuit-settled/index.html

Stelter, B. (2020, July 22). How Fox News has Changed in the Four Years Since Roger Ailes was Ousted. *CNN Business*. https://edition.cnn.com/2020/07/22/media/fox-news-trump-roger-ailes-four-years-later/index.html

TATA. (n.d.). Diamond by the Sea. *TATA Group*. Accessed on November 7, 2023, from https://www.tata.com/newsroom/taj-diamond-by-the-sea

Chapter 8

1% for the Planet. (n.d.). 1% for the Planet Network and Environmental Giving. *1% for the Planet*. Accessed on November 8, 2023, from https://www.onepercentfortheplanet.org/frequently-asked-questions

AC. (2021, February 18). Patagonia Buy Less Demand More: Customers Encouraged to Buy Used. *Alpha Commerce*. Accessed on November 8, 2023, from https://alphacommerce.xyz/sustainability/recommerce/patagonia-buy-less-demand-more-customers-encouraged-to-buy-used/

Anderson, R. C., & White, R. (2009). *Confessions of a Radical Industrialist: Profits, People, Purpose – Doing Business by Respecting the Earth*. New York, NY: St. Martins Press.

Au-Yeung, A. (2020, April 23). Outdoor Clothing Chain Patagonia Starts Selling Online Again After Unusual Decision to Pause Its E-Commerce Due to Pandemic. *Forbes*. https://www.forbes.com/sites/angelauyeung/2020/04/23/outdoor-clothing-chain-patagonia-yvon-chouinard-starts-selling-online-again-after-unusual-decision-to-pause-its-e-commerce-due-to-coronavirus-pandemic/?sh=4f425bf31c48

Bardelline, J. (2010, November 17). Patagonia Adds Reduce, Repair, Reuse to Clothes Recycling. *GreenBiz*. https://www.greenbiz.com/article/patagonia-adds-reduce-repair-reuse-clothes-recycling

Batten, C. (2020, April 21). Patagonia's Worn Wear Collection Is Saving the Planet. *The Manual*. Accessed on November 8, 2023, from https://www.themanual.com/outdoors/oatagonia-worn-wear-collection-recycled-recommerce/

Beer, J. (2019, October 16). Patagonia Founder Yvon Chouinard Talks About the Sustainability Myth, the Problem with the Amazon – And Why Its not Too Late to Save the Planet. *Fast Company*. Accessed on November 8, 2023, from https://www.fastcompany.com/90411397/exclusive-patagonia-founder-yvon-chouinard-talks-about-the-sustainability-myth-the-problem-with-amazon-and-why-its-not-too-late-to-save-the-planet

Bhasin, K. (2020, December 16). Patagonia's New CEO Plots a Post-Trump Future for the Activist Brand. *BloombergQuint*. Accessed on November 8, 2023, from https://www.bqprime.com/politics/patagonia-s-new-ceo-plans-to-keeping-up-climate-fight-at-clothing-brand

Building Transparency. (2020, July 9). materialsCAN. *Building Transparency*. Accessed on November 8, 2023, from https://www.buildingtransparency.org/programs/materialscan/

Business at the Bay. (2018, December 1). Patagonia $10m Donation. *WBHS Business & Economics Blog*. Accessed on November 8, 2023, from http://businessatthebay.blogspot.com/2018/12/patagonia-10m-donation.html

Casey, S. (2007, April 2). Patagonia: Blueprint for Green Business. *Fortune*. https://money.cnn.com/magazines/fortune/fortune_archive/2007/04/02/8403423/index.htm

Chouinard, Y. (2006). *Let my People Go Surfing: The Education of a Reluctant Businessman*. New York, NY: Penguin Books.

Chouinard, Y. (2019). *Some Stories: Lessons From the Edge of Business and Sport*. Ventura, CA: Patagonia Works.

Danao, M. (2018, February 11). How Patagonia Became A $1B Powerhouse . . . With A Heart. Accessed on November 8, 2023, from ReferralCandy. https://www.referralcandy.com/blog/patagonia-marketing-strategy

Dua, T. (2017, October 9). Dove's "Racist" Ad Might have Cost the Brand an Advantage it Spent 13 Years Building. *Business Insider*. https://www.businessinsider.com/doves-racist-ad-10-9-2017-10

DuBois, F. (2018, May 5). Patagonia v. Trump. *The Westerner*. Accessed on November 8, 2023, from https://thewesterner.blogspot.com/2018/05/patagonia-v-trump.html

Falk, T. (2013, September 3). Patagonia Encourages Less Buying, Customers Buy More. *ZDNET*. Accessed on November 8, 2023, from https://www.zdnet.com/google-amp/article/patagonia-encourages-less-buying-customers-buy-more/

Folley, A. (2018, November 28). Patagonia calls Trump Tax Cut 'Irresponsible,' says it will Donate $10M Corporate Tax Cut to Environmental Groups. *The Hill*. Accessed on November 8, 2023, from https://thehill.com/blogs/blog-briefing-room/news/418798-patagonia-calls-trump-tax-cut-irresponsible-donates-10-million/

Foreman, D. (2016, March 11). Culture Eats Strategy for Breakfast. *The Management Centre*. Accessed on November 8, 2023, from https://www.managementcentre.co.uk/management-consultancy/culture-eats-strategy-for-breakfast/

Fox, J., Tierney, L., Blanchard, S., & Florit, G. (2019, April 2). What Remains of Bears Ears. *The Washington Post*. https://www.washingtonpost.com/graphics/2019/national/bears-ears/

Gelles, D. (2022, September 21). Billionaire No More: Patagonia Founder Gives Away the Company to Fight Climate Change. *The New York Times*. https://www.nytimes.com/2022/09/14/climate/patagonia-climate-philanthropy-chouinard.html

GlobeScan. (2021, July 28). The 2021 GlobeScan / SustainAbility Leaders Survey | Report. *GlobeScan*. Accessed on November 8, 2023, from https://globescan.com/2021/07/28/2021-sustainability-leaders-report/

Gonzales, R., Siegler, K., & Dwyer, C. (2017, December 4). Trump Orders Largest National Monument Reduction in U.S. History. *NPR*. https://www.npr.org/sections/thetwo-way/2017/12/04/567803476/trump-dramatically-shrinks-2-utah-national-monuments

Greenlee, J. (2021, May 11). Dear Warren Buffett: Why the Social Responsibility "Craze" Is Here to Stay. *LinkedIn*. Accessed on November 8, 2023, from https://www.linkedin.com/pulse/dear-warren-buffett-why-social-responsibility-craze-jessi/

Gunther, M. (2017, September 8). The Patagonia Adventure: Yvon Chouinard's Stubborn Desire to Redefine Business. *B The Change*. Accessed on November 8, 2023, from https://bthechange.com/the-patagonia-adventure-yvon-chouinards-stubborn-desire-to-redefine-business-f60f7ab8dd60

Hoffman, A. (2012). Patagonia: Encouraging Customers to Buy Used Clothing (A). *WDI Publishing, W92C30*, 1–22.

Horn, J. (2014, May 1). Patagonia's New Line of Activism is Documentary "DamNation." *Los Angeles Times*. https://www.latimes.com/entertainment/movies/la-et-mn-backstage-hollywood-patagonia-damnation-20140501-story.html

Howland, D. (2018, February 22). Patagonia Doubles Down on Political Activism. *Retail Dive*. Accessed on November 8, 2023, from https://www.retaildive.com/news/patagonia-doubles-down-on-political-activism/517627/

Huckabay, C. (n.d.). More Apparel Consumers are Opting for Online When it Comes to Outerwear. *SalesFuel*. Accessed on November 8, 2023, from https://salesfuel.com/apparel-consumers-opting-online-comes-outerwear/

Interface. (n.d.). Lessons for the Future (Volume 32). *Interface*. Accessed on November 8, 2023, from http://interfaceinc.scene7.com/is/content/InterfaceInc/Interface/Americas/WebsiteContentAssets/Documents/Sustainability 25yr Report/25yr Report Booklet Interface_MissionZeroCel.pdf

Joe, T. (2021, April 27). Patagonia Will No Longer Show Corporate Logos on its Clothing. *Green Queen*. Accessed on November 8, 2023, from https://www.greenqueen.com.hk/patagonia-will-no-longer-show-corporate-logos-on-its-clothing-last-longer/

King, B. (2015, June 12). Can a Carpet Factory Run Like a Forest? *GreenBiz*. Accessed on November 8, 2023, from https://www.greenbiz.com/article/can-carpet-factory-run-forest

Makower, J. (2016, June 6). Inside Interface's Bold New Mission to Achieve "Climate Take Back." *GreenBiz*. Accessed on November 8, 2023, from https://www.greenbiz.com/article/inside-interfaces-bold-new-mission-achieve-climate-take-back

Miller, R. M. (2018, November 29). "It is Pure Evil": Patagonia Takes Swipe at Trump as it Donated $13.7m Tax Windfall to Environmental Groups. *The Sydney Morning Herald*. https://www.smh.com.au/business/companies/it-is-pure-evil-patagonia-takes-swipe-at-trump-as-it-donates-13-7m-tax-windfall-to-environmental-groups-20181129-p50j3h.html

O'Brien, D., Kounkel, S., Main, A., & Stephan, A. R. (2019, October 15). Purpose is Everything. *Deloitte Insights*. Accessed on November 8, 2023, from https://www2.deloitte.com/us/en/insights/topics/marketing-and-sales-operations/global-marketing-trends/2020/purpose-driven-companies.html

Patagonia. (2009, March 4). Closing the Loop – A Report on Patagonia's Common Threads Garment Recycling Program. *Patagonia Inc*. Accessed on November 8, 2023, from https://www.patagonia.com/stories/closing-the-loop-a-report-on-patagonias-common-threads-garment-recycling-program/story-19961.html

Patagonia. (2011a, September 7). Patagonia Launches Common Threads Initiative: A Partnership with Customers to Consume Less. *Cision PR Newswire*. Accessed on November 8, 2023, from https://www.prnewswire.com/news-releases/patagonia-launches-common-threads-initiative-a-partnership-with-customers-to-consume-less-129372068.html

Patagonia. (2011b, November 25). Don't Buy This Jacket, Black Friday and the New York Times. *Patagonia Inc*. Accessed on November 8, 2023, from https://www.patagonia.com/stories/dont-buy-this-jacket-black-friday-and-the-new-york-times/story-18615.html

Patagonia. (2014). Fair Trade. *Patagonia Inc*. Accessed on November 8, 2023, from https://www.patagonia.com/our-footprint/fair-trade.html

Patagonia. (2016, September 15). Save the Yellowstone Grizzly. *Patagonia Inc*. Accessed on November 8, 2023, from https://www.patagonia.com/stories/yvon-chouinard-save-the-yellowstone-grizzly/story-30931.html

Patagonia. (2020, November 25). Buy Less, Demand More this Black Friday. *Medium*. Accessed on November 8, 2023, from https://patagonia.medium.com/buy-less-demand-more-this-black-friday-4fd2b6c54d85

Posner, B. (2009). One CEO's Trip from Dismissive to Convinced. *MIT Sloan Management Review, 51*(1), 47–53.

Reinhardt, F. L., Casadesus-Masanell, R., & Kim, H. J. (2010). Patagonia. *Harvard Business School, 711020*, 1–29.

Robertson, G. (n.d.). Patagonia Case Study: How Their Brand Purpose Goes Against Business Norms. *Beloved Brands*. Accessed on November 8, 2023, from https://beloved-brands.com/patagonia/

Rothaermel, F. T., & Janovec, M. (2012). InterfaceRAISE (in 2010): Raising the Bar in Sustainability Consulting. *McGraw Hill Education Case, MH0005*, 1–25.

Ryan, T. J. (2020, January 16). Worn Wear Taking Off for Patagonia. *SGB Media*. Accessed on November 8, 2023, from https://sgbonline.com/worn-wear-taking-off-for-patagonia/

Schnell, H., & Azzolini, S. (2019, June 21). Patagonia has Sued President Trump. Curious to Know Why? *Sustainable Lifestyle Consultant*. Accessed on November 8, 2023, from https://www.sustainablelifestyleconsultant.com/blog-2/2019/6/19/patagonia-has-sued-president-trump-why

Stackla Survey. (2019, February 20). Stackla Survey Reveals Disconnect Between the Content Consumers Want & What Marketers Deliver. *Nosto*. Accessed on November 8, 2023, from https://www.nosto.com/blog/report-consumer-marketing-perspectives-on-content-in-the-digital-age/

Sunrise, H. (2021, June 14). 5 Examples of Companies Making a Profit with Brand Authenticity. *Instapage*. Accessed on November 8, 2023, from https://instapage.com/blog/building-brand-authenticity

Szekely, F., & Dossa, Z. (2019). Patagonia's Sustainability Strategy: Don't Buy Our Products. *IMD*, IMD790, 1–14.

Thangavelu, P. (2020, February 3). The Success of Patagonia's Marketing Strategy. *Investopedia*. Accessed on November 8, 2023, from https://www.investopedia.com/articles/personal-finance/070715/success-patagonias-marketing-strategy.asp

The Drum. (2020, September). Patagonia: Vote The Assholes Out. *The Drum*. Accessed on November 8, 2023, from https://www.thedrum.com/creative-works/project/patagonia-vote-the-assholes-out

The Harris Poll. (2021, May 13). Patagonia, Honda, Moderna, Chick-fil-A, SpaceX Top "Axios-Harris Poll 100" With the Best Reputations. *Cision PR Newswire*. Accessed on November 8, 2023, from https://www.prnewswire.com/news-releases/patagonia-honda-moderna-chick-fil-a-spacex-top-axios-harris-poll-100-with-the-best-reputations-301290515.html

Thomas, L. (2020, June 23). Resale Market Expected to be Valued at $64 Billion in 5 Years, as Used Clothing Takes Over Closets. *CNBC*. https://www.cnbc.com/2020/06/23/thredup-resale-market-expected-to-be-valued-at-64-billion-in-5-years.html

UNEP. (2019, September 24). US Outdoor Clothing Brand Patagonia Wins UN Champions of the Earth Award. *UN Environment Programme*. Accessed on November 8, 2023, from http://www.unep.org/news-and-stories/press-release/us-outdoor-clothing-brand-patagonia-wins-un-champions-earth-award

UNFCCC. (2020). From Mission Zero to Climate Take Back: How Interface is Transforming its Business to Have Zero Negative Impact | Global. *United Nations Framework Convention on Climate Change*. Accessed on November 8, 2023, from https://unfccc.int/climate-action/momentum-for-change/climate-neutral-now/interface

Weaver, A. (2020, December 3). Patagonia Encourages Shoppers to Buy Used Gear This Holiday Season. *Outside Business Journal*. Accessed on November 8, 2023, from https://www.outsideonline.com/business-journal/issues/sustainability/patagonia-buy-less-demand-more-campaign/

Wolfe, I. (2023, March 28). How Ethical Is Patagonia? *Good On You*. Accessed on November 8, 2023, from https://goodonyou.eco/how-ethical-is-patagonia/

Conclusion

Issawi, D. (2023, June 5). What to Know About the Balenciaga Ad Scandal. *The Cut*. Accessed on November 8, 2023, from https://www.thecut.com/article/what-to-know-about-the-balenciaga-ad-scandal.html

McNamee, K., Handel, S., & Kelly, M. L. (2023, January 27). India's Wealthiest Businessman Accused of Fraud. *NPR*. https://www.npr.org/2023/01/27/1152140590/indias-wealthiest-businessman-accused-of-fraud

USAO. (2022, October 5). Former Chief Security Officer of Uber Convicted of Federal Charges for Covering Up Data Breach Involving Millions of Uber User Records. *U.S. Department of Justice*. Accessed on November 8, 2023, from https://www.justice.gov/usao-ndca/pr/former-chief-security-officer-uber-convicted-federal-charges-covering-data-breach

Yuanyuan, Z. (2023, May 4). Screenwriter Hit with #MeToo Allegations, Igniting Debate in China About "Gray Areas." *The China Project*. Accessed on November 8, 2023, from https://thechinaproject.com/2023/05/04/famed-chinese-screenwriter-hit-with-metoo-allegations/

List of Abbreviations

°	Degrees
737 MAX	Boeing's 4th generation narrow body airliner
€	Euro – currency of 20 European Union countries
₹	Indian Rupee
$	United States dollar
A320NEO	Airbus 320 New Engine Option series
ABC	ABC American TV Network
AI	Artificial Intelligence
AOA	Angle of Attack
B&J	Ben & Jerry's
BDSM	Bondage, dominance, sadism, and masochism
BGH	Bundesgerichtshof, Federal Court of Justice Germany
BMW	German automaker
CAD	Canadian Dollar
CAFEE	Center for Alternative Fuels, Engines, and Emissions
CARB	California Air Resources Board
CCC	Customer Care Center
CD	Compact Disc
CDC	Centers for Disease Control and Prevention, USA
CEO	Chief Executive Officer
CFM LEAP	a high-bypass turbofan engine produced by CFM International for Boeing
ChatGPT	Chat Generative Pre-trained Transformer
CNBC	American Cable News Business Channel
CNN	Cable News Network
CO_2	Carbon Dioxide
CSO	Chief Security Officer
DEI	Diversity, Equity, and Inclusion
D&G	Dolce & Gabbana
DJSI	Dow Jones Sustainability Index
DNA	Deoxyribonucleic acid – the molecule that carries genetic information of an organism
EPA	Environmental Protection Agency, USA
EU	European Union
EUGT	European Research Group on Environment and Health in the Transport Sector
EV	Electric Vehicle
FAA	Federal Aviation Administration, USA
FBI	Federal Bureau of Investigation, USA
FDA	Food and Drug Administration
FIR	First Information Report
FLA	Fair Labor Association
FOC	Free of Charge
FOX	US News Channel
FSSAI	Food Safety and Standards Authority of India
FTC	Federal Trade Commission
FTSE4Good	UK Sustainability Index
GM	General Motors, US automaker
GM	General Manager
GMO	Genetically Modified Organism

https://doi.org/10.1515/9781501517334-012

GOP	Grand Old Party
GSM	Global System for Mobile Communication
HBS	Harvard Business School
ICCT	International Council for Clean Transportation
IHCL	Indian Hotel Company Limited
ISO	International Organization for Standardization
IUD	Intrauterine Device
J&J	Johnson & Johnson
JPY	Japanese Yen
JT	Lion Air
LGBTQ+	Lesbian, gay, bisexual, transgender, and queer. The plus sign symbolizes the other identities included under the LGBTQ+ umbrella, like *asexual* and *intersex*.
MCAS	Maneuvering Characteristics Augmentation System
MNC	Multi-National Corporation
ML	Machine Learning
MSG	Monosodium Glutamate
MSNBC	American News-Based TV Channel
NDA	Non-Disclosure Agreement
NTSB	National Transportation Safety Board, United States
NG	Boeing 737 Next Generation Series
NOx	Nitrogen Oxide
NPD	Nokia Priority Dealer
NPR	National Public Radio, American non-profit new media organization
NTSB	National Transportation Safety Board
NYU	New York University
OMB	Operations Manual Bulletin
OTC	Over-the-Counter
PCHR	Philadelphia Commission on Human Relations
PEMS	Portable Emissions Measurement System
PID	Pelvic Inflammatory Disease
PPFA	Planned Parenthood Federation of America
PR	Public Relations
QUEST	Quality Utilizing Employees' Suggestions and Teamwork
R&D	Research and Development
SAP	Systems Applications and Products
SBM	Snow Brand Milk
SMS	Short Messaging Service
SPI	SPI Group is a distributor of specialty ingredients to food, meat, and nutritional manufacturers
STARS	Special Thanks and Recognition System
SUV	Sports Utility Vehicle
T & I	Transport and Infrastructure Committee, US House of Representatives
TDI	Turbocharged Direct Injection
TV	Television
UA	United Airlines
UGC	User Generated Content
UK	United Kingdom
UN	United Nations
UNDP	United Nations Development Fund

UNEP	United National Environment Programme
UNFCCC	United Nations Framework Convention on Climate Change
UNGP	United Nations Guiding Principles on Business and Human Rights
UNICEF	United Nations International Children's Emergency Fund
UP	Uttar Pradesh, state in India
US	United States
USA	United States of America
USAID	United States Agency for International Development
VAT	Value-Added Tax
VP	Vice President
VW	Volkswagen
WF	Wells Fargo
WHO	World Health Organization

Index

https://doi.org/10.1515/9781501517334-013

About the Authors

Shailendra Pratap Jain is Bret Wheat Endowed Professor of Marketing and International Business at the Foster School of Business, University of Washington, Seattle. He has held faculty positions at Indiana University's Kelley School, University of Rochester's Simon School, Cornell University's Johnson School, University of Western Ontario's Ivey School, Cambridge University's Judge School, Indian School of Business, Hyderabad, and BITS School of Management, Mumbai. Well-known for his widely published scholarship in consumer psychology, Dr. Jain has extensive publishing and editorial experience in top marketing journals and has won many executive and graduate (MBA) teaching awards. Prior to his academic career, he worked in sales, brand management, and advertising in industry and is associated with several noted marketing campaigns in India.

Shalini Sarin Jain is Associate Professor of Management and the inaugural Director of Diversity, Equity, and Inclusion at the Milgard School of Business, University of Washington, Tacoma. She has published articles on gender representation and compensation parity in top management, allegations of sexual misconduct, sustaining livelihoods or saving lives during COVID, and corporate response to mandatory CSR regulation in leading management journals including the *Journal of Business Research, Journal of Business Ethics, Management and Organization Review, and Journal of Family Business Strategy.* Dr. Jain teaches courses in business and society, ethics, and CSR at the undergraduate and MBA level and has extensive industry, government, and non-profit experience leading and providing consulting services to state, county, and city governments.

https://doi.org/10.1515/9781501517334-014